Barry Callen addresses with admirable frankness and clarity a complex set of issues regarding the proper place of the "Foundational Testament" in Christian thought and practice. Christians who have given up on the "Old" Testament will find here many compelling reasons to pick it up again. Wesleyan Christians, who sometimes feel buffeted from both ends of the European and North American theological spectrum, will find support in these well-written pages for authentically Wesleyan (and I would say, therefore, biblical) approaches to our reading of the entire scriptural canon. As a scholar of the Foundational Testament myself, I welcome this new and stimulating contribution to a very important conversation.

    Dr. Joseph E. Coleson
    Professor of Old Testament
    Nazarene Theological Seminary

Beneath the Surface

Reclaiming the Old Testament for Today's Christians

Barry L. Callen

EMETH PRESS
www.emethpress.com

Beneath the Surface,
Reclaiming the Old Testament for Today's Christians

Copyright © 2012 Barry L. Callen
Printed in the United States of America on acid-free paper

All rights reserved. No part of this book may be reproduced, or stored in a retrieval system or transmitted in any form or by any means, electronic, mechanical, photocopying, recording, scanning or otherwise, except as permitted by the 1976 United States Copyright Act, or with the prior written permission of Emeth Press. Requests for permission should be addressed to: Emeth Press, P. O. Box 23961, Lexington, KY 40523-3961.   http://www.emethpress.com.

Library of Congress Cataloging-in-Publication Data

Callen, Barry L.
  Beneath the surface : reclaiming the Old Testament for today's Christians / Barry L. Callen.
    p. cm.
  ISBN 978-1-60947-026-5 (alk. paper)
  1. Bible. O.T.--Theology. 2. Bible. O.T.--Criticism, interpretation, etc. I. Title.
  BS1192.5.C25 2012
  230'.0411--dc23
                          2012005763

Contents

Introduction / 1

    SECTION ONE: NECESSARY JEWISH ORIENTATIONS

1. Is This Really Important? / 19
2. What Went Wrong? / 29
3. How Should Christians Read the Foundational Testament? / 51
4. The Pervasive Theological Themes / 59

    SECTION TWO: FOUNDATIONAL TRUTHS FOR CHRISTIANS

5. The "Father" of Rabbi Jesus / 75
6. Yahweh, the Truly "Open" God / 91
7. The Divine Choice of a People / 107
8. Walking the Way of Holiness / 123
9. Dealing with the Order of Things / 135
10. Living with Persistent Hope / 149

    SECTION THREE: FACING SOME OF THE HARDEST ISSUES

11. Four Inter-Testament Studies / 161

    SECTION FOUR: FURTHERING EVEN THE FINAL TESTAMENT

12. Foundations Are Always Foundations / 189
13. God's Spirit and a Surplus of Meaning / 199

Introduction

It is of the very nature of the Bible to affront, perplex and astonish the human mind.... The Bible is without question one of the most unsatisfying books ever written—at least until the reader has come to terms with it in a very special way [sometimes from *beneath the text*].... Modern man may find himself wondering, in all honesty, whether the Bible is even *readable*. So much of it is archaic. So much is seemingly exotic, utterly alien to life as we know it.[1]

When we are freed of static categories of interpretation that are widely utilized among us, we are able to see that the articulation of God in the Old Testament partakes exactly of the qualities of complexity, dynamism, and fluidity that belong to the postmodern world [today!].... Such a fresh perception of God in the Old Testament goes a long way toward letting this God be a contemporary partner in a world that is open and in process.[2]

Which is it? Reading the two quotes above could send the Bible reader in opposite directions. One could mire us in despair over the hopelessly ancient, while the other could bring fresh hope for immediate relevance of the biblical texts. The hope lies in a fresh perception of *God* that is both ancient and contemporary. Yahweh lies beneath all biblical texts. The challenge is to encounter him and really know him and his ways in this world.

When people today try to read the Old Testament, are they in an alien world or on the frontiers of where we all are living? The two writers quoted above would agree that proper biblical interpretation is

---

1. Thomas Merton, *Opening the Bible* (Collegeville, MN: The Liturgical Press, 1970), 11, 15.
2. Walter Brueggemann, *An Unsettling God: The Heart of the Hebrew Bible* (Minneapolis: Fortress Press, 2009), xii.

both critical and not easy. We need help with the "alien" part of the text so that we can focus on the fresh biblical truths so needed today.

The unusual approach of this book allows it to become an introduction to biblical studies in general, to the "Old" Testament in particular, and to Christian theology that is a natural byproduct of quality biblical study. It is an attempt to build a bridge between a far away yesterday and the fast-coming tomorrow. The bridge is *Yahweh* (God) who was, is, and is yet to come.

The approach found in these pages is not typical. Focusing on the significance of the Hebrew (Jewish) heritage for contemporary Christian faith introduces an integration of subjects not limited by yesterday's blind spots or today's sometimes arid and isolated academic specializations. We intend to be particularly conscious of today as it ought to be, that is, based on the divine wisdom of yesterday and the divine being of every day.

As Thomas Merton admits in the lead quote above, life as we know it now makes it difficult for us to even read the Bible, especially the "Old" part. I recently encountered the comments of Brent A. Strawn, a Christian professor of the Old Testament. He said that he routinely explains to his students why he teaches this particular subject matter *by choice*. "It's not that I failed the New Testament exam!"[3] After Merton's admission comes Walter Brueggemann's promise. Reading the "Old" carefully and wisely can be rewarding indeed. That reward is for today's Christians as well as yesterdays Jews and, to echo Brent Strawn, Christians should read the Old Testament often and *by choice*!

That will be the last time we will refer to the Jewish sacred Testament as "Old." In these pages, I will use the words *Foundational* Testament. "Old" sounds too much like something outdated and replaceable. In fact, the Foundational Testament is hardly outdated and, for Christians, it is not replaceable. The New Testament will be referred to as the *Final* Testament. The focus will not be so much on which Testament is newer, but on the whole biblical story that leads to the revelation of God in Jesus who is the full and final revelation of Yahweh, the one and only God.

Since this amazing biblical story is necessarily founded on the long experience of Israel, we will emphasize the interconnectedness and wholeness of the biblical revelation, with Israel taking the lead and

---

3. The professor was Dr. Brent A. Strawn, a faculty member of the "Foundational" Testament at Candler School of Theology, Emory University, Atlanta, Georgia.

becoming the essential foundation. Further, since I write as a Christian, the name Jesus will come up often—after all, that is where the long biblical story finally leads. Our goal is sensitizing Christians about the continuing importance for them of the Foundational Testament. Accordingly, we will use the Hebrew form of the name Jesus, *Yeshua*.

The reader will not find here the usual detailed discussions of the authorship of each of the biblical books. Also not addressed are some of the technical subjects that biblical scholars and Christian theologians spend considerable time exploring. We will be more basic and integrated than that. We will attempt to think like an ancient Jew and then approach Christian faith informed by the wonderful witness of the Foundational Testament and its distinctive theological perspective.

I am confident that Yeshua, a Jew, would have today's Christians do Bible reading this way. It is the biblical way of things, the way of Moses, David, Isaiah, Matthew, Yeshua, Paul, and the others. As we shall see, it comes down to the way we are to view all of reality. The view is to be dominated by Yahweh, the Lord of Lords and King of Kings, the one "Water Source" of the several "truth streams" that flow through both of the biblical Testaments. Sometimes the flow is seen right on the surface; sometimes it is found only beneath the text. We will go wherever necessary to find it.

Caught Between Truths

Gaining a proper understanding of Yahweh comes with some complexities and problems for today's biblical reader. Difficult or not, biblical understanding is something that must be sought after and gotten right. Here is a contemporary illustration that sees the complexity and helps show the way ahead.

Today's professional baseball was an unknown sport in ancient Israel, but Israel knew well a piece of wisdom that comes from one of famous players of baseball in the United States. The catcher and humorist Yogi Berra is quoted as saying: "When you come to a fork in the road, take it!" That advice lies somewhere between impractical stupidity and brilliant biblical insight. These pages champion the latter option. Let me explain.

When studying the Bible and Christian theology, and encountering a paradox, an apparent fork in the road, contemporary Christian readers are not to get frustrated or try to find a clever way around the situation. We sometimes have to accept the paradox like a good Jew would and move on. The biblical Jews accepted several important paradoxes without trying to speculate beyond their limited wisdom. They did not use the "modern," the rational, the scientific approach to "truth." Instead, they embraced simultaneously both sides of some paradoxes, an embracing that still may be the only path to true wisdom. It was the Jewish way, and it should be the Christian way. Several examples will be highlighted in the pages to follow.

My earlier book *Caught Between Truths* was written with this advice very much in mind.[4] Jewish and Christian people who are serious about their faith need to grasp the significance of what G. K. Chesterton once called the "romance of orthodoxy."[5] When the facts as we know them are paradoxical, we are to hold on with both hands! Take it all. Going with partial truths and acting like they are the whole truth can lead to serious error. "Orthodoxy," believing straight and true, sometimes requires nothing less than embracing a mystery. While not finding all of the answers or being able to reduce everything to a formula, we can open ourselves to being found by Yahweh who spans all time and truth. That will be enough!

The fact is that central beliefs of the Judeo-Christian tradition often are a joining together of two coordinate truths that form a larger whole, the higher and fuller truth. For instance, the Foundational Testament reports that this turbulent and sinful world originated with the creative act of an orderly and loving God. Yeshua is understood by Christians, based on the witness of the Final Testament, to be at once "fully human and fully divine." The Bible, composed and edited by numerous humans over several centuries, is claimed to also be fully "inspired" (initiated and inbreathed) by none other than God. The separate components of such larger wholes appear quite contradictory on the surface. And yet, taking into account what lies *beneath the surface*, each contains a vital piece of the more complex truth that pervades both the Foundational and Final Testaments.

Religious truth often defies the simplicity of "clean" and uncomplicated statements. A "propensity for paradox" was a common literary device in the thought world that lies behind the Foundational Tes-

---

4. Barry L. Callen, *Caught Between Truths: The Central Paradoxes of Christian Faith* (Lexington, KY: Emeth Press, 2007).

5. G. K. Chesterton, *Orthodoxy* (Garden City, N.Y.: Doubleday Image Books, 1959 ed.), chapter eight titled "The Romance of Orthodoxy."

tament, and the Final as well.⁶ The ancient Jews, and the early Christians who shared that Hebrew heritage and worldview, had a reverent humility in the face of the divine. They knew that the fullness of ultimate truth rarely arrives in tight rational statements readily accessible and controllable by their little and often sinful minds. They knew, and we "rational moderns" must learn, the wisdom of trusting even when we cannot fully understand.

Rather than a perplexing problem, being *caught between truths* sometimes might be exactly the right place to be, whether or not it is satisfying to our rationalistic and scientific mindset. It is important to recall that the Bible is an ancient *Eastern* and not a modern *Western* book. It also is a Jewish book. The Jewishness of the Bible remains an essential element of a proper Christian understanding of it.

Christians should proceed in their search for biblical truth by gaining an awareness and acceptance of a particular paradox. It concerns the nature and authority of their own sacred Scripture. There are two main divisions, two "Testaments." In many ways, these divisions seem rather different, sometimes even contradictory. Nonetheless, they form one whole, with each part always deeply in need of the other for its own fullest understanding. This book seeks to explain this need, illustrate its importance, and urge its acceptance.

Even if only being silly with his comment, Yogi Berra stumbled into wisdom about the Bible. When Christians come to the seemingly divergent roads of the two Testaments, Foundational and Final, they should take them! To do this successfully, however, requires some thoughtful help. One must have the patience necessary to get beneath the surface of the biblical text, see the paradox, the seeming fork in the road, and have the wisdom to take it! One must recognize and affirm the *distinctive theological base* common to both Testaments. This base is critical for biblical relevance today. These pages hope to help with such recognition and affirmation.

Our basic goal is straightforward. Contemporary Christians must hold together what must not be separated—and, sadly and tragically, so often has been separated. Jew and Gentile, Old and New, Law and Gospel, Abraham and Yeshua. The time has come to set things right. Let's remain caught between paradoxes that truly are enduring paradoxes. Why? There are several reasons, a key one being that the people

---

6. Marvin Wilson, *Our Father Abraham: Jewish Roots of the Christian Faith* (Grand Rapids: Eerdmans Publishing, 1989), 150-153. Wilson discusses the propensity to paradox under the category "block logic."

of Israel "thought differently from all the people around them.... And we [Christians] must learn to think the way they did."[7] Otherwise, the integrity of the Christian faith will be compromised seriously by the breaking of the paradox of the Bible itself.

Returning to Jewish Foundations

There is one more thing that should be said as we begin. It also may sound contradictory or at least paradoxical. On the one hand, all things that are truly biblical are necessarily Hebraic (Jewish) in their essential character. That is, the whole Bible is informed significantly by the theology of the Hebraic worldview that lay behind (or beneath) the Foundational Testament. On the other hand, some views and practices of the ancient Hebrew tradition are no longer obligatory for Christians of the Final Testament. That is true for the very Christians who necessarily are deeply indebted to that ancient Jewish tradition. All of the Foundational Testament is significant, even authoritative for the Christian, but it is not all applicable anymore—at least not everything that appears on the surface of the text. That is why we will go below.

This is a paradox that Christians must probe with care. The paradox is that today's Christians should not decide that anything in the Foundational Testament is completely outmoded and in no way meaningful for them. It all is somehow authoritative, even if no longer applicable in its cultural particulars. Just because the Foundational Testament reports that the ancient Jew practiced something or expressed something in a way clearly dated does not mean that the practice or expression can be ignored by Christians. This is true even in relation to something like the detailed ways of sacrificing animals in temple worship found in Leviticus (see my discussion of sacrifice in chapter eleven).

The dilemma appears in more than dated elements of the Foundational Testament. Sometimes the Final Testament carries over from the Foundational Testament a teaching that it does not abandon, but that Christians later, under the guidance of the Spirit of Yesuha, came to *reconsider*. For instance, the second-class status of women is assumed in both Testaments. We read this in 1 Peter 3:7. "Husbands, in the same way, show consideration for your wives in your life together,

---

7. Dennis F. Kinlaw, *Lectures in Old Testament Theology* (Francis Asbury Press, 2010), 72.

paying honor to the woman as the weaker sex, since they too are also heirs of the gracious gift of life."

Most Christians now reject the "weaker sex" status of women, a rejection they see as a natural extension of the teaching and actions of Yeshua. The extension is a better insight now being inspired by the Spirit of Yeshua. The final chapter of this book explores such a "surplus of meaning." Things assumed even in the Final Testament are not necessarily is to be taken as the last word on the subject—unless the one speaking that word is Yeshua himself.

In the fulfilling done by Yeshua, he showed a natural and heavy reliance on the Foundational Testament. He also did some reinterpreting of some of its key texts in light of his fuller revelation, or better, his more proper understanding of the previous revelation. And this process goes on. Beyond the earthly life of Yeshua and the text of the Final Testament that reports it, there appears to be some still-growing understanding of biblical truth and its present implications, but only growth in a carefully limited sense. It is growth with the ministry of Yeshua's Spirit in full control. The Spirit of God reveals nothing not fully in accord with the teachings and person of Yeshua himself. Consult chapters twelve and thirteen for the paradox of a "closed" canon that in some way remains "open."

How should Christians think of the relationship between "Old" to "New"? It is no simple relationship. For now, I will admit to being guilty of what a critic once said of a book on the "Old" Testament by Davie Napier, a Christian biblical scholar. The critic regretted that Napier's "Christian slip was showing." I also readily admit to being a Christian. In part, that means to me that there is an essential, important, and continuing relationship between the Old and the New, the Foundational and the Final. This relationship is critical, with the essential role of the Foundational to be honored, meaning that my own Christian slip may be showing. So be it.

I will state my thesis plainly. A Jew not embracing the Final Testament does not fully understand the Foundational Testament. On the other hand, and most emphatically, the Foundational Testament should not be viewed by a Christian as little more than an introduction to the Final Testament. At least at its theological base, which sometimes lies only below the surface of the text, the Foundational Testament remains absolutely essential for properly understanding the Final Testament. This is a paradox as delicate as it is important.

Christians must embrace the Bible, *all of it*. Christians also must recognize that they have added much to the complexity so far as others are concerned. Judaism, Islam, and Christianity are the three great faith communities that have the Foundational Testament in common and are committed to its central teaching, Yahweh, the one and only, the sovereign, creator God. But Christianity has added to the theological mix its classic teaching of the "Trinity," God somehow being one and also three. I will address this difficult paradox in chapter six.

The early writing disciples of Yeshua, the human authors of the Final Testament, relied heavily on their beloved Foundational Testament. However, they did so selectively, and with some refocusing of certain ancient texts in light of the dramatic events centered in the life, death, and resurrection of Yeshua. This tendency to selectivity and refocusing proved the path to the future; it also remains the source of many questions for Christians who now approach the Foundational Testament cautiously, if at all, and for Jews who judge that their sacred texts have been violated by the biased Christian reading of them.

For today's Christians, the challenge is to separate the enduring from the passing in the ancient biblical materials of the Jews. The textual surface, with its sometimes temporary cultural expressions, must be understood by the beneath-the-surface theological meanings that endure even to today. Gaining such understanding is the great challenge. To accomplish this very important task, at least four steps are required:

1. We will have to go to and then *beneath* the ancient text of the Foundational Testament, first with respect and then also with discrimination.
2. Then we will have to go to Yeshua, the Jew, taking our tentative reading to the One who finally is the measure of all things for Christians.
3. Finally, we will have to journey on with the Spirit of Yeshua to our very own times and needs and particular applications, bringing with us the past as we search for the future.
4. The above three steps must be taken with caution, humility, and sometimes repentance. There is much history between Jews and Christians that now makes the process very difficult. That sad story begins right in the Final Testament and stretches to this very day (see chapter two).

In order to be a true *biblical* Christian, in order to even really understand the finality of the "New" Testament, Christians are called to their earlier biblical foundation. We are to walk again that road to

Emmaus with Yeshua, encountering a surprising and unrecognized Jewish visitor on the way. A *fulfilled* Jewish faith and a *grounded* Christian faith equally depend on who that visitor really was—and still is. How did the two men of old, walking dejectedly on that road, come to know the real identity of Yeshua? How will we come to know him?

The report of this incident is found in Luke 24. The now resurrected Yeshua appeared by the sides of these confused and dejected Jews. He inquired about their conversation, and gently chided them for not understanding their own holy books. They were "slow of heart to believe all that the prophets have declared!" (Lk. 24:25). Yeshua corrected this situation by dipping deeply into the Jewish Scriptures: "Then beginning with Moses and all the prophets, he interpreted to them the things about himself in all the scriptures" (Lk. 24:27). We will take a similar approach here—how does one improve upon how Yeshua did it? Followers of the resurrected Yeshua should return to their Jewish foundations in order to understand their Master and their own faith journeys with him into the future.

The Jews often are thought of as the people with an exceptionally long and influential tradition, maybe the longest in human history. This is the theme of the Tevye stories popularized in the musical *Fiddler on the Roof*. Why does that fiddler sit on the roof and keep playing his fiddle? It's tradition! When the Passover is celebrated or the Torah read in synagogues still today, parents are instructing their children in the great tradition. The distinctive Jewish identity is being kept alive. Similarly, our intention here is to help keep this tradition alive and meaningful for contemporary Christians.

The *TANAKH*, the Jewish Bible, or what Christians usually call the "Old Testament," tells the story of Israel. Beneath the surface of this story is always its theological underpinnings. The surface narrative of the Foundational Testament, when viewed in light of these theological underpinnings, is what can assist Christians in knowing their own story and thus being their true spiritual selves in today's world. Sometimes it is necessary to slip beneath the text's surface to rediscover its supporting theological base.

Jews and Christians may differ in their understanding of the *outcome* of this Jewish historical drama, but they are in close agreement about the unique character of the history that the *TANAKH* records. To state that character most simply: "The man of Israel...knew that he had been addressed by One who had spoken to him in the events of the great tradition of which he was a part...."[8] In other words, God *is* and *has spoken*. To know this God and to hear and obey the divine voice is truth and life itself.

Unique or not, many Christians today quietly dismiss much of the Foundational Testament as essentially irrelevant for them. The observation of G. Ernest Wright in 1944 remains accurate: "The current fashion of thought has regarded the Old Testament as a monument of antiquity, interesting to the historian, the literary critic, and the archaeologist, but of little serious value for the life and thought of the modern Christian."[9] This "fashion" may be current, but it is intolerable.

Paul, a well-trained Jew, may have written large portions of the Final Testament in the Greek language, but the inner world of his thought was primarily his Jewish heritage. He says that "the Gentiles have become fellow heirs [with the Jews], members of the same body, and sharers in the promise in Christ Jesus through the gospel" (Eph. 3:6). Nearly all Christians are now Gentiles, and all have Israel's history as their own heritage. The Foundational and Final Testaments are divisions of the same book and carriers of the same story.

Why title these pages *Beneath the Surface*? The reason is simple given much of what's on the surface of the ancient Jewish text. When a Christian today tries to read the Foundational Testament, there is so much that appears very old and difficult to understand. For most Christians, whether they admit it or not, it is just too much. It is not just the difficulty of understanding. There is much in the Foundational Testament that, at least at the surface level of the text, seems clearly irrelevant for today, even morally objectionable to a sensitive Christian trying to follow Yeshua.

All of this would not be such a problem except that, for most Christians, the Foundational Testament is believed to be part of the Bible that remains *inspired* by God for contemporary training in righteousness (2 Tim. 3:16). What is divinely inbreathed surely is to be taken seriously, understood, and followed by today's Christians. For that to happen, however, much is needed for biblical "inspiration" to be more than a meaningless creed—except in relation to the Final Testa-

---

8. James Muilenburg, *The Way of Israel: Biblical Faith and Ethics* (N.Y.: Harper Torchbooks, 1961), 15.

9. G. Ernest Wright, *The Challenge of Israel's Faith* (Chicago: University of Chicago Press, 1944), v.

ment and the scattered "acceptable" parts of the Foundational Testament (like some but not all of the psalms).

The Bible Is Neither Flat Nor Dormant

Where can we begin in unraveling this dilemma? We need to go *below the surface* of the text of the Foundational Testament in order to discover what was so compelling for the ancient Jews, and for Yeshua himself, and what remains inspired by God for the instruction of the disciples of Yeshua in all times. This will require an understanding of the Foundational Testament that many Christians do not have.

What Christians awkwardly call the "Old" Testament was the only "Bible" of Yeshua, and he made clear that he had not come to set it aside (Matt. 5:17). It was his heart, his heritage, his "mental furniture," central to his understanding of God's nature and will. He loved, studied, and frequently quoted from the holy books of his people. Yeshua's "Bible" was essentially what Jews now call the *TANAKH*, an acronym made up of the initial consonants of the three major divisions of the Jewish Bible: *Torah* ("Law"), *Nevi'im* ("Prophets"), and *Ketuvim* ("Writings").

Yeshua obviously cherished these sacred materials. They were an indispensable resource for his coming to know himself, his Father God, and the way to live his very special life. As we noted above, after his resurrection he suddenly appeared on the road to Emmaus. He introduced himself to two unsuspecting Jewish men with three important Messianic references, one from each division of the Foundational Testament (Lk. 24:27). This clearly suggested that he was the fullness of the meaning and expectation of *TANAKH*. Therefore, to be ignorant of *TANAKH* is to be ignorant of Yeshua.

So, as we begin our approach to the ancient texts belonging to Jews and Christians, we assume that both Testaments have great and continuing value, something not always clear to contemporary Christians. The Foundational Testament is a virtual library of the Jewish heritage. It has considerable length and literary complexity, including (1) the surface text and (2) what we will identify as the critical *theological roots* that lie below the surface of the text (see chapter four for detail).

Given these points of beginning, here is an opening insight worthy of careful consideration as the *TANAKH* is approached by today's Christians. Sometimes images and metaphors communicate best when ultimate and paradoxical subjects are at hand. One image is going beneath the surface, this book's title. Another relates to topography.

The landscape of this world we call Earth is not flat, nor is the biblical text. Of course, there are many places on the surface of the Earth that are very flat. If those places were the only evidence being considered, we naturally would assume that the world is like what our eyes selectively see—flat. But the planet as a whole is not flat at all. Quite apart from the high mountains and deep valleys in numerous visible locations, there are many more that are invisible to humans because they are located far beneath the great oceans. We now know that our planet is much like a big blue ball drifting in space. Likewise, the text of the Foundational Testament has depth and movement and progress, with much of it beneath the surface of the words on the pages. Biblical materials have a rich texture. They are not *flat* and, as the final two chapters of this book will attempt to explain, neither are they *dormant*.

The ancient biblical text was written over centuries of time, by many different people, and in the midst of various cultures. At least on the surface of the text, influence from all this is quite evident. Therefore, in this and other ways, the Foundational Testament is not stagnant like an isolated pond's surface when there is no life-giving spring bubbling up from deep below. Instead, it is living water. Its life is sometimes called "progressive revelation," meaning that more was given by God than the original writers/editors understood, or at least more would be understood by faithful believers as time and reflection proceeded. Here is how one biblical scholar puts it:

> The Old Testament is a living document. It is not one-dimensional, but multi-dimensional, and sometimes you can only really understand something in its depths if it is expressed in other terms. As a result, you can find what we might call crosscurrents in the text, currents that move, as it were, against each other so that you will have to think awhile before you can get the streams consonant with each other.[10]

Reading the Bible as a "flat" book is the unbalanced approach characteristic of a narrow and rigid "fundamentalism." To level things this way is to run from the paradoxes and dishonor what God has actually provided, mystery and all. A complex and developmental biblical text, which is in fact what we have, has a dynamic to it that must be recognized and taken into account. Caution should be exercised here, however. This dynamic, with its diversity and openness, must not be exaggerated to the point of robbing the text of its distinctive claim to

---

10. Dennis F. Kinlaw, *Lectures in Old Testament Theology*, 413-414.

being *God's* Word. However, this dynamic should stop us from treating biblical texts "as pieces of a flat puzzle and trying to force them together in case there is something to be learned precisely from their not fitting neatly. Our desire for rational, propositional truth must be placed beneath the necessity to allow the text to say what it wants to and in the manner it wants to."[11]

New Wine in Old Skins?

The Christian who decides to avoid the Foundational Testament is at a great disadvantage. That Christian will be in a poor position to read well the Final Testament. How does one understand a movie when seeing only the last ten minutes? How can one appreciate a major essay if the presuppositions of the argument are laid out initially and that part is not read with care or at all? How can one understand a progressive revelation from God when it comes in the ragged clothes of our human history, with only the most recent historical events taken seriously? In short, one cannot. The fact is that the Final Testament, while a flowering of the Foundational, remains heavily dependent on it. The basis of Christian faith lies in the great insights and beliefs of the Hebrew tradition. The Foundational Testament calls Christians back to their roots that provide the potential for the proper way forward.

Followers of Yeshua today must not stop by merely glancing at the apparent clutter on the surface of the ancient Foundational writing—God asking a man to kill his son, religious people slaughtering many others to get what they were sure God had promised them, implied support for human slavery and multiple wives, animal sacrifices in worship, etc. The treasures of divine revelation lie in the theology beneath the surface of even texts like these. Christians unwilling to go after this in-depth treasure are denying the inspiration of *all Scripture* (2 Tim. 3:16) and impoverishing themselves spiritually and doctrinally. Remember that the text about divine inspiration found in 2 Timothy, at least in the first instance, did *not* refer to the Final Testament—which was just coming to exist at the time.

The subtitle of this present book, "Reclaiming the Old Testament for Today's Christians," assumes that the word "Old," when attached to "Testament," implies that the ancient Jewish writings are now to be

---

11. Clark Pinnock and Barry Callen, *The Scripture Principle: Reclaiming the Full Authority of the Bible* (Lexington, KY: Emeth Press, 3rd ed., 2009), 221-222.

viewed by Christians as outdated and preliminary material since the better, the "New," the clearer and more advanced has become available. Should we not, then, dispense with the old when the new has come? According to Yeshua in Mark 2:22, are we not to avoid putting "new wine into old wineskins; otherwise, the wine will burst the skins, and the wine is lost, and so are the skins"? These pages will attempt to answer this question by insisting that any such throw-away approach is wrongly applied to the two Testaments that now comprise the Christian Bible.

The Final Testament frequently sends one back to the Foundational Testament, often in order to clarify who Yeshua is and what he has done. He was the culmination of a long tradition of pain and persistent hope. To skip this tradition is to lose the depths and dimensions of its eventual fulfillment. The fact is that, as Christians understand things, the culminating work of Yeshua completed the actions of God "which began not on that first Christmas night in Bethlehem of Judea, but somewhere around 1750 B.C. in Mesopotamia with the first forbear of the Hebrew people [Abraham].... Christianity did not start with the events recorded in the New Testament. It started with the events recorded in the twelfth chapter of Genesis."[12]

Quoting Sigmund Freud is certainly an unusual choice when dealing with biblical teachings, but wisdom is where you find it. Born of Jewish parents, he once made an important statement on our present subject. The ironic fact is, he argued, that Christian self-interest demands that the last vestiges of anti-Semitism be eradicated. Like it or not, Jew and Christian belong to each other; anti-Semitism is a common enemy bent upon destroying the church no less than the synagogue. Freud understood that "the hatred of Judaism is at bottom hatred for Christianity."[13]

Think of it this way. The amazing functions that flash so routinely on our computer screens graphically provide the many results we want. What we take for granted is that beneath the surface of the results on the screen lies the sophisticated software that makes it all possible. Similarly, the full flowering of God savingly with us in Yeshua is now on the screen of the Final Testament. That flowering, however, functions properly and remains true to itself only because of

---

12. Paul J. and Elizabeth Achtemeier, *The Old Testament Roots of Our Faith* (Peabody, Mass.: Hendrickson Publishers, 1994), 4-5.

13. Sigmund Freud, quoted by Paul R. Carlson, *O Christian! O Jew!* (Elgin, ILL: David C. Cook Publishing, 1974), 231.

the theological "software" embedded deeply in the Foundational Testament. That is why we go *beneath the surface* of the text. There we find the theology that informs both Testaments, and what also wishes to inform our Christian lives of faith today.

Who is God? Why has God chosen to be with us so dramatically and sacrificially? What does God expect of us now? What tends to go wrong with the faith community over time? What is essential and what is only culturally passing? What does the word "Christ" even mean? Answers to all such questions lie deep in the textual currents and underlying theological themes of the Foundational Testament. Christians dare not ignore these Jewish answers, and they are to be found nowhere else.

Admittedly, there floats considerable clutter on the surface of the most ancient of the biblical texts. That is why Christians often must go below, looking for those underlying fountains of divine revelation, those basics of Jewish faith and practice that later would flower into the full-orbed Christian faith. We must learn that abruptly removing the later flower from its earlier native soil will wilt the petals, drain the flower of its brilliant colors, and push Christian faith in the direction of serious perversions, and maybe death. Therefore, these pages seek to recall the only adequate foundation on which true Christian faith can be built and sustained.

This book's presentation of the adequate foundation is organized in four sections. The first highlights the several Jewish orientations necessary for grasping this critical but complex subject. The second identifies the important undercurrents of theological truth that remain foundational for Christian believers. The third presents a series of inter-Testament case studies, testing our thesis in relation to some particularly problematic biblical texts. The fourth looks beyond the two biblical Testaments. We must not confine ourselves only to the past, a limitation God surely would not want us to impose on his ongoing work in this world.

Behind all four sections of this book lies one persistent prayer. May the God who originally inspired the whole of the Bible enliven it again, all of it, for the instruction of Christian believers in these challenging days!

SECTION ONE

NECESSARY JEWISH ORIENTATIONS

IS THIS REALLY IMPORTANT?

John Adams wrote a letter to F. A. Vanderkemp on February 16, 1809. He said that "the Hebrews have done more to civilize man than any other nation.... [They gave humankind] the doctrine of a supreme, intelligent, wise, almighty sovereign of the universe, which I believe to be the great essential principle of all morality, and consequently of all civilization."[1]

Every Christian must acknowledge an immense debt of gratitude to the Jewish people. The Gospel is the good news that Jesus is the Christ.... Those who worship Jesus as their Divine Lord and Saviour have thus received God's most precious gift through the Jewish people. Therefore they have compelling reason to show love to that people in every possible way.[2]

The original occasion for my interest in the topic of this book was an undergraduate course I taught for many years at Anderson University. I called the course "Hebrew Roots of Christian Faith." The more I taught it the more I became convinced that it was meeting a critical

---

1. Quoted by Paul Copan, *Is God a Moral Monster? Making Sense of the Old Testament God* (Grand Rapids: Baker Books, 2011), 216.
2. "The Willowbank Declaration on the Christian Gospel and the Jewish People," World Evangelical Alliance, 1989.

need of today's young Christians. Virtually all of my students identified themselves as Christians at the beginning of each semester, but rejected the category "Jew" for themselves. In an early lecture, it was my practice to ask the class why, if really Christians, they were not also Jews. Is the ideal not to be a Jewish Christian?

Few students were sure what I meant, and they doubted that connecting Jewish and Christian was ideal—or even appropriate. So the basic issue of the course always emerged quickly. The students had an aversion for the "Old" Testament. "Wasn't the Old somehow replaced by the New?" "Jesus is quite enough for me." Of course, they were not alone, likely having acquired their attitudes from parents and preachers and Sunday school teachers.

My students had to be helped to recognize the problem they had—and that numerous Christians today also have. They readily affirmed divine inspiration of the whole Bible, but in practice devalued and virtually ignored the meaningfulness and contemporary authority of the Foundational Testament--the ancient text they usually carried around with them. Actually, some of them avoided the carrying task. They had only the Final Testament, with a few having one that at least included the Psalms. The rest of the Foundational Testament was out of sight and certainly out of mind—until they saw the demands of my class syllabus.

The Issues Are Not Optional

A central goal of that college course of mine became replacing a sometimes toxic vacuum of awareness with an appreciation for what it should mean to be a "Jewish Christian." I insisted that Christian faith is significantly impoverished and even distorted by ignorance of and especially an aversion to its Jewish roots. As I sought resources for my "Hebraic recovery task," I soon became indebted to particular individuals and organizations whose writings and ministries became particularly helpful to me. I express my debt to Rabbi Jeff Adler, Zola Levitt, Dwight Pryor, Clark Williamson, Marvin Wilson, Brad Young, and many others, along with organizations ranging from "Jews for Jesus" to the "National Conference of Christians and Jews."

In recent generations, there have been several "quests" to discover the real Yeshua. Albert Schweitzer and Rudolf Bultmann emphasized respectively the apocalyptic context and the perceived need to demythologize Yeshua. The "Jesus Seminar" scholars more recently have come to question the historical accuracy of the Gospels. They look for the real Yeshua elsewhere. Joachim Jeremias insisted that the teachings of Yeshua must be understood in their original Jewish context, heralding a new "quest" for the real Yeshua that now has been carried on by E. P. Sanders, N. T. Wright, James Charlesworth, Robert L. Lindsey, David Flusser, and the Jerusalem School of Synoptic Research. The consensus view of this latter group is that "we must situate Jesus fully within Second Temple Judaism and we must draw upon Jewish sources if we are to more fully understand the historical Jesus of Nazareth."[3]

An alma mater of mine, Chicago Theological Seminary, has sponsored for decades its "Center for Jewish-Christian Studies" (now including Islam). This seminary recognizes the urgent need for religious leaders to understand and appreciate differing faith communities. In fact, the peace of the world now appears to depend in large part on such understanding. This fact alone should make the case for the importance of the subject at hand! With this importance comes a key clarification.

To understand and appreciate a differing faith community is not necessarily to agree with it. Peace and diversity can co-exist when nurtured by mutual understanding. In our kind of world, this must be the case. Even so, several contentious issues certainly remain. One is whether or not Christians should join inter-faith dialogues with the ultimate purpose of trying to *convert* others to Christianity.

Many Christians are respectful of others, but are convinced nonetheless that they have good news that must be delivered to others needing it. One example of a strong "yes" to the conversion goal in relation to Jews is the Center for Judaic Studies at Liberty University in Virginia. Its founder, the late Jerry Falwell, was lauded by many Jewish leaders for his staunch support of the contemporary State of Israel; he also was feared for his uncompromising evangelical commitment to converting Jews to Christian faith.

Other Christian leaders strongly criticize an evangelistic agenda like that of Falwell. But if the goal is not converting Jews to Yeshua, should not Christians at least be fully supportive of the modern State of Israel? On the other hand, if they do support it, do they not thereby alienate much of the Arab world? Is friendship with Jews more important than friendship with Moslems? Politics, evangelism, and the desire for world peace can be a volatile mix these days, all complicating the Christian's proper reading of the Foundational Testament today.

---

3. Dwight A. Pryor, *Behold the Man!* (Dayton, Ohio: Center for Judaic-Christian Studies, 2005), 3.

The issues at hand obviously are numerous, large, and not easily avoided, nor are they located only in the past. They demand center stage in today's highly interconnected world. We will not address at length the major issue of Islam. We will address the issue of the contemporary State of Israel in the section "The Gift of Land" in chapter seven. We will confine ourselves primarily to the first task of Christians, reaffirming their own roots in the Bible, *all of it*.

If the Christian community does not restore its essential Jewishness, she will continue struggling without a key dimension of the gospel of Yeshua, its historical context and the groundwork for its fundamental doctrinal concepts. When the church proclaims a gospel removed from its native soil, it risks failing to proclaim "the whole counsel of God" (Acts 20:27). It easily can be reduced to communicating what Paul once called "another gospel" (Gal. 1:6-9). Such risks constitute more than a marginal concern!

To push the "Jewish issue" brings with it an obvious danger, one that echoes throughout the pages of the Final Testament itself (see chapter two). The danger is the reappearance of the ancient heresy of "Judaizing," meaning an insistence that a non-Jew cannot be "saved" only by believing in Yeshua the Messiah; there also must be conversion to the religion of Judaism and faithfulness to a range of Jewish cultural and religious practices. The problem is that having to be a Jew before becoming a Christian implies a legalism that falsely sees God's law as a set of inflexible rules and practices, like circumcision (see chapter seven). By clear contrast, today's call for the restoration of the Jewish roots of Christian faith is *not* a new Judiazing.

What, then, is it? It is primarily the re-establishing of one central fact: "The Old Testament is the theological key for opening the door to the New Testament. The theology of the early church was Hebraic to its very heart; it was the Old Testament theology now raised to its ultimate spiritual significance in the coming of Yeshua."[4] To think and witness as Christians without conscious connection to the Jewish base of the faith is to wander in a dangerous vacuum and finally resurrect the old heresy of Marcion that dispenses with the Jewish base altogether (see chapter two).

So the questions come, both from my university students and from large numbers of believers who now fill the pews of Christian churches. Why should today's Christians care about relating more closely and constructively to their Jewish roots? Why care about the "Old" when

---

4. Marvin Wilson, *Our Father Abraham*, 113.

the "New" is here? Why even carry around the thick Foundational ("Old") Testament if in practice its meaning often is not clear and its relevance is questionable at best? Why go back when forward seems the most natural thing to do? I often hear this: "The Jews are yesterday; we are the future people of Jesus." These questions deserve answers.

And there are many more questions. Is Judaism an adequate faith on its own, conveying full "salvation" to its faithful, or is it merely Christianity without Christ, a good preface with the rest of the book missing? Is Christianity an adequate faith on its own, having no more need for what went before? Was it not the Jews who turned on Yeshua and had him killed? On the other hand, did not Yeshua die willingly with beloved words of the Foundational Testament on his lips and his Father (Yahweh) filling his consciousness?

This book assumes that there are satisfying answers to all such questions. They are compelling answers that lead to a more whole and effective identity for the people called Christian. They reject any reversion from two Testaments back to one. The true circumstance is clear and extremely important. Judaism without Christianity is unfulfilled; Christianity without Judaism is rootless, definitionless, and open to easy distortion.

If an essential relationship between the two biblical Testaments is not enough to make the subject of critical concern, there are other reasons why this subject is timely today. Just turning on the television or reading a newspaper or an internationally sensitive blog should make this graphically clear. Christians, Jews, and Moslems are locked in dangerous conflicts around the world. The conflicts are social, political, economic, military, and religious in nature, even though these three faith communities all stem from the same Abraham tradition and the same Foundational Testament of the Jews and Yeshua. Any hope of lessening misunderstanding and heightening mutual respect and trust among these religious communities could be very important for the whole world.

Christianity's most solemn events, the life, death, and resurrection of Yeshua, began with a Jewish Passover meal in Jerusalem. Rabbi Yeshua was both honoring his Jewish heritage and opening the door to its fulfillment and widening future. As Passover and Easter now are closely connected, so are the light of hope for God's persecuted people (celebration of Hanukah) and the true light that has come into this world (celebration of Christmas). Before the eventful last week of his earthly life, Yeshua had been "transfigured" with Moses and Elijah (Matt. 17:1-13), great representatives of the Jewish Law and Prophets.

It is obvious that the Jewish reporter of this unusual event, Matthew, saw great significance in who these two men had been and who Yeshua now was in relation to them. Even so, many of today's disciples of Yeshua seldom do much careful reading of the Foundational Testament where the stories of Moses and Elijah are found. The significance of it all gets lost for them.

The site of the Jewish temple in Jerusalem, revered by Yeshua and now a pilgrimage goal of many Christians (the location only, of course, since the temple is gone), is also the general site of the Al-Aqsa Mosque and the Dome of the Rock, regarded by the majority of Moslems as the third holiest site in the Islamic faith. In that pivotal place, the three Abrahamic-rooted faith communities find common roots, and often collide, threatening and not enriching each other. If Christians are to speak a word of credible witness to Jews and Moslems, they first will need to know the Abrahamic tradition well, and do some confessing.

Confess what? Chapter two will detail some of what needs to be confessed. The histories and sacred writings of these three Abrahamic faith communities are interwoven in many ways. Their actual relationships, unfortunately, have been troubled and even tragic. Blame belongs to all three. The facts must be known, faced, and somehow resolved if peace is to be found in today's world. Accomplishing this will not be easy.

Some Christians say that it is an insult to tell Jews that accepting Yeshua as their Messiah and Lord is necessary for their salvation when millions of Jews have been brutally persecuted by people professing to follow Yeshua. One Christian theologian judges that a Christian who cannot look a Jew in the face and deal credibly with the Christian complicity in the Holocaust of the 1930s and 1940s has no integrity in his or her own believing—and certainly no hope of or right to successful witnessing to that Jew about Yeshua.[5]

If Christian integrity has been lost and is to be regained, the conversion question still remains. Do Jews who are faithful to their divinely-inspired tradition need to hear and accept the good news of Yeshua to supplement their faith? The testimony of the Final Testament is that Yeshua came to his own people as well as to the rest of the world (Jn. 1:11). To withhold from Jews a witness to Yeshua as Lord seems to some Christians to single them out for a significant disservice. To in-

---

5. Clark Williamson, *A Guest in the House of Israel: Post-Holocaust Church Theology* (Louisville: Westminster/John Knox Press, 1993).

sist that they be converted to belief in Yeshua as their Messiah seems to other Christians a sign of disrespect for Jews and the significance of their heritage.

Christians trying to share their faith with Jews usually have great difficulty, partly in light of the many past sins committed by Christians against Jews (see chapter two). Here is a clear statement of the complexity being faced by Christians:

> Some have protested that it would be anti-Semitic (anti-Jewish) to desire for Jews to be evangelized with the gospel of Jesus. One theologian has said that if Jews said "yes" to Jesus, there would be no more Jews—that Hitler's goal would be accomplished. However...many Jewish believers in Jesus embrace their Jewishness more so than they did prior to believing in Messiah.... Not to witness to Jewish people would be anti-Semitic, because that would exclude them from opportunities to respond to the gospel of Messiah Jesus.[6]

Very difficult issues intertwine—evangelism, anti-Semitism, historical sin, current political realities, etc.

And there is even more. Terrorism is now a daily fact of international life. Hundreds of millions of Moslems have a faith that is deeply rooted in the Foundational Testament and its Abrahamic tradition, the common spiritual ancestor of Jews, Christians, and Moslems. They have a strong conviction. It is that Christianity and Judaism are enemies of *Allah* (different from *Yahweh*?)? Radicalized Moslems think so and sometimes strike back with violence.[7]

The numbers "9/11" now are burned into the American psyche. The stakes obviously are high indeed, and solutions are not being found easily. Christians falling in love again with their Jewish heritage is one place to start, and without necessarily taking a particular political stance in relation to the current State of Israel (see chapter seven). And yet, many will view any Christian realignment with Jewish roots as a stand against Islam, and even a diminishing of Christianity.

---

6. James R. Leaman, *Faith Roots: Learning from and Sharing Witness with Jewish People* (Nappanee, IN: Evangel Press, 1993), 21-22.

7. It should be recognized that Islam in general is committed to peace, as are most of its adherents. This is why I say "radicalized" Moslems. As the extremists, they represent the minority of the faithful.

Jew and/or Gentile?

Jews typically assume that all Christians are Gentiles (non-Jews). They reject the claim of today's "Messianic Jews" that one can be a true Jew and at the same time a fully committed follower of Yeshua. Some Christians assume that Yeshua was the first "Christian." He is acceptable because, they wrongly assume, he repudiated his Jewish heritage and became something other than the Jew he was.

A Jewish reporter once interviewed Edith Schaeffer about her Christianity. Her explanation of her deep faith in Yeshua caused him to say, "It sounds like a Jewish religion to me." Her reply? "Christianity *is* Jewish."[8] I join Schaeffer by arguing in the following chapters that the wholeness of biblical faith might properly be called "Judeo-Christianity." It is, if you will, the Yeshua form of Judaism.

Since Yeshua said he came to *reform* and not *replace* his Jewish heritage (Heb. 9:10), Christians today surely are to champion, with understanding and joy, the work Yeshua so sacrificially completed. Christians also need to consider this thoughtfully: "If Judaism were to cease to be...then Christianity would be poorer, more open to distortion. I as a Christian need Judaism to be Judaism lest the ultimate truth of God be compromised or even lost in the shallowness of a rootless Christianity."[9] Christians also should consider this:

> [Christian] theologians have read the Gospels as Christian literature, written by the church and for the church. When Jesus is viewed among the Gentiles, the significance of Jewish culture and custom is minimized, or forgotten altogether. But when Jesus is viewed as a Jew, within the context of First Century Judaism, an entirely different portrait emerges.[10]

The Final Testament certainly sheds fresh light on the witness of the Foundational Testament. Without the Foundational as the base, the Final is adrift and clearly in increased danger of distortion as it moves through alien cultures and multiple centuries. Christians are less able to interpret properly their own Scriptures when they fail to see them in their original Jewish context. They do not realize that the Final Tes-

---

8. Edith Schaeffer, *Christianity Is Jewish* (Wheaton, IL: Tyndale, 1975), 11.

9. John Shelby Spong, "The Continuing Christian Need for Judaism," in *The Christian Century* (September 26, 1979), 918.

10. Brad Young, *Jesus the Jewish Theologian*, as quoted by Dwight Pryor, *Behold the Man!*, 63.

tament is a flowering of ancient Jewish theological themes and the fulfillment of Jewish historical precedents and prophetic expectations.

Definitions, goals, and historic relationships are confusing to all parties, and they easily become sources of conflict. Consider the following as one proposed way to walk carefully through this maze. "The witness about Jesus is not an invitation to convert from Jewishness to Christianity, but to turn from sinfulness to salvation in Jesus. Jewish believers in Jesus are still Jewish-Messianic Jews.... Whether Jewish or Gentile, all believers in Messiah Jesus are 'Messianic' believers."[11] For some, this is a viable way ahead. For others, particularly Jews, it is doubletalk that leads nowhere good.

Previewing What Is To Come

We will look carefully in the following pages at a series of particular beliefs that originate in the Foundational Testament, find fulfillment in the Final Testament, and remain critical for a necessary Jewish influence on the integrity of Christian faith today. As a brief preface to these considerations, consider this:

> To recapture the Jewish sense of a God who is made known in history, a God who calls us to lay down our fears and step boldly into tomorrow, to reclaim that Jewish sense of God's ultimacy so that we can see all other religious symbols as less than ultimate and therefore subject to change, to rediscover our Jewish roots which time after time unlock the doors of Holy Scripture, all of these can become the fruits of the dialogue between Christian and Jew.[12]

To enter into inter-faith dialogue is important, but not enough. Christians engaging Jews in dialogue need to know, value, and profit from their Foundational Testament.

The content and organization of this book is designed to assist with this knowing, valuing, and profiting. Christians today need to know how much is at stake (chapter one), understand and confess what has gone so wrong in the past (chapter two), learn how to read the whole Bible properly (chapter three), identify the great theological themes that underlie both biblical Testaments (chapters four through ten), grapple with case studies of select troubling texts of the Foundational Testament (chapter eleven), and be filled with God's Spirit in

---

11. Leaman, *Faith Roots*, 33.
12. Spong, *op. cit.*, 921-922.

order to keep the meanings of the past relevant for the living of these present days (chapters twelve and thirteen).

Christians, of course, are Christ people, faithful followers of Messiah Yeshua. While the pages to come gladly affirm this Yeshua centeredness, they will do so with the following key assumption always in mind:

> We see [in Yeshua] a man who was thoroughly Jewish and operated comfortably and creatively within the Hebraic culture, traditions, and worldview of Second Temple Judaism. The Scriptures of Israel defined his identity, charted the course of his ministry, and served as the inspired source for his teachings. The Sages of Israel bequeathed to him a rich legacy of learning and wisdom and interpretative tools with which to explicate and illuminate the Scriptures for us.[13]

---

13. Karen H. Pryor, ed., *A Continuing Quest: The Dwight A. Pryor Legacy Collection* (Dayton, OH: Center for Judaic-Christian Studies, 2011), 55.

WHAT WENT WRONG?

I will make those of the synagogue of Satan who say they are Jews and are not, but are lying—I will make them come and bow down before your [Yeshua's] feet... (Rev. 3:9).

"The Holocaust of the twentieth century stands as an unparalleled event. Nazi propaganda stated that the human race must be "purified" by ridding it of Jews. The "final solution" to the Jewish "problem" was camps, gas chambers, and crematoria.... Some six million Jewish lives were destroyed. It is to the shame of Christians everywhere that the established [Christian] Church did so little to prevent or protest the slaughter.[1]

How sad and even tragic that something went very wrong in the relationships among the three Abraham-rooted faith communities. Today's deep divisions among Judaism, Christianity, and Islam are bringing great danger to the whole world. Beyond the political, economic (oil), and military dangers, there is the possibility of Christianity virtually losing its true identity as a *Judeo*-Christian faith tradition.

The history of these deep divisions makes the present need for recovery both urgent and most difficult. The Islamic dimension is very

---

1. Marvin Wilson, *Our Father Abraham*, 100-101.

important, as anyone knows who is aware of current world events. Unfortunately, dealing with this is beyond the scope of this book. We will focus on the serious divide between Jews and Christians—enough of a problem for one book.

Often there is a mixture of strong emotions between parents and their children. They frequently include cycles of dependence and rebellion, sometimes even love and hate, especially during the teenage years. Judaism is Christianity's parent. Unfortunately, the potential of a negative relationship has become so real and has marred most or all centuries since the time of Yeshua. Both overt and covert acts of rejection and even violence have soiled the pages of history with unforgettable amounts of both blood and shame. Some of the shameful things came from the Jewish side early; most of it since has been an anti-Semitism coming from Christians and others. The European Holocaust of the twentieth century stands as possibly the worst of all, happening in the midst of Martin Luther's "Christianized" Germany.

Recent years have seen the dawning of a somewhat better time in Jewish-Christian relations. One intent of this book is to extend and deepen this dawning. But the improvement cannot be accomplished easily and the motives for attempting it need careful scrutiny. Advancement in a positive direction depends in part on understanding what went wrong in the first place. The more we know the less we are likely to repeat the sins of the past.

One Heritage Ruptured Into Two

The earliest Christian communities faced the struggle of dealing with the fundamental issue of their identity. Who were they? What were they to believe? How should they understand who Yeshua was in relation to their Jewish messianic expectations? What was to be considered dependable authority as they dealt with such questions? How should their communities be administered and relate to each other and their synagogues? Most of all, who were they in relation to their previous identity as Jews of the great Abrahamic, Mosaic, and Davidic tradition? These questions were being debated and decided very early, with the process highly visible in the Final Testament itself.

We apparently can say with assurance that the first big struggle of the Jewish believers in Yeshua as Lord was their continuing relationship with Judaism. Soon the tension-filled process of deciding led to a nearly complete separation of the two groups of Jews. The pain and irony of this separation would be great. After all, the Christian church was born and reared in Judaism. Yeshua, his disciples, the earliest converts to Yeshua, and the great Christian theologian Paul were all Jewish.

It has been well argued that it is proper to refer both to Yeshua and Paul as "Jewish theologians."[2] Most of the early Christians likely understood themselves to be Jewish, with their belief in Yeshua as the Messiah embraced as a welcome addition to and the fulfillment of their treasured Jewish heritage. They understood themselves to be no less Jewish because of their belief in Yeshua. They were "completed Jews" as some today would put it.[3]

Initially, Jewish people seem to have accepted the "Christians" among them as another variation in the multifaceted Judaism of the first century after Yeshua. These Jewish Christians typically continued their worship in the Temple in Jerusalem until its destruction by the Romans in 70 C.E. Then they had to gather in synagogues in the Jewish homeland and in neighboring nations where Jewish communities existed. They adhered to at least most of the traditional Jewish practices and understood their divine Savior primarily through the teaching tradition of the Foundational Testament (the only one they had).

Differences quickly developed, however. The "Yeshua Jews" naturally began reading their beloved Foundational Testament through the eyes of the messiahship of Yeshua. They readily accepted a rearrangement of the biblical materials that to them appeared to better highlight the recent fulfillment in Yeshua. The traditional arrangement was Law, Prophets, and Writings, ending with the book of Chronicles. The new arrangement put the Prophets at the end, concluding with the book of Malachi. This prophetic ending seemed to the followers of Yeshua a perfect preface to the story of the coming of Messiah (Mal. 3:23). This translation of the Foundational Testament into Greek (the *Septuagint*) had been completed prior to the birth of Yeshua, likely in Alexandria, Egypt.

Letters from Paul and others began circulating among the churches trying to explain the significance that Yeshua had for reading the

---

2. See the books of Brad H. Young, especially *Jesus: The Jewish Theologian* (Hendrickson, 1995) and *Paul: The Jewish Theologian* (Hendrickson, 1997).

3. The organization "Jews for Jesus" was founded in 1973 by Martin Rosen (1932-2010), son of immigrant Jewish parents. He converted to Christianity in 1953 and became a Baptist minister. Most Jewish leaders opposed vigorously Rosen's claim that one can be Jewish and Christian at the same time, and certainly resisted his relentless attempts to evangelize Jews for the Christian faith.

Foundational Testament. Some of these writings gained wide respect for their spiritual helpfulness. Soon they were collected, supplemented by the Gospels that told the story of Jesus and by collections of the teaching of Yeshua himself, all leading to the eventual formation of the Final Testament.

Tension was in the wind very early and major change seemingly could not be avoided. The followers of Yeshua, especially as instructed by Luke, John, and Paul, had a much broader vision of the mission of God's people than was typical of the traditional Jews of that day. These leading disciples of Yeshua looked to their Foudational Testament and saw in it a call to carry God's redeeming activity to the whole world, Jewish and otherwise (Gentile). God, after all, was one God *for all* (see chapter four). Yeshua had made that dramatically plain, as had previous Jewish writings like Isaiah, Jonah, etc., all now reconsidered by the disciples of Yeshua.

Luke was a prominent Final Testament writer likely responsible for both the Gospel of Luke and the Book of Acts—seemingly one continuous work. He had a clear agenda in his writings. He wanted his readers to know that Yeshua is the redeemer *of the world*, not only of Israel. Typical of a Jew, Luke was deeply God-oriented. He saw God's creating and guiding hand in the whole range of human history. He understood God's work to have culminated in the history of Yeshua. Luke's reading of history "is the story of that new reality which has turned the world upside down, revitalized all existing relationships, and enabled believers to live as people 'between the times'—between the end of an old age held by the powers of death and evil and a new age where the future is still to be fully realized, still open-ended to the movements of the Spirit."[4]

Luke saw Israel coming under judgment because of its failure to comprehend properly the will of God through its own prophets. He does not go so far, however, as to separate the nature and mission of the church from its Jewish base, and certainly not from its Jewish Messiah. He only scolds harshly the failure of those who had a special relationship with God and yet misread God's saving work and persecuted his Son (Acts 7:51-53). Even so, Luke proceeds to hold up those same Jewish prophets as very important for Christians, although insisting that they are properly read only through the life, teachings, death, res-

---

4. William H. Willimon, *Interpretation: A Bible Commentary for Teaching and Preaching, Acts* (Atlanta: John Knox Press, 1988), 20.

urrection, and world mission of Rabbi Yeshua, the Christ *from* the Jews *for* the whole world.

The non-Yeshua Jews looked to the same Foundational Testament, but their eyes were fixed more on the necessary purity and threatened survival of their own traditional communities of faith. They actively resisted a ministry like Paul's that was *rooted in* but not *fenced in* by his rich Jewish heritage. The success of the early Christian mission to the non-Jewish world created an additional and particularly volatile context for Paul's relationship with Jews who did not accept Yeshua as their Messiah. Soon there emerged among the followers of Yeshua a series of social and theological innovations that led toward separation of Jewish and non-Jewish Christians—and eventually to things even worse than that.

Despite the common historic root system and underlying theological "software" shared by Judaism and what would become Christianity, the Final Testament letters of Paul and the Book of Acts were already portraying the tension and conflict that began to develop almost from the beginning of the Jewish-Yeshua movement. Acts reports that Peter, John, and other followers of Yeshua were arrested, imprisoned, and even stoned by or at the instigation of Jewish leaders. Why? Because of their relentless preaching about Yeshua (3:1—4:22; 5:12-42). Stephen, for example, denounced the Jews because of their rejection of Yeshua and then was stoned to death by them (Acts 6:8—8:1). Before he died, he made quite an historical speech about the Jewish tradition and how Yeshua had culminated it on behalf of all people. He saw the Jewish and Yeshua stories as one continuous whole. Those throwing the killing stones did not.

Whether the execution of Stephen was spontaneous mob violence or an official action of the Jewish Sanhedrin is not clear. What is clear is that significant tension was present that soon led to the active persecution of the followers of Yeshua in Jerusalem. Paul, a Jewish Pharisee and theologian, led the way. Then came, even for him, the big reversal. He met the resurrected Yeshua while on his way to Damascus (Acts 9:3-6). After that, he often preached in Jewish synagogues and convinced many Jews of the validity of the claim that Yeshua was the Jewish Messiah. His preaching angered members of various Jewish communities. He and his companions were imprisoned on occasion or driven out of towns by antagonistic Jews (see 1 Thess. 2:14-16).

Two primary causes of this volatile relationship are evident. The first was the conviction that Yeshua of Nazareth was resurrected from the dead and none other than the Christ of God, the expected Messiah foreshadowed in the Foundational Testament. This conviction substantially redefined the common Jewish perception at the time about the nature of their expected Messiah. The Yeshua-Jews, and soon many non-Jewish (Gentile) disciples of Yeshua were championing a Savior who was not the hoped-for political and military figure come to defeat the enemies of the Jews and reestablish Israel as a free nation under God. Instead of the Jewish common expectation, and with emphasis on other parts of the Foundational Testament (Isa. 53, etc.), Yeshua had chosen voluntarily to suffer and die at the hands of the Roman enemy. This was his acting out of of his understanding of Yahweh's way of bringing salvation to the world. For Jews, the question was obvious. How could somebody like that be the true Messiah? The shame of a cruel Roman cross was not a symbol and memory that many Jews could accept as the divine way to the future. It was like a humiliating Exile all over again.

The second cause of the conflict was the inclusiveness of the Yeshua movement. This also ran counter to the Jewish mindset at the time of Yeshua. Jews who believed in Yeshua as God with us humans in the flesh were saying that saving faith was directly accessible to all people through Yeshua and his Spirit. That was true even for non-Jewish people and apart from an acceptance of some of the treasured rituals of Judaism. The Final Testament says that, in Yeshua, distinctions among people groups are abolished. Why? Because "in one Spirit we were all baptized into one body...and we were all made to drink of one Spirit" (1 Cor. 12:13). This flew in the face of the historic exclusiveness of Jewish chosenness (see chapter seven).

The more inclusive world vision of Yeshua is a wonderful restatement of the overarching paradigm of all Jewish belief—one God *for all* (see chapter four). True covenant relationship with God was now to be based on response to God's initiative of amazing grace in Yeshua, and without necessary regard for the circumstances of one's birth or faithfulness to the Jewish religious system. Such a conviction made a growing rupture between the two Jewish groups nearly inevitable. "Conservative" Jews saw the Yeshua movement as dangerously "liberal." The "liberal" Yeshua Jews saw a broader vision as essential to the good news of Yahweh made known in Yeshua. It was the collision of contrasting visions—both Jewish.

One trigger for creating the deep division between the Jewish and early Yeshua-Jewish faith communities was the Jewish-Roman War of 66-74 C.E. The trauma of the destruction of the Temple in Jerusalem by the Romans was awful for all Jews (see Lk. 21:20-24). Eusebius reports that many of the Yeshua Jews fled Jerusalem prior to its fall and went to Pella across the Jordan River. Likely, some of them did fight the Romans alongside the Jews of Jerusalem. Nonetheless, traditional Jews would readily interpret any "defection" from the fight as traitorous to their embattled tradition.

The same would have been the case when, about sixty-five years later, Jewish followers of Yeshua refused to support Bar Kochba's disastrous revolt against Rome. He had designated himself the Jewish Messiah, something disciples of Messiah Yeshua obviously could not accept. Whatever the exact facts in these troubled circumstances, later Christian writers would turn the tables, interpreting the fall of Jerusalem as divine punishment for the Jewish rejection of Yeshua and the execution of James.

In the Gospels of the Final Testament there already were strong indications of this harsh judgment against non-Yeshua Jews. The separation of these two sectors of Judaism was also coming from cultural factors. Increasingly, there were Gentile leaders in the growing churches of Yeshua located outside the Jewish homeland. They found it easy to be at home with the Final Testament and its Greek language. The Jewish roots of the faith were fading in significance for many of them. Others had not known it well in the first place.

The actual break between the two communities of Jews, one embracing Yeshua and one not, has no precise date or single event. Nonetheless, it clearly occurred on a broad scale by the end of the first century—even before the Final Testament as we know it was finally formed and officially accepted by the Christian community. What was happening can be glimpsed in the Final Testament itself, certainly in Acts 15, throughout the four Gospels, and in the writings of Paul. It was happening despite the fact that all who belong to the Messiah were being claimed as the spiritual seed of Abraham (Gal. 3:29). Christianity at first understood itself as the fullest flowering of Judaism. The Final Testament is a work full of Jewish content, even if in "Greek dress" (the Greek language and to some extent its audience and culture).

The rupturing process suddenly became quite complete in 312 C.E. when Constantine, the Roman emperor, adopted a positive attitude toward Christianity, probably in part as a political strategy for holding together the aging empire. Whatever his motives, his action elevated and also soon compromised Christianity. When Christianity became a state religion, Jewish Christianity was outlawed, with the Jewish Messiah becoming the nationally honored Gentile Christ. It was a long road from Romans crucifying Yeshua to Romans adopting Yeshua, the Jewish Messiah, as their own religious ideal!

Seeking Middle Ground

There tend to be peacemakers in every family. While dramatic changes in the larger world were pulling the Jewish-based communities apart, forces from within the young Christian church were seeking a stable middle ground. The more the young community of Yeshua spread into the Gentile world, opening its arms to new and often non-Jewish believers, the greater became the pressure to weaken further the formal ties between Yeshua believers and traditional Judaism.

Followers of Yeshua still living in Palestine, particularly those remaining loyal to the customs of the Pharisees and the "traditions of the fathers," were deeply concerned about this growing pressure to "broaden" the faith. They were trying to avoid a virtual break with Judaism. They insisted on a strict and necessary tie between Yeshua's followers and the historic Jewish tradition.

In the view of the more conservative Jews who had accepted Yeshua as their Lord, integrity lay in all believers in Yeshua observing faithfully the historic Mosaic law. Luke records that this view raised a vigorous debate (Acts 15:2). Positions were hardening. Only two general options for a way out of this impasse appeared available. The hoped-for middle ground looked dangerously unstable to each group. Unfortunately, the two options tended to be extremes.

How would the world mission of the new Yeshua community ever be accomplished if it were to function as merely a sect of Judaism? On the other hand, how would it ever have integrity if it were cut off from its historic Jewish roots, from its essential interpretive context, the Foundational Testament? Fortunately, some believers in Yeshua were committed to finding a workable middle ground.

The first hardened option was the more exclusive approach of the "Judaizers." Unless Gentile believers in Yeshua submitted to the Jewish rite of circumcision, for example, they could not be considered legitimate believers in the historic Jewish tradition now claimed to be fulfilled in Yeshua. The argument was that the Foundational Testament was the revealed Word of God, and the "traditions of the Fathers" added critical supportive meaning. Therefore, this combined tradition should be obligatory on all who sought to live in accord with the will of Yahweh. The Foundational Testament did teach that Gentiles one day would share in the promises made to Israel (Gen. 22:18; Isa. 49:6, 55:5-7); nevertheless, Israel continued as God's appointed agent for the administration of these blessings. Only through Israel, with its sacred institutions, religious practices, and interpretive traditions could Gentiles have a part in God's gracious redemption.

The second hardened option was the much more inclusive argument. The good news in Yeshua belongs to the whole world. It appears necessary to shed the weight of many Jewish particulars and explore the meaning of Yeshua in wider religious and philosophic contexts—this would be seen shortly in the Greek "logos" concept used at the beginning of the Gospel of John. Most people had no knowledge of Judaism and likely would not be accepting of Yeshua if he were forced into a narrow Jewish mold. Any such forcing was unnecessary and much too costly to the prospects of world outreach.

Fortunately, Paul was one of those believers in Yeshua who was committed both to taking the good news of Yeshua to the world and finding middle ground with the more conservative Jewish believers. For him, in light of his own dramatic experience with Yeshua on the way to Damascus (Acts 9:1-19), salvation was now understood to be *by faith alone*, making many of the Jewish external observances unnecessary. Paul earlier had practiced such observances as strictly as any Jew, and for him they had proven themselves inadequate apart from his personal relationship with the Christ.

If not strict observance of the traditions of the fathers, what remained for Paul of the continuing significance of the Jewish believing tradition for the new Yeshua believers? He now was saying that the Foundational Testament, beloved by himself and all Jews, spoke of Abraham as having been justified before God *by his faith* long before the Mosaic law had been given (Rom. 1:16). Paul and some Gentile converts to faith in Yeshua came willingly to Jerusalem to confer about all this with the leaders of the more conservative "mother church" (Acts 15:1-29; Gal. 2:1-10). They came respectfully and hopefully, but not prepared to compromise their new theological insights.

It was significant that Peter, so close to Yeshua himself, sided with Paul and the others who had come from Antioch to Jerusalem. Peter recalled the time when he had preached the good news of Yeshua to Cornelius, a Roman centurion. That entire Gentile household had received the gift of the Holy Spirit and been admitted into the believing Yeshua fellowship by baptism, all without undergoing the rite of circumcision (Acts 10:44-48). That event heralded something truly new that Peter, a loyal Jew, at first had not welcomed. But his visit to the home of Cornelius and the dramatic events that followed had convinced him that God was guiding in a new and broadened path, one that valued Judaism while also leading outward to the whole world (Acts 10:1--11:18). That was the paradox that had to be understood.

This Jerusalem meeting was a pivotal point of decision. James presided and sided with the position of Paul and Peter. He pointed out that the Jewish prophets had foretold the calling of the Gentiles (Isa. 45:21; Jer. 12:15; Amos 9:11-12). When this meeting was over, their viewpoint prevailed. A letter was written recognizing Gentile converts as true Yeshua believers without their submission to Jewish rites like circumcision being mandatory. This countered the rigid position of the "Judaisers." Rather than an ethnically closed exclusivity, God now was making no distinction between Jew and Gentile in the outpouring of his inclusive grace (Rom. 2:11). There was, however, a "compromise," probably characterized better as a loving gesture to the "conservatives" whom Paul later would describe gently as "weaker brothers" (1 Cor. 9:22).

The letter carrying the conclusions of this historic meeting did call for minimum restrictions in the interest of harmony between the two wings of the young Jewish-Yeshua community (the early church). These restrictions apparently were judged reasonable by James, Peter, and Paul. They were temporary, agreed to in the face of understandable Jewish sensibilities, and stated for the sake of maintaining fellowship among believers in Yeshua who had differing cultural and religious backgrounds (cf. Gal. 2:11-21). The restrictions may not have been enforced anywhere except in Jerusalem, and they did not violate the *faith-only* basis of a truly saving relationship with Yahweh through Yeshua. Nor were they intended to sever the Yeshua faith from its rich Jewish foundations. They intentionally kept the young church rooted in theological Judaism and yet free from many of its formalized restrictions. This allowed for the church's mission to the whole world.

These restrictions were limited to how believers would relate to certain practices of the paganism of the time that were particularly abhorrent to Jews in general. They were:

1. Abstention from eating food previously sacrificed to idols and then made available for human consumption. To the traditional Jew, such meat was contaminated with idolatry.
2. Abstention from eating any meat that had been slaughtered without a draining of the blood. Jews saw in the blood the essence of life, and life belongs only to God.
3. Remaining apart from all sexual laxity (Acts 15:29), something often seen in relation to pagan worship practices and clearly abhorrent to God.

Outside that time and setting in Jerusalem, Christian believers easily misunderstood these restrictions and why they were so crucial to believers steeped in the Jewish tradition.

The point goes back to what in the next chapter we will call the "overarching paradigm" of Jewish theology, *One God for All*. By the time of Luke's writing, the Jewish king, the Jerusalem temple, and even the land had been destroyed. What remained was *Torah*, the beloved teaching from God. Loyalty to it, obvious and unbending loyalty to it, was the joyful and often dangerous witness of the Jews to the one true God in a world of idols. No one, the followers of Yeshua included, wanted that line of God-faithfulness blurred.

One question is important yet today. Had the "Judaisers," the ultraconservatives, emerged victorious? Would Gentiles first have to become Jewish practitioners before becoming recognized as legitimate believers in Yeshua? "No" is the clear answer. If the Judaisers had prevailed, the early Christian church would have remained an adjunct of the synagogue, a mere sect of Judaism. Instead, the historic Jerusalem meeting leaned toward an open future with the God of all people. It did so, however, without Jewish root-cutting or a failure to recognize legitimate Jewish sensibilities. The meeting's conclusions kept open the way for the universal missionary reach of Christianity—the "for all" part of the overarching paradigm of Jewish belief, while also retaining important ties to the significance of the long Jewish tradition.

The growing community of Yeshua's disciples was destined to be based on historic Judaism *and* its fulfillment in Yeshua, the Jewish Messiah. However, it would not be tied to any one ethnic, national, or cultural people, place, or pattern. The Yeshua core of the faith would be non-negotiable; the Jewish base of the faith, with its distinctive history and underlying theology, would be unending. Many other things would be flexible, secondary to honest faith and saving grace from God. Unfortunately, this delicate tension, this carefully crafted middle ground was soon under assault from multiple directions and would be substantially lost over time. Paul represents well the approach of the Final Testament in general.

The Word of God in the Foundational Testament is the sacred beginning of God's truth—not merely a preface but an essential part of the truth itself. However, later interpretations of that beginning by many Jews collided with the great messianic event in Yeshua, which had created fresh insights into the now-extended meanings of the teachings of the Foundational Testament. These fresh insights left Paul and many other Jews breathlessly excited about sharing them with the whole world. The Foundational Testament had been freed to function as a vital servant of the gospel of Yeshua. It was still extremely important, but no longer to be read on its own apart from its fulfillment in Yeshua. It certainly was not to be eliminated from the sacred Scriptures of Christians.

Divorce Becomes Disaster

How tragic that two groups of Jews, both rooted in the Foundational Testament and at first equally powerless in the face of the dominant Roman Empire, would turn their frustration and anger on each other. Unfortunately, the work of the special Jerusalem meeting and its carefully crafted both/and position may have helped to hold together the two communities of Yeshua-believing Jews for a time, but the rest of the Jews became more distant than ever from the Yeshua believers. Hostility kept growing and can be seen in the Final Testament writings that were developing at the time.

It was an ironic and sad situation. As Rabbi Perelmuter puts it, "the siblings, equally impelled by their scriptural and messianic roots, blaze new trails in the highways of history, starting from a common origin and moving forward in diverse routes."[5] All of these Jews were siblings with different personalities and plans, and now with belief in a different Messiah—one come and one yet hoped for.

It is important to remember both the background of persecution and the sense of alienation and vulnerability that early Christian writers felt. This makes a difference when one comes to an abrasive verse like Revelation 2:9—"I know the slander on the part of those who say that they are Jews and are not, but are a synagogue of Satan." By the time that followers of Yeshua first appeared, Judaism already was a well-established religion in the Roman Empire. Although Jews were considered strange by the general populace and often were harassed, the Empire had learned to tolerate them and even had accorded them a measure of respect—so long as perceived danger to the Empire did not exist. The Jewish Sadducees seen in the Final Testament had become skilled at working with the Romans.

These siblings, loyal Jews not accepting Yeshua and other Jews gladly accepting Yeshua as their Lord, had begun to stereotype and separate from each other. They were natural family members, having

---

5. Hayim Goren Perelmuter, *Siblings: Rabbinic Judaism and Early Christianity at Their Beginnings* (NY: Paulist Press, 1989), 20. He further observes that Rabbinic Judaism and early Christianity received their basic forms at about the same time, each using a different reading of the messianic force at work among the Jewish people. This is why he calls the two "siblings" (2).

in common father Abraham, the Torah, and a messianic hope. Even so, they were finding themselves increasingly in a family struggle. On one side were those fully committed to what was developing into Christianity; on the other side were those continuing to put priority on certain classic structures of Judaism and still looking for a messiah more like their expectation, someone who would liberate them from Roman domination. These groups, both Jewish, were on different paths headed in apparently competing directions.

Early Christian writings like Matthew, Mark, Luke/Acts, Hebrews, and Revelation are filled with references to the Foundational Testament. They explain, highlight, and justify the direction of the Christian community of Jews with their allusions to the history of Jewish expectations—often at the same time reacting defensively and speaking sharply about other Jews. This sharpness soon would turn to misconceptions and stereotyping, even hatred and violence, what now is called anti-Semitism.

Bishop Ambrose, prominent Christian leader of the fourth century, advocated burning Jewish synagogues as a proper treatment of Jews because of their rejection of Yeshua. Saint Jerome translated the Foundational Testament into Latin for the Roman world (the Vulgate Bible). Rather than this process increasing his appreciation for the essential Jewish roots of Christianity, he became famous for referring to Jewish synagogue worship as "the grunting of pigs and the braying of donkeys."[6] With such acidic views sinking deep into and poisoning the Christian psyche over the centuries, the separation between Jews and Christians moved from divorce to disaster.

The twentieth century would be filled with violence against Jews, sometimes called pogroms (a Russian word). Earlier it had been Christian crusades against Jews and Moslems, all "children of Abraham." The first crusade ended in Jerusalem in 1099 with the burning of a synagogue filled with Jews. Such disasters led to this sobering assessment. If one counts the pogroms against Jews in Czarist Russia and the Holocaust carried out by Nazi Germany, scholars estimate that Christians have killed about half of all Jews born into this world in the last eight hundred years![7] That is a pathetic display by followers of the Prince of Peace.

---

6. This unfortunate quote is cited by Dwight A. Pryor in *Behold the Man!*, 64.

7. Irwin J. Borowsky, "Foreword," in *Jews and Christians*, ed. James Charlesworth (Crossroad, 1990), 9. To identify the Nazis as "Christians" is

Both Jewish siblings carry some guilt for what has happened. Probably about 85-90 C.E. the standard synagogue liturgy of the Jews, known as the *Eighteen Benedictions,* came to include one section of prayers that had a curse. That section asked God that "the Nazarenes and the heretics perish quickly; and may they be erased from the Book of Life; and may they not be inscribed with the righteous." The reference to "Nazarenes" certainly meant believers in Yeshua as the Jewish Christ. Such believers could hardly remain faithful to synagogues with a benediction like that! By then there was obvious hostility among many "Christians" to the reactionary institutions of Judaism.

Matthew's Gospel begins with a genealogy that deliberately ties the Yeshua story to Israel's long tradition. But it also refers to the synagogues of Matthew's time as "their" and "your" synagogues, reflecting a widening separation of the Yeshua community from Judaism (Matt. 4:23, 9:35, 10:17, 12:9, 13:54, 23:34). The Gospel of John is more pointed (Jn. 9:22). The emergence of this religious estrangement can be seen in the different stages of the Final Testament's own development. Understanding these stages is crucial to understanding properly the references to Jews and Judaism in the Gospels.[8] The three stages are:

> Stage #1: materials dating from the actual ministry of Yeshua in the early 30s of the first century.
>
> Stage #2: materials dating from the post-resurrection preaching of the early apostles—the first decades of the young Christian community.
>
> Stage #3: materials dating from the time of the actual composition of the written Gospel texts. One may have been as late as the early 100s C.E.

---

not altogether accurate, of course. Germany at that time, however, was a highly "Christianized" nation by traditional measures, and much of establishment Christianity allowed itself to be used by Hitler, at least through its silence and relative inaction. Various Christian groups now have admitted this.

8. See Philip A. Cunningham, "The Synoptic Gospels and Their Presentation of Judaism," in David P. Efroymson, et. al., eds., *Within Context: Essays on Jews and Judaism in the New Testament* (Collegeville, Minn.: The Liturgical Press, 1993), 41-66.

The general pattern appears to be that the later the time the more strident the Christian view of traditional Jews and Judaism, the more hardened the competing positions, and the closer to an outright rupture of relationship between them. This happened despite the fact that the "Jesus Movement" originated within first-century Judaism and many of its adherents, for generations, even centuries, placed a premium on continuity with the Jewish tradition that remained central to their worldview.[9] Today's "Messianc Judaism" movement is essentially an attempt to recover this "apostolic" circumstance of early Christianity. It is a fresh celebration of Yeshua in the context of his natural Jewish matrix.

Despite the early emphasis on continuity between the originating Jewish base and the new Yeshua reality, the forces pushing toward increased separation grew stronger and stronger as time went on. One of the first great anti-Jewish threats to Christianity, a threat finally judged a "heresy," was the teaching of Marcion. A rich merchant in what now is Turkey, he taught that this evil world must have been created by a "Demiurge," a cruel god of wrath and bloody battles. Marcion decided that the god of the Foundational Testament was this cruel creator, concluding that the book of the Demiurge was of little or no value to the people of Yeshua. In fact, several overly "Jewish" books of the Final Testament were also discredited. At worst, they were offensive, at best unedifying. The true God of love revealed by Yeshua is the Final Testament God.

Marcion insisted that Christians are free from the Jewish Law (Gal. 5:1), meaning done with Judaism and its old books and negative views and ways. He was extreme in his view to the degree that the Christian church in Rome excommunicated him in 144 C.E. Even so, that hardly ended the influence of his thought. God may be the overarching paradigm of the Foundational Testament, One God for All, but Marcion did not think so. The "god" he saw there is not worthy of Christian worship. The shadow of Marcion still spreads quietly across much of the Christian community, by default if not by declaration.

Many Christians today function as "quarter-of-the-Bible" believers (the Foundational Testament has 929 chapters and the Final 260). The Revised Common Lectionary is one now widely used in North America. While it is understandably Christ-centered, the Foundational Testament is significantly disadvantaged by the choice of passages

---

9. This was well documented in the 2011 manuscript *After Israel* by Jeffrey L. Seif, Professor, Christ for the Nations Institute, Dallas, Texas.

suggested for consideration in Christian worship. Not including the Psalms, this lectionary contains some 435 readings from the last twenty-seven books of the Bible and only about 270 from the first thirty-nine books. In the weeks of the Christian year following Easter, the Foundational Testament disappears altogether from the lectionary, at least symbolically weakening the taproot between the Jewish heritage and the Yeshua community. Christian worship is thereby impoverished.

This is in great contrast to the original writers of the Final Testament who clearly had their Foundational Testament constantly in mind. There are over sixteen hundred references, direct or implied, to the Foundational in the Final Testament. Richard B. Hays describes how this operates for Paul:

> The vocabulary and cadences of the Scripture—particularly of the *LXX* [Septuagint, Greek translation of the Foundational Testament]—are imprinted deeply on Paul's mind, and the great stories of Israel continued to serve for him as a fund of symbols and metaphors that condition his perception of the world, of God's promised deliverance of his people, and of his own identity and calling.[10]

Here is another way of making this very important point:

> The First [Foundational] Testament furnishes the basic vocabulary and the conceptual framework within which to understand the nature and purpose of God's presence in Christ and the church. Further, the First Testament is larger than the Second [Final] Testament. It was written over a much greater span of time and deal's with a broader range of life's situations and concerns. Therefore, the First Testament helps enlarge the church's understanding of the divine presence and its effects in the world.[11]

Despite this important contribution of the Foundational to Final Testament believers, a neo-Marcionism lives on. It tends to be advanced "when a church communicates to a nearby synagogue the impression, 'We don't have anything to learn from you and your dead, legalistic religion, but you've got everything to learn from us.'"[12] In the face of this, good instruction comes to us from the late C. H. Dodd:

---

10. Richard B. Hays, *Echoes of Scripture in the Letters of Paul* (New Haven: Yale University Press, 1989), 16.

11. Allen and Holbert, *Holy Root, Holy Branches: Christian Preaching from the Old Testament* (Nashville: Abingdon Press, 1995), 62.

12. Wilson, *Our Father Abraham*, 110.

> What is certain is that while the theology of the New [Final] Testament contains a substantial Hellenistic [Greek philosophic] element, its fundamental structure...is not Hellenistic but biblical.... If [Christian] theology seeks an accommodation with contemporary fashions of thought by cutting loose from its firm [biblical] foundations...it declines into insignificance, and has in fact nothing to say to the world which may not learn elsewhere. The challenge of a new period, with its peculiar problems, should force us back to the pit from whence we were digged and the rock from whence we were hewn.[13]

In spite of Dodd's wisdom, Christians traditionally have done quite other than drink again for the fresh water of their Hebrew heritage, their essential root system. They have dug other wells and carved rock other than from the one whence they were originally hewn.

A glance at Christian church history quickly fills in the sordid details. We learn much from the medieval cathedrals built by Christians in Europe. Like Christianity itself, the cathedrals are inescapably Jewish, in both positive and negative ways. There was an architectural overlapping of the Christ-in-the-shadows of the Foundational and the Christ-in-the-light of the Final Testament. This is seen, for instance, on the north porch of Chartres Cathedral in France. A series of beautifully preserved statues of Jewish figures is arranged on either side of the portal. They are on the north side of the building "because this is the side that receives less light in the course of the day, and they are the shadowy anticipations of the light of Christ."[14]

While recognizing and even celebrating the Jewish prefiguring of Christ, the cathedrals also express a disdain for Jews and their rejection of the Messiah. On many of the windows in the Gothic cathedrals, Jews are depicted with ugly features and even portrayed as villains. Anti-Semitism obviously had become institutionalized. It was solidly embedded in the very artwork of the great houses of Christian worship, so that "the Jewish aspect of the cathedrals is in part their glory and in part their shame."[15]

Pope Innocent III (1198-1216) issued a Christian decree forcing Jews to wear a distinctive badge making it easy for them to be identified and avoided. Jews were forced to live in crowded ghettoes in many large European cities. Unfortunately, Martin Luther (1483-1546), the

---

13. C. H. Dodd, *According to the Scriptures: The Sub-Structure of New Testament Theology* (N.Y.: Charles Scribner's Sons, 1953), 11, 13, 14, 136, 138.
14. Robert Barron, *Heaven in Stone and Glass* (N.Y.: Crossroad, 2000), 65.
15. Barron, 69.

great Protestant Reformer, attacked Jews in writings near the end of his life. Why? For one reason, they had not responded positively to his "Protestant" reforming efforts. Some of his harsh words were: "Burn their synagogues and schools; what will not burn, bury with earth, that neither stone nor rubbish remain. In like manner, break into and destroy their homes."[16] Though surely never Luther's intent, the day would come when Adolf Hitler would proclaim Luther a German hero and quote his anti-Jewish words to support his "final solution" to the "Jewish problem."

Hitler even made Jews the scapegoat for Germany having lost World War I. Elie Wiesel, a Jewish death-camp survivor, wrote *Night*, a vivid account of Nazi executions of helpless Jews. He posed a painful question. Where was God in all this horror? Apparently, at least in Wiesel's view, God also had been executed, helpless as the others in the face of overwhelming evil. The divorce between Christians and Jews had become a total disaster, with God himself seeming to be one of the victims!

I mentioned earlier the university class I taught for years called "Hebrew Roots of Christian Faith." One lecture was keynoted each semester with this question: "Who killed Yeshua?" "The Jews!" was a common first answer from students. "But," I would respond, "not all Jews rejected Jesus. The common Jewish people are said to have heard him gladly; the opposition came mostly from Jewish leaders in Judea. Only one of the disciples betrayed Jesus, and it was only the Romans who had the authority to actually crucify him. It was a Roman governor who sentenced Yeshua, even though the governor was convinced of his innocence. Jew and Gentile joined to bring Yeshua to the cross."

I would go on to quote from the song that asks, "Were *you* there when they crucified my Lord?" I suggested that, in a real sense, we all were there at the cross, our sins being the root cause of it all. But there is even more. It also is true that Yeshua went to his terrible death voluntarily. He had an option. One student blurted out, "You mean it was suicide?"

"Not exactly," I responded. "The sovereign Father of Yeshua was pouring out his loving heart, and his Son's blood was flowing on our behalf. It was a divine Self-revelation, God choosing to suffer for us humans and thereby reveal the great divine heart. To single out Jews as 'Christ killers' is much too simplistic and a most unfair assessment."

---

16. Quoted by George H. Stevens, *Strife Between Brothers* (London: Olive Press, 1979), 33.

We all are to blame, and potentially we all are able to benefit by God's amazing grace. In the end, the death of Yeshua was God's saving initiative. God's own heart was broken. God voluntarily opened himself to absorb our sin and shame, enabling our cleansing and rebirth to occur. We will explain in chapter four that a proper understanding of God lay at the heart of all Jewish understandings of truth and life— and Yahweh is quite other than what Marcion thought.

So must be the understanding of today's Christians. Viewed in light of Yeshua, God the sovereign is the God of amazing love who suffers on behalf of a creation gone very wrong. Chapters five and six will probe at length the nature of Yahweh come to be with us in Yeshua. The Foundational and Final Testaments carry a single and interconnected story of the one God, Yahweh, the loving Father of Yeshua, come for the salvation of us all.

Hope in Christian/Jewish Relations

Some aspects of Jewish-Christian relations have changed in recent decades, and clearly for the better. These pages are intended to continue this improvement. It is significant to note that Abraham, so important to the opening chapters of the story of God's people, virtually disappears from that story's literature until the period of the Exile. Once humiliated in a foreign land, that troubled period of Jewish history seemed to need its imagination fired again by the "father" of the Hebrew tradition. Abraham somehow had once found his way by faith into the future from that same foreign land. Likewise, historical and religious developments in recent decades have seemed to need Abraham's story again.

A seminal 1965 document from the Second Vatican Council of the Roman Catholic Church set the pace for improved Jewish-Christian relations in modern times. It deplores "all hatreds, persecutions, and displays of anti-Semitism leveled at any time or from any source against the Jews." It gladly affirms "the spiritual ties which link the people of the new covenant to the stock of Abraham." This fresh stance of appreciation and dialogue did not involve to any significant degree the large "Evangelical" community of Protestantism, at least not at first. That soon could change.

The formation of the modern State of Israel in 1948 eventually would bring substantial moral and financial support to that nation from millions of American "evangelical" Christians, many of whom came to view this regathering of Jews as a dramatic fulfillment of biblical prophecy. At least until the 1970s, however, Evangelicals "were often perceived by many Jews as unenlightened 'Elmer Gantrys', even bigoted anti-Semites. Conversely, many Evangelicals defined Jews as 'Christ killers,' 'deniers of Jesus,' and 'scribes and Pharisees'."[17] Then Marvin A. Wilson, an Evangelical Christian, began his significant ministry of reconciliation that came to include a close personal and professional relationship with Rabbi A. James Rudin. He and others began bridging the very wide gorge.

Progress has been real, but should not be overstated. Jews continue to find particularly odious the evangelical tendency to seek the "conversion" of Jews and then call converts "completed Jews," implying that Judaism is an "incomplete" religion.[18] Even so, progress has been made. The Synod of the Evangelical Church of the Rhineland in Germany is a good example.

In 1980 this Synod announced: "We confess with dismay the co-responsibility and guilt of German Christendom for the Holocaust."[19] Then in 2000 the Jewish statement *Dabru Emet* (Heb. for "Speak the Truth" from Zech. 8:16) appeared. It was signed by numerous Jewish rabbis and intellectuals from all branches of contemporary Judaism. One of its purposes was pointing out the considerable common ground that exists between Jews and Christians. It says on the one hand that, without the centuries of Christian oppression and contempt of Jews, "Nazi ideology could not have taken hold [in Germany] nor could it have been carried out." However, on the other hand it also says that "Nazism itself was not an inevitable outcome of Christianity.... We applaud those Christians who reject this teaching of contempt, and we do not blame them for the sins committed by their ancestors."

Moving beyond the sometimes sordid past, many Christian denominations now have made official pronouncements affirming the crucial importance of the Jewish tradition for a true understanding of the Christian faith. What God did in Jesus Christ is said to be virtually unintelligible apart from the story of Israel's prior election told in the

---

17. Rabbi A. James Rudin, "Evangelicals and Jews: The Unfinished Agenda," in Steven Hunt, ed., *Perspectives on Our Father Abraham* (Grand Rapids: Eerdmans, 2010), 313.

18. On the lighter side, see Zev Chavets' 2007 book *A Match Made in Heaven*. It is a breezy and insightful look at the Evangelical Christian community through Jewish eyes.

19. Found in *The Theology of the Churches and the Jewish People* (World Council of Churches Publications, 1988), 93.

Foundational Testament. Paul's image of Christians being grafted to the good olive tree of Israel (Rom. 11:17-18) clearly pictures the gracious divine inclusion of Gentiles in the scope of God's saving work, but certainly not the blanket repudiation of the original Jewish tradition—the tree itself. Gentile believers now share in the nourishing sap of the ancient Hebrew tree. Christians must not be so arrogant as to be disrespectful of the root that still graciously supports and feeds them.

If the heritage of Yeshua, the Jewish Messiah, is indeed crucial for an understanding of Christian faith today, how are Christians to read properly the Foundational Testament known and loved by Yeshua himself? The next chapter will address this important "how" question, and chapter eleven will attempt four case studies to illustrate proper Christian interpretation that shows respect of the Foundational Testament, even for its most "difficult" passages.

The possibility of a proper and useful Christian reading of the Foundational Testament has increased because of the improved climate noted above, and because of recent innovations in scholarly approaches to the ancient Jewish text. These changes have tended to admit more than the technical "experts" into the process. This opening now allows multiple persons and perceptions to help identify the direct relevance of the text for the actual life of today's believers and churches. Scholars like Walter Brueggemann, Brevard Childs, and Dennis F. Kinlaw have helped lead the way to this opening.

HOW SHOULD CHRISTIANS READ THE FOUNDATIONAL TESTAMENT?

With what conviction should Christians read the Foundational Testament? "My strong conviction is that the Lord is restoring the Hebraic foundations of the Church so that together we all can move forward in greater faithfulness and maturity in the service of the Messiah and the Kingdom of God. Toward that end we should be Father-focused, Christ-centered, and Spirit-saturated."[1]

We have established that Christians have an important stake in their rich Jewish heritage. Despite the tragedy and shame of much of Jewish-Christian relations over the centuries, the fact remains clear. For Christians, God has inspired the *whole Bible*, including both the Foundational (Old) and Final (New) Testaments. A key problem persists, however.

There are challenges facing a contemporary Christian who attempts a serious reading of the Foundational Testament. After all, for nearly all Christians there now is a great distance between themselves and the language and cultures that lie behind (beneath) the ancient

---

1. These words represent well the thinking and writing of Dwight A. Pryor, founder and president of the Center for Judaic-Christian Studies in Dayton, Ohio, and founding board member of the Jerusalem School of Synoptic Research.

text. Even so, since the earlier Testament is believed to be foundational and authoritative for Christians, these challenges must be faced. Christians must overcome the historic Jewish-Christian tragedies of the past and address with new care the problems faced when trying to read the Jewish materials with spiritual profit. The Foundational Testament, after all, is an essential part of the Christian faith. We must learn how to read it properly and profitably.

Critical Assertions

How can Christians read the Foundational Testament with understanding and spiritual profit? Since the text is ancient, the language unfamiliar, and the cultures involved very different and long gone, it will take some hard work. Even so, the Jewish roots of Christianity are so strong, and the history and customs of the Jews have done so much to shape the entire Bible. To profit from all this is God's intent. There is little choice. As it was once put: "If Jesus had been an Eskimo, we'd be studying Inuit (Eskimo) language and culture, learning about igloos, ice fishing, and polar bears."[2] In fact, Yeshua was a Jew and his "Bible" was thoroughly Jewish.

We begin with this assumption: "It is clear that the Old Testament provides the categories of faith and interpretation through which the New Testament is to be understood and without which the New Testament cannot be faithfully and intelligently read."[3] This central assumption contains three critical assertions. They are key to an effective strategy for reading the Foundational Testament by Final Testament believers. They are:

1. Every text of Scripture is there not simply to take up space, but because it is given by the Spirit of God and contains some *theological concern* which prompted it to be taken, by God's providence, into the canon.[4] Chapter four will identify the pervasive theological themes of the Foundational Testament that later also would underlie the Final Testament. Our eyes must learn to focus on such theological concerns.

---

2. Ann Spangler and Lois Tverberg, *Sitting at the Feet of Rabbi Jesus* (Grand Rapids: Zondervan, 2009), 8.
3. Walter Brueggemann, *An Introduction to the Old Testament: The Canon and Christian Imagination* (Louisville: Westminster John Knox Press, 2003), 3.
4. Marvin Wilson, *Our Father Abraham*, 115.

2. What is of primary concern for Christians in the Foundational Testament? What remains normative? It is precisely in the underlying *theology*—not always the details of Israel's history or the historically and culturally conditioned forms in which Israel's faith sometimes found expression.[5] There is *God's Word* always behind (beneath) all of the *human words*. The Bible, after all, and paradoxically, is a *divine-human* book.

3. God's Spirit must be given center stage in the reading process. A colleague of mine and I once wrote: "We should not think of God as giving to believers private information about the original meaning of a text and denying it to others. If he did that, the locus of revelation would shift to subjective experience and away from its connection with the Bible.... Even so, there is still a crucial role for the Spirit in the interpretation of the Bible."[6] That role is sometimes said to be the current *illumination* of the Bible reader by the Spirit, the same Spirit who originally *inspired* the Bible. What once was *infolded* in the text by the Spirit of Yahweh now needs to be *unfolded* for the current Christian reader by the same Spirit, now known as the Spirit of Yeshua. See chapter thirteen for an extended exploration of this ongoing unfolding.

A Reading Strategy

We now have one assumption and three assertions in place. They highlight (1) the importance of the Foundational Testament for today's Christian, (2) the underlying theological structure of one Testament that is critical for the interpreting of it and the other Testament, and (3) the central role of God's Spirit in the process of proper reading and current interpretation. We now will develop the resulting reading strategy by first going back to the imagery informing this book's title.

Contemporary Christian believers should imagine themselves sitting in a small boat and looking out over the surface of the whole text

---

5. John Bright, *The Authority of the Old Testament* (Nashville: Abingdon Press, 1967 ed.), 147.
6. Clark H. Pinnock and Barry L. Callen, *The Scripture Principle: Reclaiming the Full Authority of the Bible* (Grand Rapids: Baker Academic, 2nd ed., 2006), 194.

of the Foundational Testament. It is a diverse library with various forms of literature dating from different centuries and cultures. It is a vast sea of words, concepts, and images. Some of this biblical sea's surface is made up of strange little waves that are confusing; some is quiet and lovely in the sunlight; and some is littered with floating debris that appears to be of no continuing value.

How should the Christian reader proceed, knowing that all of this text is supposed to be "inspired" by God for contemporary use? The three assertions above tell Christians a series important things that together form an appropriate approach to reading and interpreting the Foundational Testament. From these assertions come five core elements of an appropriate reading strategy.

1. When a Christian looks at a passage of the Foundational Testament, the first thing to do is be patient and open to God's voice. Avoid hasty judgments and refuse to focus attention only on what appears to be the "good stuff." Christians are to believe and be encouraged by the following. While ancient Israel lived "amid the glorious ruins of Egypt, Syria, and Mesopotamia, one still must stand amazed at the literary, poetic, and religious genius of Israel. The other nations had nothing which can be placed on the same level with the Bible. Israel lived in that ancient world, borrowed widely from it, and yet transformed all that was borrowed. Her literature, while produced *in* that world, was never quite *of it*."[7] We are reading something truly unique.

2. Christians are called to believe that, in God's gracious providence, the Foundational Testament is the inspired text that God *intends us to have*. It is to be valued as an indispensable aid for Christians seeking an encounter with the face of God. *In its entirety*, the Foundational Testament is authoritative for Christians, despite the strange waves and unsightly debris sometimes seen on the surface of the text (see samples in chapter eleven). One caution is obvious. There is great danger in *individualistic* biblical reading. Christians, in fact, face a double danger. They can be the victims of the uncontrolled practice of subjectivism; they also can be closed to what the Spirit may be

---

7. G. Ernest Wright, *The Challenge of Israel's Faith* (Chicago: University of Chicago Press, 1944), 14-15. Emphasis added.

saying to the churches today because of the fear of subjectivism. Reading should be with all of one's head *and heart*, and in the midst of the wisdom of the larger community of faith—Christian and Jewish.

3. Christian readers are to focus on the *great theological themes* that inform the whole of the Foundational Testament text (and then that of the Final Testament also). Often these themes only become visible when one searches *beneath the text's surface*. They are to be sought out as primary truth guides, no matter how deep one must go and despite the languages in which the guides first were articulated and the cultures through which they were originally expressed and lived out. These theological themes will be identified in the next chapter and then be explored in detail in later chapters.[8]

4. Once respecting every text of the Foundational Testament on its own terms and seeking to understand each of them in light of the informing theological theme that lies beneath the textual surface, there is still more. Two interactive truths are to be honored by Christians. We also are then (and only then) to employ *the final revelation in Yeshua* as critical for helping to sharpen understanding of whatever theological theme is basic to the "old" text in question. This approach assumes two things. (1) The Foundational Testament is the base and larger context of the Final Testament. (2) The Final Testament becomes the ultimate context in which the Foundational is most fully understood—and occasionally adapted or even altered in some ways. To use a book title as a good picture of this reading strategy, Christians are to give attention to *Israel's Scripture Traditions and the Synoptic Gospels: Story Shaping Story*.[9] The

---

8. This approach is similar in some ways to the influential work of the early Christian scholar Origen of Alexandria (185-254 A.D.). He assumed that all of the Scriptures are intended to be taken seriously by Christians, even Old Testament texts that seem repulsive or meaningless. His approach to interpretation was that not all of the Bible has literal meaning, but it does have a "higher meaning," either spiritual or moral. "Spiritualizing" the meaning of the ancient text, however, too easily pulls it from its original historical setting and makes it into whatever the modern reader wishes.

9. Willard M. Swartley, *Israel's Scripture Traditions and the Synoptic Gospels: Story Shaping Story* (Hendrickson Publishers, 1994).

Foundational and Final Testaments are story one and story two—actually, one continuous story. They probe each other. Each informs the other, with neither wholly itself or really understood when cut off from the other.

5. One other thing is important to realize, but it must be handled carefully since it is misunderstood and abused constantly. With the above core elements firmly in place, and only then, the Christian has the liberty in the Spirit of Christ to build upon and even beyond the Jewish foundations. The *upon* always should precede and inform any *beyond*. There is need in changing times and cultures to seek fresh insights, meanings, and truth applications. However, any supposed freshness should remain solidly situated on the ancient foundations of Abraham, Moses, David, Matthew, Peter, Paul, and the others, especially Messiah Yeshua. They all share a core set of theological assumptions (see chapter four). Whatever the changes of expression in language and application to contemporary life, these theological assumptions do not change from the Foundational to the Final Testament, or on to today. Even so, Christians must be willing to "link the mind and the Spirit, study and prayer, in the work of interpretation.... There is a level of understanding that only comes through involvement with the text *and* a walk with the Lord."[10]

The full and current understanding of a biblical text cannot always be limited to the immediate setting and exact meaning of its original biblical appearance. There often is a "surplus of meaning" that, while fresh, is meaning never to be disconnected from the original meaning. However, neither is it ever to be completely imprisoned by that original meaning. This interpretive assumption is explained in chapter thirteen. It affirms that the most careful attention must be given to the original historical, cultural, and linguistic expression and canonical setting of any text under consideration. What it then does is go on to link mind and Spirit, study and prayer, recognizing the ongoing ministry of the divine Spirit. There is "progressive revelation" that is seen clearly *within* the Bible, and sometimes even *beyond* it—although never separate *from* it. What always remains stable are the *core theologi-*

---

10. Clark H. Pinnock and Barry L. Callen, *The Scripture Principle*, 195.

cal themes. They persist from Testament to Testament, and then from biblical times to today.

As will be explained in chapter six, Yahweh (God) is wonderfully and amazingly "open" to his creation, and is relational in nature. God grants a partnership role in the creation's ongoing and often troubled life. God enters into "covenant" with a people. God interacts with this people lovingly and even vulnerably, by choice, of course, certainly not by necessity. As Christians study God's Word in both Testaments, they must be open to God's voice, even as God is open to them. Some aspect of Yahweh's being, working, and eternal truths lies somewhere just beneath every biblical text.

Disciples of the Final Testament must read their Foundational Testament with patience. They must be open to the wisdom of paradox, welcome the insights that sometimes come only from worship, and not rush to premature closure on a subject that strikes them as strange, offensive, or just incomprehensible. In short, they should be "Jewish" in their reading, reading as disciples of Yeshua the Jew whose Spirit continues to open the biblical text to contemporary readers.

It is typically Jewish to recognize that "our readings are always provisional, because there is always another text, always another commentary…. Jewish reading knows that 'final readings' are toxic and eventually lead to 'final solutions'."[11] The relational God inspires an ongoing dialogue with the text that slowly deepens understanding and keeps refreshing the best current application. Martin Buber contributed greatly to this emphasis on dialogic reading with his classic 1937 book *I and Thou*. The great Thou of the ages honors and engages with the human reader, the "I."

Seven of the early Christian congregations were having trouble managing the reading of their biblical texts and discovering how best to live out their faith in Yeshua. Strange theologies were all around them, and at points were perverting them. John shared with them some very pointed messages from their Lord who was anxious to re-engage with them. The messages are capped with one common warning: "Let anyone who has an ear listen to what the Spirit is saying to the churches" (Rev. 3:22). Christians must have eyes to read with care, and also ears to hear with equal care when the Spirit of Yeshua speaks.

Once all of the above is understood and personally affirmed, the Christian reader of the Foundational Testament is ready to proceed.

---

11. Walter Brueggemann, *An Unsettling God: The Heart of the Hebrew Bible* (Minneapolis: Fortress Press, 2009), 6.

Historians and language experts will be needed to help with the details of the ancient cultures that surrounded and influenced Israel, and certainly with the original meaning of words that the writers used to form the biblical text. Biblical scholars can also assist in showing the placing of a text in relation to the texts immediately around it and to others of a similar kind that may be found in distant parts of the Bible. Many specialties make their particular contributions.

What will be of additional and critical assistance is a clear identification of the basic theological themes that form the base of the whole text of the Bible, and the particular one that informs the text under consideration at any given time. Since these themes often lie beneath the surface of the text, finding them requires a sharp eye and clear awareness of the themes being sought. These theological foundations are relatively few in number, and yet are of paramount importance to all proper biblical reading and believing. We now proceed to their identification.

THE PERVASIVE THEOLOGICAL THEMES

The Old Testament...is unable and unwilling...to think outside the categories and boundaries of its own sense of YHWH and YHWH's partner [covenant Israel]. As a consequence, the primary categories of Israel's faith, sovereignty, fidelity, covenant, and obedience, pertain for this topic as well. Israel makes this claim for all human persons, including those well beyond its own community.[1]

The historical study of New Testament theology...is faced by the difficult task of discovering the true starting-point.... In describing the contents of the *kerygma* [core proclamation of the early Christian church], I have distinguished the *events* which it announces...and the *significance* which it attaches to them.... The significance is indicated mainly by reference to prophecies of the Old Testament.... Thus the Church was committed, by the very terms of its *kerygma*, to a formidable task of biblical research, primarily for the purpose of clarifying its own understanding of the momentous events out of which it had emerged....[2]

The earliest Christians looked to Yeshua and the Foundational Testament to discover their core beliefs. The pervasive theological theme discovered was Yahweh as now known best in Yeshua.

---

1. Walter Brueggemann, *An Unsettling God*, 57-58.
2. C. H. Dodd, *According to the Scriptures: The Sub-Structure of New Testament Theology* (N.Y.: Charles Scribner's Sons, 1953), 11, 13-14.

When Christians today also look at the Foundational Testament, what do they see? Is there a proud and still relevant tradition of monotheism (only one sovereign, holy God)? Or is there more of what Marcion long ago, and now the "new atheists," claim to see, a god unworthy of anyone's worship or no god at all? One of new atheists, Richard Dawkins, deems God's commanding Abraham to sacrifice his son Isaac (Gen. 22) "disgraceful," making the divine a "moral monster." Dawkins sees religion as the "root of all evil" when recalling Joshua's destruction of Jericho. He judges that this event is "morally indistinguishable from Hitler's invasion of Poland or Saddam Hussein's massacres of the Kurds and the Marsh Arabs."[3] A response to this is found here in chapter eleven.

A view like that of Dawkins is a harsh but not uncommon judgment. Many Christians struggle with various parts of the Foundational Testament as they seek God's wisdom in its pages.[4] Delwin Brown says, "It is silly to claim that the Bible can be made to say anything.... The Bible has a distinctive if complex perspective on the world and how life is to be lived in it."[5] It is true that people grossly misuse the Bible out of their own ignorance and for their own personal ends. Taking verses out of context and twisting them to strange new meanings does not result in "what the Bible says"—the actual result is what the interpreter says with the misuse of a few biblical words. Regardless, Bible readers often are confident about what they read, and they sometimes read very differently.

Brown's main point is of paramount importance. There is beneath the entire Foundational Testament, and then also beneath the Final Testament, a consistent view of life and the world. This view, in its various dimensions, is expressed through a set of pervasive theological themes that express this single but yet multifaceted view. When these themes are recognized, it indeed is silly to say that the Bible can be made to say anything. In fact, it has a singular and wonderful message—God *is* and God *is with us* for our good, first in Israel and then in Yeshua. Diversity on many subjects within the biblical materials is admitted, but the diversity is overshadowed by a consistent worldview

---

3. Quoted by Paul Copan, *Is God a Moral Monster?*, 20-21.

4. Andrew Sloane has written a fine book for Christians with this very problem in mind. It is titled *At Home in a Strange Land: Using the Old Testament in Christian Ethics* (Hendrickson, 2008).

5. Delwin Brown, *What Does a Progressive Christian Believe?* (N.Y.: Seabury Books, 2008), 16.

that is quite singular throughout. It is this common perspective and the resulting theological themes that should be key to a Christian reading of the Bible, both its Foundational and Final Testaments.

Chapter three attempted to sketch the key elements of an appropriate strategy for Bible reading. For Christians seeking to read their Foundational Testament with contemporary meaning, these elements help to maintain the original integrity of that earlier Testament and also allow the later Testament to be informed both by what went before and what came after in Yeshua. He is the Messiah of the Jewish tradition whose person, actions, and teachings spread the brightest light on all aspects of biblical theology. Now we will elaborate on this reading strategy through identification of the pervasive theological themes.

The Permanent and the Passing

It was only a quick TV ad I saw in 2011. It was squeezed strangely between beer and car commercials. Three older men sat down together at an outdoor café. As one opened a box of donuts he had brought, they each reached for one, clearly happy to be together again. As they visited, the ad announcer reported that one was a Jew, one a Christian, and one a Moslem—already obvious from their clothes. Further, it was made clear that they had more in common than a taste for donuts. They shared *friendship*. That was a good message for today's divided and suspicious public, but the ad was quickly over without having gone far enough.

These men shared a common religious tradition, a common spiritual "father," Abraham, and a common belief in the one, creating, fully sovereign God. That belief is more basic than the many things across history that have come to divide these three branches of the Abrahamic tradition of monotheism. That much meaning, of course, does not make it into a thirty-second ad. Given what these men were representing, however, and the associated turmoil in today's world, the greater meanings should be given attention in some public venue, and certainly when one reads the Bible.

Two things should be clear when we approach biblical revelation. First, the Foundational Testament takes human history very seriously. Its pervasive theological convictions grow out of the real history of Israel. Second, this Testament is not limited to the recounting of mere historical "facts" (are there such things?), nor is it "theological" in the typical modern sense of an academic discipline. The biblical story of God with Israel is *interpreted history* (is there any other kind?). It is not philosophical speculation, but a particular reading of actual history that took Israel's remembering and reflecting far beyond human history for ultimate explanations. Therefore:

> Old Testament history is even further removed from the rubric of history by the emphasis on the event as a witness in Israel to *the One in whom all life has meaning*, to whom belong the earth and its fullness, the world, and those who inhabit it. Ancient Israel takes for granted in its story that the determinative factor in all human events and in all creation is *outside and above event and time*. There is no history merely of people and events, since these are determined by the impingement of God's life and will on the plane of human history. Thus, the Old Testament remains essentially existential and supra-historical.[6]

When reading the Bible, there is need to distinguish between what it sometimes *reports* and what it intentionally *teaches* from the richness of its distinctive theological depths. The deliberate and intentional teaching is what remains authoritative for the Christian, and often this teaching lies beneath the surface of the literal biblical text. Here is a helpful statement: "A text of the First [Foundational] Testament makes a *surface* witness expressed in its own culture, worldview, and idiom, but can be understood on a *deeper level* to contain values [theological truths] that transcend its particular cultural expression."[7]

Sometimes the full reality is more than what immediately meets the eye. For instance, Mauna Kea is a volcano on the island of Hawaii that stands nearly 14,000 feet above sea level. Impressive as is this highest point in the state of Hawaii, what is not seen makes it more impressive, more fully understood for what it really is. Much of this mountain is under water. When understood from beneath, looking upward from its oceanic base, Mauna Kea is over 33,000 feet in total elevation, much more than Mount Everest. As we read the Foundational Testament, we need to comprehend the ancient theological base in order to interpret the upper, more visible, and sometimes more passing structures that got reported—as opposed to being *taught*.

Further, because of the dramatic shift in cultures from the Bible's times and places of formation to its many current places of interpretation and application, we must be on the lookout for the *permanent* in the midst of (or beneath) the merely *passing*. From Genesis to Revela-

---

6. Davie Napier, *Song of the Vineyard: A Guide through the Old Testament* (Philadelphia: Fortress Press, rev. ed., 1981), 2. Emphasis added.

7. Ronald Allen and John Holbert, *Holy Root, Holy Branches,* 35. Emphasis added.

tion, the Bible is essentially a Jewish document. Once read with appreciation from that perspective, "our experience of it will be transformed, as though we have just swopped an old black-and-white TV...for the latest flat screen, high-definition set. Suddenly, the Bible takes on new depth and color...."[8]

An effective Christian strategy for reading the Foundational Testament, therefore, should be based on a *beneath-the-surface* assumption. There are critical theological themes underlying all texts of this Jewish Testament and they must be identified clearly. One excellent way to do this is to picture the truth understood by the ancient Jews as a major *Water Source* that flows in various *truth streams* to cover and nourish the entire biblical landscape. Water was precious in the arid Near East. To abuse it could spell the difference between life and death. The streams of truth and their one source (Yahweh) dare not be ignored or abused by the Christian reader.

My wife and I visited En-Gedi a few years ago. Located in southern Israel near the Dead Sea, it is surrounded by some of the driest and barest landscapes on the planet. But En-Gedi itself has bubbling springs. It is a wonderful oasis teeming with life. The one difference between this amazing ravine and its surrounding desolation is *water*. The Bible originates from this dramatic area of the world and is highly sensitive to issues related to the presence or absence of water.

A water imagery is employed as a warning by the Hebrew prophet Jeremiah. Jeremiah's imagery is set forth as the way to secure right belief, and the only way. God's people had committed two evils, says Jeremiah on God's behalf. They "have forsaken me, the fountain of living water, and dug out cisterns that can hold no water" (Jer. 3:13). So now, as in ancient times, we are to seek *the fountain*, the only adequate truth fountain, and we are to do so determined not to dig useless dry holes of our own.

The singular water source is Yahweh God, and the essential truth streams that flow from God's being and heart comprise the theological framework that underlies the Foundational Testament, and appear again in their fullness in the Final Testament. Each stream is an expression of the same Water Source. Each carries the same living water, just in varying ways and sometimes over different arenas of our lives. Each affirms in its unique way the pre-eminence of the one living God. Each truth stream spreads its distinctive nuances of the presence and work of God in this fallen world. When received and honored, the wa-

---

8. Ann Spangler and Lois Tverberg, *Sitting at the Feet of Rabbi Jesus*, 19.

ter from these streams brings and nourishes life both now and hereafter.

All truth streams are important because each is an organic extension of the one originating fountain, God, who defines all that deserves to be called "truth." Christians reading this Jeremiah 3 text and thinking about flowing water in truth streams cannot help but recall something Yeshua once said to a Samaritan woman near a well: "Everyone who drinks of this water will be thirsty again, but those who drink of the water that I will give them will never be thirsty. The water that I will give will become in them a spring of water gushing up to eternal life" (Jn. 4:13-14). That water is none other than the life of Yahweh streaming into the lives of his people through the present Spirit of Yeshua.

Ephesians 4:1-6 exhorts young Christian congregations to maintain their unity. The "oneness" theme permeates the passage—one body, one Spirit, one hope, one Lord, one faith, one baptism, *one God*. The hearer of this text who is steeped in the Jewish tradition will immediately recall Deuteronomy 6:4-9. It states that the most basic tenet of the Hebrew faith tradition is this: God *is*, and God *is one*, one *for all*. The oneness of the Christian church is rooted necessarily in the shared oneness of God made known in the one, integrated story told in succession by the two biblical Testaments. Here is where, at their very taproot, Judaism and Christianity share a common core. This remains true even when the "Trinity" doctrine of Christians is introduced (a multiplicity related to the one God!). See chapter six for a discussion of this difficult but important Christian doctrine.

Theology in Ancient Israel

Before we identify the pivotal truth streams, it is important to clarify the status of "theology" in ancient Israel. The prophets of Israel were not systematic theologians. They appear to have cared little about abstract principles of philosophic truth. What they claimed to have received was a *Word from God*, a gifting of Self-revelation from the divine and received in the midst of the concrete and often very troubled events of their world. For them, "history is no mere story of human activity to be viewed, dissected, and described as one would analyze mathematical statistics. It is the arena of the creative activity of the living, righteous, holy God—a God whose works permit no description apart from a clarion call to repentance and conversion...."[9]

Israel approached history as *His-Story*, God's unfolding drama played out on the scene of human history. History is significant because God *is*, God *launched it*, and God chooses to be *redemptively involved in it*. It is through this involvement that the truth streams arise and flow. It is exactly here that wisdom and authority lie for the contemporary Christian.

Israel's understanding of God as we have it in the Foundational Testament did not appear in a vacuum. There was a rich believing tradition in the ancient Near East. However, something quite distinctive appeared among the Jews. It was a believed Self-revelation of the one high God. What was so new? It was that "while the character of YHWH reflects the common theology, Israel's own peculiar articulation of God takes YHWH's *readiness to relate*—with all of its problematic—*as definitional*."[10] The God who is, the sovereign and singular One, is *by nature* the reaching, relating, redeeming God. God is as God does. And what does God do? God actively relates to the creation. This readiness to relate to a fallen world, with all its risks, becomes the biblical basis for such dramatic things as a covenant partnership with a people and, later, an actual incarnation in Yeshua. There may be two "testaments," but it is the ongoing story of the same God active on the human scene.

It is important to understand the nature and function of theology in the context of the Foundational Testament. Marvin Wilson puts it well: "The Semites of Bible times did not simply *think* truth—they *experienced* truth...truth is as much encounter as it is propositions.... To the Jew, the *deed* was always more important than the *creed*."[11] Returning to the acceptance of paradoxes, Judaism "is never afraid of contradictions...it acknowledges that full reconciliation...is possible only in God. He is the coincidence of opposites."[12] Theology represents *paths* of truth more than *propositions* of truth highly defined rationally.

The voices of ancient Israel, if not ones of systematic theologians, certainly were ones of singers. When ultimate matters are in view, poetry seems to rise above prose, music above the mechanics of plain

---

9. G. Ernest Wright, *The Challenge of Israel's Faith*, 28.
10. Walter Brueggemann, *An Unsettling God*, 5. Emphasis added.
11. Marvin Wilson, *Our Father Abraham*, 153. Emphasis added.
12. Quoted in Paul R. Carlson, *O Christian! O Jew!* (Elgin, Ill: David C. Cook, 1974), 142-143.

language. The song of the Jews was always about the one God who reaches far beyond the mere notes and words of humans. Two of the great singers were women, one from the Foundational and one from the Final Testament. Each sang essentially the same song.

Hannah, mother of prophet Samuel, sang: "There is no Holy One like the Lord, no one besides you; there is no Rock like our God" (1 Sam. 2:2). Mary, mother of Yeshua, sang what seems to be verse two of the same song: "My soul magnifies the Lord, and my spirit rejoices in God my Savior...for the Mighty One has done great things for me, and holy is his name. His mercy is for those who fear him from generation to generation" (Lk. 1:47, 49-50). More recently, but with the same singing, it was Charles Wesley. In 1739 he wrote the great hymn "O for a Thousand Tongues to Sing." It is about "my great Redeemer's praise" and the "triumphs of [God's] grace."

Whether Hannah or Mary or Charles, the song true to the biblical tradition is always the same. It is about the truly amazing God, sovereign over all and actively for all people, the One beyond all time and also the One relationally engaged in the midst of our present times. Rather than only being out there somewhere in the distant heavens, Yahweh chooses involvement where we are, transforming our troubled history into *His-story*. From that involvement comes our understanding of the pervasive theological themes that underlie and inform both biblical Testaments.

The Most Important of All Truths

An ancient Jewish prophet points the way ahead. Jeremiah once was called by God to speak to wayward Jerusalem, and now he speaks to today's Christians as they seek the very center of truth, the water that is eternal. The Water Source for the Foundational Testament, the "overarching paradigm" of all its intended teaching, the one distinctive and all-encompassing Jewish belief is *"One God For All."*[13] We are not so much to believe *something* as we are to believe *in Someone*.

Every reading of history and every major piece of religious writing works from some premise. So, for the Foundational Testament, there is a clear historical interpretation that arises from a deep theological conviction, the prevailing conviction basic to all else. It is made clear in the very first line of the Testament. The final editor(s) of this large composite work were surely intentional with this opening statement:

---

13. Ronald Allen and John Holbert, *Holy Root, Holy Branches*, 36-38.

"In the beginning, *God*..." (Gen. 1:1). Here is the one all-encompassing belief that sheds its divine light on all else. If we stay with the water analogy, then the premise of all other beliefs, the overarching paradigm—to use a contemporary phrase, is as follows.

> **The Water Source**: All is God's creation; all people are intended to live in harmony with God and each other. The whole history recounted biblically is the story of God creating and then searching for renewed *shalom* (peace, harmony) in all creation. Israel's life is to be a reflection of the God who lives for the sake of all people and the entire creation. Whatever appears on the textual surface of the Foundational Testament, one thing is always sure. Beneath the surface, it all relies on and somehow intends to reflect belief in the amazing God who is holy, sovereign, the only God who is searching and loving and working for the redemption of all people in all times.

By way of illustration, note the *Shema* (Deut. 6:4). It is one of the more theologically crucial of all texts in the Foundational Testament. The Hebrew word literally means "Hear!" There is an urgent call to listen, to pay primary attention. Listen to what? Listen to the affirmation of the truth that is the context for all else: "Hear, O Israel: The Lord is our God, the Lord alone." God *is*, God is *our* Lord, and our Lord is *one* (*ehad*). This Hebrew word, especially taking into account Israel's existence in the midst of Near Eastern polytheism, is proclaiming that there is one and only one true God (cf. Deut. 4:39). Therefore, Yahweh claims and deserves the love and loyalty of the entire creation. To the Jewish mind, everything derives from God and thus everything is "theological." No distinction is made between "the sacred and the secular arenas of life. They see all of life as a unity. It is all God's domain."[14]

What were faithful Jews to do with what they heard? They were to teach the *Shema* to their children and write it on the doorposts of their houses and gates. In other words, they were never to let this great message get out of sight or mind. They were to keep it in front of every coming generation. As the two-Testament story goes, this constant remembering finally reached the coming of Yeshua, who adopted the words of Deuteronomy 6:5 as the first and greatest of all commandments. What did Yeshua and his Jewish heritage say we ought to do once we are aware of the message about this amazing God? We are to

---

14. Marvin Wilson, *Our Father Abraham*, 156.

"love the Lord your God with all your heart, and with all your soul, and with all your mind" (Matt. 22:37).

And what have the followers of Rabbi Yeshua learned to emphasize most of all? I checked the hymnal of my particular Christian tradition. It contains 734 entries, nearly all hymns and spiritual songs. Composed by numerous Christian poets and musicians from recent centuries, and covering nearly every imaginable aspect of Christian faith and life, what did the editors of this hymnal choose as entry *number one* in the book? That hymn's title is "Praise to the Lord, the Almighty" and the keynote biblical reference cited below the hymn's title is Revelation 4:11—"You are worthy, our Lord and God, to receive glory and honor and power, for you created all things, and by your will they existed and were created."[15]

Here are the words of verse one of this hymn number one: "Praise to the Lord, the Almighty, the King of creation! O my soul, praise Him, for He is thy health and salvation! All ye who hear, Now to his temple draw near, Join me in glad adoration!" Echoing the Jewish *Shema*, Christians likewise are summoned to *hear*, hear the good news of the one God, and receive, celebrate, and gladly repeat it to all others who will hear in all generations and places.

Four Streams That Carry the One Truth

We have established that, for the Foundational Testament, Yahweh God is the Overarching Paradigm, the Water Source, the bottom line of all truth. From that single source there flow four primary truth streams.[16] As the Jewish mindset would have it, these streams do not so much combine to form a creedal statement; instead, they express the core faith of the biblical Jews in *story form*. Knowing God is perceiving God at work in the history of the chosen people. It is there that Israel learned who God is and how they should be as his people in the world.

The four truth streams carry the central aspects of grace-full gifts that enable redeemed lives to be lived under God. Here is an important insight for contemporary Christians. At least one of these streams un-

---

15. *Worship the Lord: Hymnal of the Church of God* (Anderson, IN: Warner Press, 1989), 1.

16. The identification here of the four "truth streams" is similar to four "Trajectories" of Ronald Allen and John Holbert, *Holy Root, Holy Branches* (Abingdon Press, 1995), 38-56.

derlies *every passage* of the Foundational Testament. Each textual passage is understood best in relation to the living stream that flows beneath it. In its own time, place, and way, every surface passage is attempting to grapple with and express the immediate meaning of what lies below.

When these four truth streams are viewed together, they inform each other, bringing the fuller truth to light. Together they reveal the being and nature of the one God by recounting the story of God with Israel. In short, the four streams tell the one story in four stages. It goes this way:

1. God acts to choose a people for a divine redemptive purpose;
2. God sanctifies this people so that they can properly carry out the purpose;
3. God stands with his people in their questions, suffering, and even despair.
4. God grants a radical hope that sustains the people as they move toward God's intended future.

God chooses, sanctifies, stands with, and grants sustaining hope. Each element of this divine story interacts with each of the others. Each is clarified in the Foundational Testament as the life of God's people proceeded. These four truth streams or the four "ways" are:

1. The Way of Covenant
    God has acted to choose a people with a special mission in the world. God's choice is made out of love, not because any are deserving of being chosen. In an important sense, the choice is of *all* people, with a particular people responsible for spearheading the reaching of all others. God partners with unworthy people for the most worthy of all purposes.

2. The Way of Holiness
    All life is intended to be holy and pure in light of the holiness of the God who created and sustains all life. God has called a people to separate from the floundering world and reflect his own life among themselves and to others. Belonging to God's people should lead to a reflecting of God's life and world mission. God transforms into his own likeness those unworthy people with whom he partners.

3. The Way of Ordering and Questioning
   There is an order and purpose in the world created by God. Life is lived properly only in accord with that order that is God-ordained. Since the freedom of choice given by God to humans has been abused badly, the natural order of things is now disrupted and virtually invisible. Serious questioning to find and understand that order is a natural and acceptable part of the life and faith of God's people. Doubts and complaints are understandable, divinely welcomed, and need not lead to despair. God receives the doubts and questions of his people who remain only partially transformed and understand only in part.

4. The Way of Radical Hope
   God's enables a radical hope that can sustain faithful believers in the face of apparently hopeless circumstances. This hope transcends the present time, with its fragile institutions and practices that too often seek to maintain the status quo in opposition to God's will and way. God is always faithful. One day God's messiah will come! Those in covenant with God, those still in the process of being purified by God, will have a persistent hope, even in the midst of their frustrations and unfaithfulness.

There they are, the one Water Source (God) and the four truth streams that graciously flow from it. Again, each passage of the Foundational Testament in best read by Christians today only when: (a) it is understood textually in its original place, time, language, culture, and author/editor intent; (b) it then is understood theologically in relation to the overarching perspective, One God For All; (c) it also is understood in relation to the particular theological stream of which it is a part—and finding it often requires going *beneath the surface*; and (d) it finally is understood in relation to Yeshua who pre-eminently reveals the divine presence, nature, and redemptive purpose and is the fulfillment of the hope of the ages, past and future.

Occasionally in the following pages we will attempt to illustrate how best to handle for today's Christians what appear to be the most troubling passages of the Foundational Testament (see particularly chapter eleven). Necessarily, we will revert to the Water Source and to one or more of the truth streams that flow from this generous divine fountain. First, however, we will expand on what is truly important, the Water Source of all truth and the four streams of eternal truth that flow from it. We will devote two chapters to the Source, God, and one each to the streams of truth that flow forth from the divine to inform and potentially redeem all of the creation.

Listening again to Jeremiah 2:13, we dare not forsake the one and only fountain of living water, the one God for all people. We dare not risk digging for ourselves cracked cisterns that turn out to hold no water at all. To be truly Christian, belief about God must claim with reverent joy the Jewish perspective. On the one hand, Paul is correct. In light of Yeshua, there no longer is "Jew or Greek...for all of you are one in Christ Jesus" (Gal. 3:28). On the other hand, all who claim Yeshua Christ as Lord are necessarily joined through their Jewish Lord to some ancient paths that lead us back to David, and then to Moses, and then to Abraham, our common spiritual father. And, beyond Abraham, we come to Yahweh, the originator and center of it all.

The Christian doctrine of "Trinity" highlights the person and central role of Yeshua in God's larger plan for human redemption. Despite vigorous insistence to the contrary, this doctrine in no way conflicts with the core monotheistic belief of the Foundational Testament. In light of the theologically rich Hebrew tradition, what the Gospel writers and Paul were doing in the Final Testament was "to say a *logos*, a word about what God has done in Jesus of Nazareth. Their 'theologies'...are not primarily rational, philosophical investigations of the nature of God, but instead efforts in the direction of life transformation, re-presentations of the energy of the original Word."[17] Rabbi Yeshua, the Messiah, points us directly to the fountainhead from whom all truth streams flow. "Hear, O Israel: The Lord is our God, the Lord alone" (Deut. 6:4). From him come the four "streams" or "ways" to believe and live.

---

17. Robert Barron, *And Now I See: A Theology of Transformation* (N.Y.: Crossroad, 1998), 10.

SECTION TWO

FOUNDATIONAL TRUTHS FOR CHRISTIANS

THE "FATHER" OF RABBI YESHUA

If God has come to us, what is reliably known of God? To Whom do we address our prayers? What sort of language can one ascribe to this mysterious, wholly exceptional, transcendent reality? Who is this Holy One, which is to say, by what name shall we call Him? (Ex. 3:13-16).[1]

Abba, Father, for you all things are possible; remove this cup from me [the crucifixion]; yet, not what I want, but what you want. (Yeshua, in Mk. 14:36)

The faith of ancient Israel was characterized by one dominant reality. These chosen people knew themselves to have been addressed by Another, the only Other there is, the One who stands before, above, and beyond all else. There is God, they believed, and there is a Word from God to be heard and obeyed. This Word was spoken by Yahweh in direct relation to Israel's understanding of the formative events of its great tradition as a people. The God *behind* all human history was the God very much *in their particular history*. The belief of the later Final

---

1. Thomas C. Oden, *The Living God*, Systematic Theology: Volume One (Prince Press edition, 1998), 41.

Testament would be no different. Nor should it be for today's Christians.

We have made clear in previous chapters that the fountainhead of all faith in the Foundational Testament is the distinctive belief in the existence and particular character of God. There is one God for all people, the One who eventually came as Messiah to be the world's Redeemer. The earliest Christian community, thoroughly Jewish in its origins, understood itself to be continuing this tradition of belief and expectation when it told the dramatic story of Yeshua. The expected had been fulfilled. Yeshua was the apex of God's redeeming involvement in the ongoing life of the wayward creation. The Final Testament tells the whole world to look to Yeshua, the embodiment (incarnation) of the eternal heart of God. Yeshua regularly directed attention to his "Father."

With Us, But Not *Of* Us

As it had been with the ancient Jews, so it was with the Jews who first learned of the resurrection of Yeshua and accepted him as God's Messiah. Without denying his humanness, these amazed Jewish disciples came to know Yeshua as the One having come from God—so much so that he was really *God with us* for our salvation. Yeshua is the ultimate Word from God. Yahweh, the "Father" of Yeshua, is the transcendent One now come to be known by us in the stories of Israel and the divine Son. The story of Yeshua is the flowering of the earlier story of Israel. It is deeply rooted in and freshly expressive of the most radiant colors of Israel's story. God the Sovereign had stooped as God the Son to make the one and only divine being known, accessible, and redemptively effective.

Christian theology frequently addresses the doctrine of God by use of the terms "immanent" and "economic." The first word refers to the character of God's very being when considered apart from creation. Who is God within God's private and eternal self? Considerable caution is required here since our human knowledge is so limited and speculation is very undependable. After all, how can we have such ultimate, divinely intimate knowledge? The standard Jewish answer, continued in the story of Yeshua, is what is meant by "economic." More will be said about the importance of these terms when we address the "Trinity" doctrine in the next chapter. In short, "economic" means that the knowledge of God comes in the process of experiencing God working among us in our history.

From a Christian viewpoint, the continuous Israel-Yeshua story is the "economic" path to certain knowledge of the divine. The same loving heart of the divine known in ancient Israel now shines in the being of Yeshua. He taught his disciples the way they should pray. Christian prayer should begin majestically with "Our Father in heaven, hallowed be your name" (Matt. 6:9). That God-centered prayer, however, would always be Yeshua related. Something truly startling happened to those first Jewish disciples of Yeshua.

Despite their close contact with the humanness of Yeshua and their staunch heritage of Jewish monotheism, these first "Christians" came to believe that God was really with them in Yeshua. At the risk of their lives, they refused to stop announcing publically that worshipping God could not be separated from the holy presence in Yeshua of God among humans for our salvation. Paul made clear to the Colossian believers that the sovereign God will not be manipulated toward any selfish ends of superstitious humans. Spiritual alternatives to God-in-Christ are no alternatives at all. Only God is God, and only Yeshua is Lord! The ultimate that is conceivable was declared confidently to have become fact. In Yeshua "are hidden all the treasures of wisdom and knowledge" (Col. 2:3). In him "all the fullness of God was pleased to dwell," and through him God had acted "to reconcile to himself all things" (Col. 1:19-20).

This man Yeshua, who had appeared on the human scene in an especially humble way, "is said to have intersected grace-fully, lovingly, and decisively with human history and culture, and continues to do so, never being locked in any past."[2] Here is the bold declaration of the Final Testament—Yeshua is the full and final Self-revelation of God. And how is this to be understood in the larger context of God's economy? The answer had become obvious to those first Jewish believers. While not captured by any limitations of the Foundational Testament, the mission and identity of Yeshua would be incomprehensible without the enduring witness to God long at work in this broken world, and especially at work among the people of Israel.

The Gospel of Matthew begins the Final Testament materials with exactly this assumption of the continuity of Yeshua and God's previous work in Israel. It explains the true identity of Yeshua by reference to the story of God's preparation for the Christ in the history of the Jewish people. Matthew begins with a Jewish genealogy that leads to

---

2. Barry L. Callen, *God as Loving Grace* (Nappanee, IN: Evangel Publishing House, 1996), 172.

Yeshua, "Israel's new David," the "fulfillment and zenith of God's history with His people Israel."[3] Rooted in and understood by the Jewish past, this Yeshua also came to be seen as the very presence of God's intended future with all humanity. The "Christian" claim is dramatic and fully consistent with the "overarching paradigm" of all Jewish theology that lies beneath the surface of the entire Foundational Testament text. There is one and only one God, and God is lovingly for all creation!

Yeshua arrived as a *ben brith*, a son of the covenant. He sat as a boy at the feet of rabbis (Lk. 2:46-47). In later life, it was his custom to go "into the synagogue on the sabbath day" (Lk. 4:16). The Final Testament witness is an extension of the Foundational Testament, not a contradiction of it. Yeshua, the Jewish Christ raised from the dead by God, is another—actually the ultimate—Word of God. It flows from, is consistent with, and fulfills all previous words.

Here is the situation as the Final Testament paints the scene. We have two questions before us, and which we choose is crucial. Was Yeshua the son of Mary, somehow becoming the Son of God during his lifetime? Or was Yeshua the eternal Son of Yahweh who temporarily became the son of Mary as a redemptive act of God in our human history? The Christian witness is a dramatic "Yes!" to the second question. If Yeshua merely emerged *from us* humans as one of us, even the very best of us, that would be the usual way among human religions, only an admirable projection of our greatest fears and fondest hopes. But if Yeshua came *to us* from the loving heart of the Eternal, then his coming has the potential of doing for us what only God can do.

The Gospels of Matthew and Luke report that no human male was the biological father of Yeshua (see an expanded study of this in chapter eleven). It had been a "virginal conception." It has not proven helpful to press the scientific "Western" questions about how such a thing could have happened. The Bible simply says that the conception of Yeshua resulted from the overshadowing of God's creative Spirit. So the heart of Christian faith lies in the following: "God the Father stresses the *ultimacy* of the Divine...the mystery, the ineffability, as well as the primacy and finality of Deity.... Yeshua Christ defines the *character* of God.... God is the life-transforming, life-redeeming Energy of the character of Yeshua of Nazareth.... The Holy Spirit affirms the *intimacy*

---

3. Michael Lodahl, *The Story of God* (Kansas City: Beacon Hill Press, 1994), 129.

of omnipotent Power."[4] Three? Yes, in one sense. And yet, made so clear in the Jewish tradition, God is always only one! See more on this in the next chapter.

The most central of all subjects in the Foundational Testament is God. God is the eternally *Prior One* who also is the immediately *Present One*. To know this God is less a successful intellectual exercise and more the result of a transforming communion with the Holy One heard, remembered, and obeyed. To "know" requires a yielding to a oneness with God's presence, will, and way. To remember this God is more than not forgetting; it is "to activate the past in such a way as to influence present decision and present conduct."[5] This faith of the ancient Israelite was so very different from the many other ways humans seek to believe and live.

The goal of all life, as viewed in the Foundational Testament, is not to conform to the laws of nature; it is not to grasp deep philosophical principles that presumably lie behind all human thinking; it is not to maximize the joy of each moment, distracting from the ultimate meaninglessness of existence; nor is it to placate perceived powers that control our little lives unless we can figure out how to control them first. All these goals are typical ways of the world, characteristics of "pagan" religions.

It was not so for the people of Israel who were the people of Yeshua. For them, the goal of life is to hear God's voice and obey, to realize that God is, has acted, and is speaking and redeeming. It is to "know" God, not merely in the rational way of "knowing about" God, but in the biblical sense of knowing God by way of personal experience of a relationship with God as part of his chosen people. The goal is not mere *information about* the divine, but *communion with* the divine. God is *relational by nature*. When viewed in and through Yeshua, Yahweh is intensely, lovingly, even sufferingly present and active on our behalf.

The person especially representative of what is most distinctive about the whole tradition recorded in the Foundational Testament is the *prophet*, not the philosopher. The prophet does not emerge with his own intellect, insight, and claimed religious genius. He comes to speak to the people because he has *heard* and has been *sent* by Another. Yahweh is the Speaking One, the Sending One in whom Israel found her life and destiny, that is, when she heard and obeyed.

---

4. Laurence W. Wood, *Truly Ourselves, Truly the Spirit's* (Zondervan, Francis Asbury Press, 1989), 175-176.

5. James Muilenburg, *The Way of Israel*, 17.

There were many times when Israel hardly heard and refused to obey; there were times when the prophets proved to be false, speaking only for themselves or their political superiors. Yes, even this great tradition of the chosen people is filled with such waywardness. But the false only makes clearer the true. Behind everything that the faithful prophets proclaimed was this assumption: "Hear the word *of the Lord*!" The prophets of the Final Testament were announcing that God had spoken again and most fully in the coming of Yeshua. They had heard and now were commissioned to proclaim (Matt. 28:18-20).

Truth Emerges in Worship

My undergraduate years at Geneva College in Pennsylvania introduced me to the practice of using the Psalms in Christian worship. We would sing in chapel without instrumental accompaniment. On the most formal occasions, like a commencement ceremony, our singing often used these great words of Psalm 100:

> Make a joyful noise to the Lord,
>   all the earth.
> Worship the Lord with gladness,
>   come into his presence with singing.
> Know that the Lord is God.
>   It is he that made us, and we are his;
>   we are his people, and the sheep of his pasture.

Here again is the centerpiece of the faith of the Jews—knowing that *the Lord is God* and we are his sheep.

Recall that, biblically speaking, "knowing" is less rational comprehension and more an engagement with and a transformation by. The Jews were a passionate people who preferred the concrete to the abstract, the historical to the speculative, the relational to the creedal. True godliness was understood to be tied more to a *relationship with* than to a *formal teaching about*. Sheep can do without a map and answers to many questions; what they require is knowing and being close to their shepherd!

As heirs of this tradition, Christians today "must not forget that the earliest theology in the New Testament is relational or existential rather than propositional or creedal."[6] Many "Evangelicals" read the

---

6. Marvin Wilson, *Our Father Abraham*, 138.

Bible mostly to find and support particular "doctrines" precious to them. Typical of the Jews was an early action of Rabbi Yeshua. In order to increase knowledge—an experienced awareness--of his person and mission, he appointed the twelve disciples "that they might be *with him*" (Mark 3:14). The deepest "knowing" is in the "being with" and becoming like Yeshua.

Psalm 100 instructs us to come into God's presence with gladness and singing. Given this instruction and the whole tenor of the ancient approach to "theology," it likely is best to think of the first chapter of Genesis as mostly a hymn, the joyous witness and poetic celebration of people thinking relationally about ultimate things, including about the origins of the creation itself. These were things well beyond their comprehension in any technical, scientific, or geological sense. To read this chapter looking for such "information" is surely to read it wrongly. The result of doing that is basically the reader of today *bringing* to the text what is not truly *found* there.

As the ancient Jews pondered such things as the creation in light of their own experienced history with God, they naturally focused on and celebrated the amazing God who must have been behind it all. They soon were lost in wonder and praise. They worshipped with a song of beginnings, exactly where the Foundational Testament begins. "In the beginning when God created... (Gen. 1:1).

Moving on from Genesis 1, Dennis Kinlaw suggests that the book of Psalms is the right place to begin reading the Foundational Testament *theologically*. He explains: "If the goal of theology is the knowledge of the true God, the end result of that experience ought to be adoration and praise and prayer.... Here is where we find what Israel really believed, and how it affected their daily lives.... You will know you have found him [Yahweh] if you find yourself on your face before him."[7]

Although there is no systematic theology in the book of Psalms, there is a vibrant worshipping of God. The worshippers are people opening their hearts to Yahweh, the One to whom they are related by his unmerited grace through what he had done for them and what they hoped he would do. It was not only experience and emotion, however. In all the variety of ideas and emotions and shifting cultural settings, there is in the Psalms and throughout the Foundational and

---

7. Dennis Kinlaw, *Lectures in Old Testament Theology*, 13-14, 16.

Final Testaments "a coherent set of ideas about God, humanity, and the world...."[8]

Yahweh, the personal name for God, appears nearly 7,000 times in the Foundational Testament. Its root meaning is "to be" and likely intends to convey at least two critical truths. (1) God *is* and (2) God is the One who *causes to be*. Virtually everything from Genesis to Malachi is somehow rooted in this assumption of the existence, character, and working of Yahweh. Psalm 146 begins with "praise the Lord" or *hallelu-Yah* (praise God). When God is met and known, the natural human response is an experience of worship, of joy and praise that transfers into English as "hallelujah!"

One could not easily construct a systematic theology based on the Psalms. They were not intended for that. What they express is a wide range of spiritual reflections, introspections, questions, and affirmations based on personal and community experiences. Nonetheless, there is a central focus running through the Psalms. It is *Yahweh* and a discernable set of crucial theological assumptions related to Yahweh and his interaction with the creation. Primary among these assumptions is that Yahweh is God alone, lacking any rivals. Psalm 115:1-4 is a good example:

> Not to us, O Lord [Yahweh], not to us,
> but to your name give glory,
> for the sake of your steadfast
> love and your faithfulness.
> Why should the nations say,
> "Where is their God?"
>
> Our God is in the heavens;
> he does whatever he pleases.
> Their idols are silver and gold,
> The work of human hands.

With the lack of rivals comes a related theme. Yahweh, the incomparable and only God, transcends all things, in fact is the Creator of all that is—except for evil which derives from the creation's own choosing.

At this point comes an important paradox, a necessary theological balance point to be affirmed carefully in all its complex fullness—so typically Jewish. Failing to achieve balance loses the Jewish perspective

---

8. Dennis Kinlaw, 88. See chapter four of this present book for an identification of this "coherent set of ideas."

and introduces an alien view that elevates the creation beyond its actual status in the order of things. One side of the theological paradox is this. There is a significant discontinuity between God and the creation. The creation is not self-generating and did not emerge out of God in the sense of being an extension or part of God's being. To the contrary, God voluntarily spoke the creation into existence, having himself eternally existed prior to creation.

The other side of the paradox is this. Yahweh, the wholly Other, the Creator of all from what had been nothing prior, is the same Yahweh who involves himself deeply, even vulnerably in the now-fallen creation's life. The purpose of this involvement is enabling a loving partnership, not absolute control or manipulation of the human partners in the covenant. The involvement is redemptive in intent and is because of no necessity brought to God from anything external to the divine being; it is only because of a voluntary divine choice flowing out of the love that characterizes God's very being. God acts in accord with the nature of his being, which we have learned is relational and loving.

Three words are central in order to keep this essential paradox whole and representing well the ancient faith of the Jews. The first is "sovereignty." Yahweh is clearly sovereign over the creation, being its Creator. Sovereignty, however, cannot be the highest attribute of God. In the beginning, when there was nothing but Yahweh alone, there was nothing for God to be sovereign over. Instead, the primary word of the Foundational Testament is that Yahweh is "holy." Being holy is not just a lofty adjective attached to the being of God. It is descriptive of the very nature of God's essence. Here is a key tie between the two biblical Testaments: "Since the distinctiveness of God has been established in the Old Testament, the New testament is concerned to show by Whom and in what way the people of God will share that holiness."[9]

After "sovereign" and "holy" comes the word "jealous." Yahweh is said to be a jealous God. This is not a green-with-envy jealousy. How could it be? Yahweh has no rivals, none to be jealous of. Jealousy can be a bad or good thing. It is bad when selfish and protecting the petty, like weak humans striking out at others when feeling threatened; it is good if guarding what is precious, and doing it out of an unselfish love.

The biblical idea of divine jealousy appears in Exodus 20:1-6, the classic statement of the "Ten Commandments." Yahweh's people,

---

9. Dennis Kinlaw, 218.

newly liberated from slavery, are told to have no "gods" before God. Why be concerned about other gods when there are none, only false pretenders and human self-delusions? It is for the sake of Yahweh's people. They are instructed to avoid building or symbolizing anything that tempts humans to bow the knee in worship to what, in fact, is not real. Yahweh is jealous—*for his people!* Jealousy can be a vice (Gal. 5:20) or quite the opposite. Yahweh's jealousy is like when Paul was deeply concerned about the well being of the believers in Corinth (2 Cor. 11:2).

Yahweh is other than all the "gods" we humans create and then worship. In fact, "there is a categorical distinction between Yahweh and all other gods. The gods of all the ancient pantheons were simply projections of you and me...regional particularities of the natural world that Yahweh created."[10] None of them transcends the creation. People imagined them, projected them, feared them, tried to keep them happy and gain from them protection and favors.

The sad fact is that people do build images of their gods and often place them on high hills. Therefore, Yahweh directed that his people "demolish completely all the places where the nations whom you are about to dispossess served their gods, on the mountain heights, on the hills, and under every leafy tree.... You shall not worship the Lord your God in such ways" (Deut. 12:2-4). Yahweh is not looking for favors from his people. To the contrary, Yahweh is jealous *on behalf of his people*, a concerned lover paining over his beloved who is in danger of selling her soul to that which is false and deadly.

Praying "Our Father"[11]

The biblical psalmists celebrate what was considered the foundational truth of this world. There is one and only one divine being who is beyond the whole creation as sovereign, holy, and rightly jealous. "I lift up my eyes to the hills—from where will my help come? My help comes from the Lord who made heaven and earth" (Ps. 121:1-2). The help is not from the hills themselves, but from what is beneath and beyond and prior to them. The help is Yahweh who created the hills and all else.

---

10. Dennis Kinlaw, 50, 53.

11. For an extended commentary on the Lord's Prayer, see Barry L. Callen, *The Prayer of Holiness-Hungry People* (Francis Asbury Press, 2011). This subsection relies in part on material in this source.

Israel's deliverance from Egyptian bondage, the "Exodus," is an historical highpoint of the Jewish tradition. But the theological center of this pivotal event was less a conflict between Moses and Pharaoh and much more between Yahweh and a false view of God. Pharaoh was worshipped as a god. In fact, he was not, nor is any other, then or now. There is none except Yahweh.

The one and only God who is sovereign Creator, truly holy, and rightly jealous for his people, is the God encountered dramatically by the prophet Isaiah in the year that King Uzziah died. The Lord was sitting high on a throne and his robe filled the temple. The surrounding seraphs were calling to each other what humans always should: "Holy, holy, holy is the Lord of hosts; the whole earth is full of his glory" (Isa. 6:3). Moses had learned this earlier when Yahweh told him to lead the people out of Egypt into freedom and their intended destiny. Moses had responded nervously by insisting on knowing God's name. He judged that both the people and the pharaoh would want to know what god had dared to launch such an audacious redemption strategy.

What Moses was told by Yahweh left him with a paradoxical and almost speechless awe. "I am who I am" (Ex. 3:14). Yahweh is beyond all categories that can be named. He is what he is and will be what he will be. What he does is what he does, and he need answer to no one. That ineffable God is the One who had decided to save the people of Israel! God is *holy*, which literally means "other," beyond all we can know in normal ways. God is wholly *sovereign*, and yet still the One who was about to become the savior of an enslaved people. This is a paradoxical vision of God, the far-beyond One who also is the very-near One, the One in the heavens who also is the One intervening in the crisis of our sin and suffering. Such a vision naturally leads us to grateful prayer.

Yeshua later urged his disciples to pray in a particular way, now called the "Lord's Prayer." It begins with deep reverence, and also the warm relationality of "Our Father...." Traditional Judaism made occasional references to God as "Father" (e.g., Isa. 63:16), but only occasionally. The concept of divine fatherhood often had divine-human physical connotations among surrounding polytheists. The Jews, in order to avoid idolatry, resisted the potential awkwardness of "Father" language. Yeshua, a Jewish teacher in a considerably changed environment, expanded the modest Jewish "Father" tradition, using this unusually personal manner of addressing God no less than six times in his classic high priestly prayer (John 17). Yeshua knew himself to be God's "Son," a unique relationship indeed. He judged that "Father" was an appropriate God reference that expresses both the salvation and mission of Israel. Salvation (freedom) had come to Israel, God's first-born son (Ex. 4:22–23). Slaves were released from their bondage to sin and transformed into children of the divine on mission in this world.

When Yeshua called God "Father," historic memories and meanings would have been shaken awake in his Jewish disciples. For Yeshua to call God our "heavenly Father" was to make the most audacious theological statement that could be made. The God who created the world and cast the nebulae into space, who heard the prayers of the first man and woman on earth and who sees the intricacies of the future, the God whose majesty is seen from the highest mountain and inhabits the depths of the darkest ocean, the God who led the Hebrews out of captivity in Egypt and brought Yeshua from the grave is the very God who can and should be addressed as "Father." If the word Father gathered up all this Jewish history, frustration, and expectation, then Yeshua was saying to his disciples, "Let it be *now*, and let it be *us*!"

Begin prayer, instructed Rabbi Yeshua, with "Our Father."[12] The Father of Yeshua is also the Father of Israel. He is Lord of Lords, King of Kings, the author of time, the bringer of salvation, and the master of eternity. This Father "in heaven" is Yahweh. By addressing God as "our Father" who is "in heaven," we place emphasis on twin realities that too often are separated in Christian church life. There first is the intimate reality of our dear and loving Father who is so present with us in healing, gifting, and empowerment. Second, there also is the sovereign reality of the God who is utterly different from us, whose ways are higher than our ways, whose being is beyond our theological formulas and "sacred" church institutions. Yeshua makes clear that the prayer life of his disciples must balance these twin realities. God is in heaven, yes, but also very close at hand. He is in heaven, yes, but nonetheless a very present help in time of trouble.

The opening and closing verses of Psalm 8 are identical: "O Lord, our Sovereign, how majestic is your name in all the earth!" This One "in heaven" had now become most

visible in Yeshua. Affirming this Jewish foundation and Yeshua fulfillment spells death to all human "isms" that divide when God does

---

12. At the time of Jesus, the designation "Rabbi" was not a formally ordained religious office but a term of honor, essentially meaning "great teacher." Many Jews considered Jesus at least a master teacher before some of them came to know him as "the Lord."

not—nationalisms, racisms, classisms, and the ugly rest. The Holy One is gathering a family of equals. All members of this divine family are undeserving; all are reborn and adopted by divine grace; all people are invited to join this family of God.

According to Rabbi Yeshua, "hallowed be your name" is to be our heart-cry toward God. "Hallowed" draws on the Greek *hagios* (holy), essentially meaning "different from other things." God's name is different from other names. It is not to be "taken in vain," used glibly, selfishly, harshly, to no effect. To hallow God's name goes beyond being respectful of it. It necessarily involves actual transformation of the one who prays with proper awareness and respect. The one praying must become what the name implies and makes possible.

In the Jewish culture of biblical times, a person's name often indicated that individual's nature, character, or special trait. So praying for God's name to be "hallowed" means gladly granting to God the unique place that his nature, character, and actions deserve. In effect, Yeshua asks his disciples to surround all that they affirm or ask in prayer with the spirit of psalm 111: "Praise the Lord!... Great are the works of the Lord.... Holy and awesome is God's name!" (vss. 1, 2, 9). The psalmist asked God two humbling questions. "Where can I go from your Spirit? Or where can I flee from your presence?" (139:7). The obvious answer to both questions is "Nowhere!"

What, then, is true holiness? It is a life-reshaping reverence. It is seeing and submitting to the invisible, spiritual reality of God. It is the outcome of a life that truly sees and properly submits to the eternal God. Thus, Rabbi Yeshua says to pray, "Hallowed be *Thy* name!" And what of his own name? The Master's name in Hebrew is *Yeshua*, or Joshua in English. The name's meaning is "Yahweh's salvation" or "Yahweh is salvation." Why this particular name? Joseph had a vision in a dream. It was of an angel who instructed him to give the new baby this name Yeshua because "he will save his people from their sins" (Matt. 1:21).

Early Christians, worshippers of Yahweh through the Son Yeshua, were sometimes called "saints"—the holy ones, the ones set apart for God, those "who are sanctified" (Acts 20:32). They knew that "hallowing" is a disciple's proper stance toward God. The Greek word for "saints" in the Final Testament comes from the same root word as the verb meaning "to hallow." This suggests that, as we hallow God's name, he hallows us. God answers the first petition of the Lord's Prayer by "sanctifying" those who pray, making them "saints." Believers are holy only because of who Yahweh is and what Yeshua has done for them. They must continue to be holy by the enablement of what God's

Spirit will do in them with their willing cooperation. The heart of the matter is this:

> For thus says the high and lofty one who inhabits eternity, whose name is Holy: "I dwell in the high and holy place, and also with those who are contrite and humble in spirit, to revive the spirit of the humble, and to revive the heart of the contrite" (Isa. 57:15).

A Parade and a Folk Tale

The prophecies of Isaiah do more than describe a critical understanding of the necessary balance between Yahweh's present *nearness* to creation and Yahweh's eternal *beyondness* from it (57:15). At one point this prophet paints a picture of public stupidity when something far less than Yahweh is actually worshipped out in the open. It is a sad picture of idolatry at its most embarrassing.

The Jews were deep into their long captivity in Babylon. Their captors staged a periodic parade featuring their gods riding on floats being dragged through the streets by large animals. The prophet of Yahweh first explains the absolute absurdity of idol worship (Isa. 44:9-29). Then he imagines that he was watching the parade and wanting to encourage the depressed Jews who were forced to line the streets to witness this silly spectacle. Isaiah let his sarcastic side take over. He could no longer contain his mixture of amusement and disgust in the face of such a public display of idolatrous arrogance.

"Bel bows down, Nebo stoops, their idols are on beasts and cattle; these things you carry are loaded as burdens on weary animals. They stoop, they bow down together; they cannot save the burden, but themselves go into captivity" (Isa. 46:1-2). What a scene! Idols cannot walk for themselves. Rather than saving their people, they are a great burden for weary animals. Then it happened! It may have been only a bump in the road, a problem on the parade route, but a sudden crisis developed, one that Isaiah found so ironic that it was laughable.

An animal lost its balance or was just exhausted. It began to collapse, and with it the god on its back or on the cart it was pulling. Handlers rushed to help, but it was too late. The beast was down and the helpless idol quickly joined it, splattered all over the street, maybe its head flying off and injuring a child standing in the front row. How different it is with Yahweh, announces Isaiah! Yahweh speaks:

> Listen to me, O house of Jacob, all the remnant of the house of Israel, who have been borne by me from your birth, carried from the womb; even to your old age I am he, even when you turn gray *I will carry you.* (Isa. 46:3-4)

What did the exiled Jews need to know when surrounded by pagan gods who seemed to give Babylon its power? They needed to know that...

--the word of Yahweh stands forever (Isa. 40:7-8);
--Yahweh neither faints nor is weary (Isa. 40:28);
--Yahweh is always involved with current history (Isa. 41:4);
--Yahweh one day will render all divine pretenders meaningless (Isa. 40:17);
--one day soon the exiles would leave Babylon with joy (Isa. 55:12).[13]

One could imagine a much earlier time in the very same area. There is an old Jewish folk tale that goes back to none other than Abraham, the man who would become the father of the Judeo-Christian faith tradition. He is the one who was willing to believe in God's future despite the rampant idolatry around him, and with no understanding of exactly what that future might involve. Keeping in mind Isaiah's prophecy based on the silly parade of idols, consider a Jewish man gathering his family soon after the fatal parade, focusing especially on the children, and telling this little Jewish folk tale.

"You know, of course," he would say to his family, "that Abraham was the father of our people. He began his life around here among the *goyim*, those non-Jews who worshipped idols like you saw in the streets today. His father Terah owned a little store that made and sold small idols. According to *Midrash Rabba*, it happened like this." Then the story would proceed about as follows.

One day Abraham, then a teenager, was entrusted to mind the store while his father Terah went on some errand. A man came in to buy an idol. Instead of hurrying the sale process and getting the precious money, Abraham asked the man how old he was. The answer was fifty, to which the young man responded surprisingly: "Why would a mature man like you buy an idol that is made only of clay?—in fact, Dad made this one in our back room only last night." So much for that sale. There were other shops nearby where one did not have to face hard questions.

Soon a woman came in ready to buy. Abraham recognized her and asked why she needed to buy another idol. She'd been in just the week

---

13. Barry L. Ross, *Our Incomparable God* (Pune, India: Fountain Press, 2006), 8-10.

before and bought one. "Thieves stole it" was her sad report. The young man's mouth let loose with something that immediately lost his father another valuable sale. "Why would you pray to and entrust your own safety to an idol that can't even keep itself from being stolen?" Since the woman had no answer, that neighboring shop soon got another new customer.

As soon as she had walked out empty-handed, Abraham locked the door and went to work. He had convinced himself of the sheer stupidity of idolatry. He took his father's axe and cut off the feet of the smallest idol on the shelf. Then he chopped off the hands of another one, put out the eyes of another, and finally placed the axe in the hands of the biggest idol, the only other one on the shelf. Terah soon returned and had to unlock the door of his own shop—which was supposed to be open for business. He saw the carnage on the shelf and demanded an explanation from his son, who now was sitting quietly in the corner.

Abraham calmly said to an angry father, "The largest idol did it all. See, the axe is still in his hands!" Terah looked at the big idol in disbelief. "Impossible. That thing can't use an axe!" Abraham's reply was this: "Sure it can, Dad, just ask it." That being impossible, the story was over, the powerful point made.

Once Terah cooled off and did some heavy thinking, his conclusion was: "If that is the best the gods of this world can do, maybe it is time to move on. I've been hearing from Yahweh, the God above the mute little gods. He is calling us into some unknown future." Then it happened, a pivotal event that set the Judeo-Christian heritage in motion. The call had come from Another, the one true God not made with human hands, the one who could actually answer when addressed. Soon Terah, Abraham, and the rest of the family began their historic journey of faith into a future known only to Yahweh. At least Yahweh was not subject to being lost, stolen, or the victim of street accidents and public humiliation! Instead, he was choosing a people and forging a future.

YAHWEH, THE TRULY "OPEN" GOD

Exodus 34:6 reports that the "merciful and gracious" God is "abounding in steadfast love and faithfulness." Psalm 136 says repeatedly that "the steadfast love [of God] endures forever."

"Self-giving love is an essential attribute of God's eternal nature.... Because of love, God provides freedom to creatures—as well as agency, value, and relationship.[1]

Who really is the holy God, and how does God relate to a fallen creation in order to encourage and enable a corresponding holiness at the human level? What does the word "perfect" mean when applied to God? How does the God of *holy love* relate to the God also known as truly *sovereign*? Does God ever change, being responsive to and possibly even impacted by developments in the creation? Can God be eternally perfect and still change in relation to the temporal scene of humans?[2]

---

1. Thomas Jay Oord, *The Nature of Love: A Theology* (St. Louis: Chalice Press, 2010), 124-125.
2. See a set of stimulating and frank conversations on these questions by twenty-one prominent Christian thinkers, in Barry L. Callen, *Heart of the Matter* (Lexington, KY: Emeth Press, 2011).

There are no more basic questions than these. They are exceedingly demanding, much debated, and their answers carry major implications for how Jewish and Christian believers carry on their lives of faith. These questions should be approached humbly, reading both biblical Testaments, and doing it together as a body of believers seeking to gain the wisdom of the Spirit and reflect the holiness that is God. The questions should be approached as the great reformer John Calvin advised, even though at points his theology appears to violate his own advice.

What is the good advice? Allow God to reveal himself in Scripture rather than predetermine our knowledge of God by the use of some philosophical principle or pre-set theological system. Let the Bible say what it does, not what we think it should have said. Unfortunately, Calvin and many "Evangelical" Christians today appear to begin with a principle (not clearly biblical) that God's "perfection" necessarily means that there can be no change in God—any change, they say, would have to be for the worse. So, when statements of change related to God appear in the Foundational Testament, and many of them do, the statements are disallowed and read some other way.

I am convinced that the Foundational Testament seeks to convey God's "perfection" within its broader view of God's loving relationality—which implies an openness to change of certain kinds. The eternal Yahweh chooses to relate to his people openly, flexibly, even vulnerably.

God *Is* as God *Does*

Yahweh's existence, nature, and ultimate will for the creation are "perfect" and never change. However, Yahweh's loving concern and ways of working with the creation are characterized biblically as a dynamic, interactive process involving flawed covenant partners. The Bible reveals "a *sufficient* God, not necessarily an *efficient* one."[3] How is this revealed? It does not come from some prior set of philosophic principles derived from human rationality. That was not the Jewish way. God *is* as God *does*. We come to know God as God becomes increasingly apparent to us through his actions in human history.

Who, then, is God? The creation accounts in Genesis refer to an absolute beginning of the creation, with God already being before

---

3. Paul Copan, *Is God a Moral Monster? Making Sense of the Old Testament God* (Grand Rapids: Baker Books, 2011), 166.

that. Granted, it is difficult and likely impossible to fathom who God was without reference to the creation that he freely chose to set in motion. We must be careful not to speculate rashly about who God is within God's own eternal self. Only God defines God. What we are told in Genesis, however, reveals aspects of the "providence" of God.

Full dominion over the creation belongs to God. However, exactly how God chooses to exercise that dominion ("providence") depends on God's creating nature and purpose. We come to know who God is by what God chooses to do in actually superintending this creation.

Lacking independent knowledge of ultimate things about God, the Jews of old turned to the lessons of their own actual history. They were not philosophic speculators; they were students of history, products of history, the gracious result of amazing things that Yahweh had chosen to do. Did the Jews learn from their history that divine "almightiness" means that Yahweh sees to it that everything turns out just as Yahweh desires as ideal? The answer had to come from the experienced story of God-with-us, God-with-Israel, later God-with-Yeshua, God acting and reacting in the actual give-and-take of history as biblically recorded.

Looking at the historical record of the Foundational Testament, apparently Yahweh is prepared to allow room for the creation to become what it chooses, for good or ill. Yahweh granted freedom and agency to humans, a partnership, a relationship that carried a dignity for the human partner—along with the potential danger of the freedom being abused. It was that way from the beginning:

> The creation stories depict divine providence as creating an environment for the sustenance of the creatures, granting divine blessing on them, establishing communities of relationships and bestowing tasks to be accomplished. The divine sovereignty has decreed that it should be this way rather than one of exhaustive divine control. God creates significant others and gives them "space" to operate.... It is a world in which he grants integrity to his creatures and singles out human beings for a special relationship, involving genuine give-and-take dynamics.[4]

Since God is known to us humans primarily through what God does, it is natural that the Foundational Testament features much historical reporting. History is taken seriously as the arena in which God comes, expresses openness to the creation, judges, saves, and suffers in the process. Yes, God suffers, a consequence of a loving God entering

---

4. John Sanders, *The God Who Risks: A Theology of Providence* (Downers Grove, ILL: InterVarsity Press, 1998), 45, 88.

into real relationships with free creatures who often choose to sin against God's will. Consider this strong statement:

> The God and Father of Jesus Christ is compassionate, suffering, and victorious love. The god of philosophy is immutable, timeless, and apathetic.... Augustine was wrong to have said that God does not grieve over the suffering of the world; Anselm was wrong to have said that God does not experience compassion; Calvin was wrong to have said that biblical figures that convey such things are mere accommodations to human understanding.[5]

An important assumption that lies beneath both the Foundational and Final Testaments. The sovereignty of God is awesome, but also beautiful because of the amazing openness of God to genuine relationships with us fallen humans. It is an openness knowable to us because of God's intentional and redemptive activity in human history.

William Willimon puts it well in his Christian context: "Scripture thinks that our greatest need is to be with the God who, in Jesus Christ, has shown such remarkable determination to be with us. Richard J. Foster and others worked for years in intensive biblical study and then reported being profoundly struck by two great realities:

> First, we found that the unity of the Bible is discovered in the development of life *with* God as a reality on earth, centered in the person of Jesus. Through Scripture we heard God whispering down through the centuries: "I am *with* you!" "I am *with* you!" "I am *with* you!" Then we heard God asking a question that searches the human person to the depths: "Are you willing to be *with* Me?"[6]

A vision of God, rather than helpful hints for everyday living, is what Scripture seeks."[7] To understand such a vision of the sovereign and "beautiful" God, we must do as the Foundational Testament directs. We must begin with a vision of God, not of ourselves, and find that vision in God's actual dealing with the creation, especially God's gracious seeking of and working with Israel.

We begin, then, with the Jews and their experiences with Yahweh over time. We do not begin with any philosophic tradition of humans. If we must choose between Athens and Jerusalem, accepting as prima-

---

5. Clark H. Pinnock, *Most Moved Mover: A Theology of God's Openness* (Grand Rapids: Baker Academic, 2001), 27.

6. Richard J. Foster, *Life With God: Reading the Bible for Spiritual Transformation* (HarperCollins e-books, preface).

7. William H. Willimon, *Proclamation and Theology* (Nashville, TN: Abingdon Press, 2005), 46.

ry either the Greek philosophic tradition or the biblical approach of the Jews, as biblical believers we choose Jerusalem.

The "Openness" of God

This choice of interpretive traditions for understanding Yahweh lies at the heart of the current debate about God in the "Evangelical" Christian community. I join my late friend Clark H. Pinnock in insisting that the biblical record is the proper source for developing Christian thinking—not a heavy reliance on the Reformed (Calvinistic) theology. Dwight Pryor and others have shown that "our view of Jesus invariably is filtered through the lenses of our culture, such as through Byzantine spectacles, Protestant Reformation spectacles, or American spectacles." He cautions that we need to "put on Hebraic [Jewish] lenses to see Jesus of Nazareth more clearly and to understand Him more fully."[8] The resulting thesis of this book is that going "Hebraic" and being "biblical" in our central perspectives are the same thing.

The parable of the "prodigal son," as told by Yeshua in the Final Testament, is a good case in point. When read through Hebrew-sensitive eyes, the eyes of Yeshua who told the story, the parable is not intended primarily as a commentary on the actions of the younger or older brother. Typical of the Jewish tradition, it is about the *amazing father*. In the Oriental world of the ancient Near East, children were expected (required) to show the utmost respect to their parents. For the younger son to have asked for his inheritance while his father was still alive was in effect to say to his father, "I wish you were dead! Treat me now like you were!" (Lk. 15:11). The hearers of Yeshua would have been shocked by the young son's request and wondering what the father would do to this awful child. This father did surprising, even amazing things. He gave, waited, and finally welcomed home the terribly wayward child.

What a picture of Yahweh! Yeshua was saying by this "prodigal" story, "Here you see the Father I know, the true God of Israel. Yahweh surprises us with grace and mercy when only judgment is deserved." Such a Father is the God who is celebrated by the prophets Jeremiah, Isaiah, and the others. He is the One who brought a people out of Egyptian slavery (Exodus), would later bring them out from Babylonian Exile, and still later would bring Yeshua from the dead. Yahweh is the One greater than all the would-be gods of the nations, the One

---

8. Dwight A. Pryor, *Behold the Man!*, 13.

who holds the reigns of life and death. The Jewish prophets give us a picture of the loving and forgiving God in action. Yahweh is the holy sovereign who functions as active love and expresses love by granting a dynamic partnership with his chosen people.

I gladly join today's "Messianic" Jewish and "open-theology" Christian communities in calling for a reclaiming of key aspects of the Jewish foundation of Christian faith. For the biblical authors, God is understood *functionally*. God acts, and thus is known through his actions. The Hebrews thought of God primarily in terms of personality and activity, not in abstract terms of pure and perfect being. God is as God does. Thus, the Foundational Testament shows little interest in many of the issues the Christian church has debated over the centuries, issues like the supposed aseity, immutability, and impassibility of God. Rather, Moses, Isaiah, Amos, Jeremiah, and the others saw God creating a people, saving a people, calling for holiness, implementing justice, and offering hope for the future. Their understanding of God grew out of these perceptions of divine activity. These perceptions, they believed, were inspired by God to ensure their accuracy and allow us to rightly call them "revelation."

Reviewing the Foundational Testament, we see that Yahweh had become known within the ancient Jewish community as the One who is living, holy, jealous, righteous, gracious, and purposeful.[9] Yahweh is a loving person, sovereign, communal, faithful, and also relational and resourceful in shifting circumstances.[10] All of these descriptions are limited human understandings, of course. They are analogies employed to describe what is finally indescribable. Nonetheless, they speak meaningfully of the One who has become known as active in these particular ways among and for his people. Taken together, these descriptions of Yahweh were believed by the biblical writers to constitute a basic and balanced understanding of the divine being. Especially when many Jews later added Yeshua to the revelational mix as its apex, God was even more intensely understood to be holy, gracious, self-giving, redemptive love.

This composite understanding of God brings us back to the important issue of divine providence, a subject of considerable disagreement in the current Christian community. How does Yahweh choose to govern the ongoing life of the creation? When we look to the Foun-

---

9. Barry L. Callen, *God As Loving Grace* (Nappanee, IN: Evangel Publishing House, 1996), 85-92.

10. Clark Pinnock, *Most Moved Mover*, 79-104.

dational Testament for an answer, we learn that the dominating motivation of divine providence, the way Yahweh chooses to work in this creation, is stimulated more by the motive of *love* than the maintenance of *full control* of all things at all times. Here is the apparent paradox of divine sovereignty in relation to divine providence: "Suffering is not inherent in God, but God freely wills to enter into our suffering so that it can be overcome. God cannot be changed by either heavenly or earthly powers, but God can change himself. He remains unchanging in his will for the world, but he alters his ways with his people in conjunction with their response to his gracious initiative. God enters into a reciprocal relationship with his people so that we can have a role in the realization of his plan and purpose."[11]

What sometimes is called "classical" Christian theism, the Calvinistic/Reformed tradition so influential in today's "Evangelical" community, has introduced a major theological difficulty. It has made it difficult to speak meaningfully of a God who covenants with humanity, makes humans significant partners in introducing the reign of God in human affairs, and interactively loves all creation. If God is changeless and invulnerable to human evil, as this tradition insists, one wonders what was really going on as Yeshua hung on that old rugged cross—unless one separates God the Father far enough from the event that the real divinity of Yeshua is compromised. Better than this wrong direction, Christians should follow the lead of the Foundational Testament.

Was not Yahweh, *as God in Christ*, reconciling the world to himself on that cross? Was not Yahweh, *as God in Christ*, in the midst of this world-shaking and suffering incarnational act? Was the self-giving of Yeshua not Yahweh's own Self-giving love? Was there not a Self-giving cross lodged deep in the heart of Yahweh before it was driven a few feet into a hill called Golgatha? Did Yahweh not suffer on our behalf in the agony of Yeshua? Was the imagery of Psalm 85:10 not lived out wonderfully in the Yeshua event? "Mercy and truth are met together; righteousness and peace have kissed each other" (KJV).

In the cross of Christ "we see best the living God so present in our world, the holy and jealous God, so singular and different from us, the righteous God, so committed to what is right and just despite the high cost, and especially the gracious God with a clear purpose being real-

---

11. Donald G. Bloesch, *God the Almighty: Power, Wisdom, Holiness, Love* (Downers Grove, ILL: InterVarsity Press, 1995), 95.

ized by a redeeming love beyond compare."[12] Yahweh suffers for us sinners because Yahweh so chooses—not out of any necessity external to the divine self. Yahweh is "open" to this suffering because of his relating, reaching, and redeeming nature.

Today's Christian "process" theologians accept this view of God at work, but tend to hesitate at conceiving God "as distinct from the world."[13] This distinction is critical, however. "Openness" theologians affirm *both* the loving vulnerability of God and the absolute sovereignty of God. This is not viewed as a contradiction, but a necessary paradox. Process thought tends to deny that God absolutely controls much of anything. It argues that God does not act unilaterally and coercively. Openness thought finds the paradoxical middle ground more adequately, representing well the whole of the Foundational Testament. While God freely chooses not to determine everything, God can and sometimes does act unilaterally, even coercively, although relational love keeps such times to a minimum.

The ultimate impulse of Yahweh's life is love; respect for the freedom and integrity of humans is basic to Yahweh's general way with the world. The origin, interim life, and ultimate destiny of the creation exist because of divine initiative. They never lie outside the potential of full divine control. Yahweh's loving ways are usually persuasive and not coercive, but coercion for significant cause is always a possibility for the One who remains transcendent in the midst of loving immanence. God is "completely reliable and true to himself and, at the same time, flexible in his dealings and able to change course as circumstances require."[14] As with that father in the story of the prodigal son told by Yeshua, our heavenly Father responds, grieves, always loves, always waits to welcome home.

The "Trinity": Still *One* God

We have noted that the Foundational Testament presents a range of challenges for contemporary Christians. But, for most of church history, introducing even more challenges to the Jewish-Christian relationship has been a key Christian doctrine. There is the reference to the "Trinity," quite a challenge for strict monotheists like Jews and

---

12. Barry L. Callen, *God As Loving Grace*, 92.
13. John B. Cobb, Jr., and Clark H. Pinnock, eds. *Searching for an Adequate God* (Grand Rapids: Eerdmans Publishing, 2000), 93.
14. Clark H. Pinnock, *Most Moved Mover*, 85.

Moslems who naturally wonder if Christians have left the one-God fold. Christians have insisted that the one God, now known best in Yeshua, is somehow three. Has the overarching paradigm of the Foundational Testament, *One God for All*, been violated?

Rabbi Bentzion Kravitz certainly thinks so. On the occasion of the death in 2010 of Moshe Rosen, founder of the Christian evangelistic organization "Jews for Jesus," Kravitz said that all denominations of today's Judaism agree that the number one reason Jews can't believe in Yeshua is that such belief would contradict "our fundamental Jewish belief in the absolute unity of God."[15] Why, then, was a multiple about God added by Christians to the singularity of God, risking at least the perception of a subtle polytheism?

The Trinity doctrine is not found in the Bible, at least not as an obvious and formal teaching. The initial impetus for the development of this Christian doctrine came from a theological puzzle. Out of the Jewish context of absolute commitment to one God emerged a spiritual experience and then a resulting confession that seemed to necessitate a trinitarianism. The experience was the indwelling of the Holy Spirit and the confession was the lordship of Yeshua. The Jewish way is that we know who God *is* largely by what God *does*. Thus, the humanly experienced Self-revelation of God, as Christians have argued, yields some modest understanding of the interior divine life prior to the creation. This is known because of the experience with Yahweh in Yeshua, and then with Yahweh in the Spirit of Yeshua who has continued with us.

Our limited human understanding of the mystery of God cannot be separated from our experience of God's redeeming work among us. The good news of the Final Testament involves Father, Son, and Holy Spirit. This Trinity concept is an attempt at a comprehensive way of affirming how the *one* God stands (Sovereign), stoops (Savior), and stays (Sustainer). The one God "provides our salvation by originating, expressing, and actualizing it. The Son is God *for* us. The Spirit is God *with* us."[16] The Christian doctrine of the Trinity is less a matter of numbers and much more an expression of the humanly perceived divine relations to our salvation, that in turn influence our human understanding of God's eternal nature and present intent.

Two of the more helpful ways of entering into the mystery of God involve affirming God as *personal* and *loving*. These two divine de-

---

15. On the web site www.rickross.com, accessed 8/18/2011.
16. Barry L Callen, *God As Loving Grace*, 186 and note 31.

scriptors point to God's sharing, mutuality, and community building. There is in God a "genuine diversity as well as true unity. The Christian God is not just a *unit* but a *union*, not just *unity* but *community*."[17] What is the goal of the spiritual life as Yahweh intends it and Yeshua understood it? It is that we be ingrafted by God's grace into the eternal circle of love that always exists within the divine being of the one God. Yeshua prayed this way: "...may all be one. As you, Father, are in me and I am in you, may they also be *in us* so that the world may believe that you have sent me" (Jn. 17:21).

Paul exhorts believers to pray to God through the power of Christ in the love of the Spirit (Rom. 15:30). Each member of this "Trinity" is fully present in the being and acts of the others—after all, Paul was a Jew who believed staunchly in the one and only God. Even so, he had come to understand that God had been fully present with us in Yeshua. God the Father, reaching, risking, dialogical in nature, had suffered deep pain as the Son was nailed to that cross. Jürgen Moltmann's explanation of this amazing, relating, redeeming God follows what Abraham Heschel had earlier seen in the Jewish prophets.[18]

Stanley Grenz has surveyed the considerable Christian theological work on the Trinity doctrine done across the twentieth century. He features Karl Rahner as the consensus figure in this work. Rahner saw God's self-communication to humans as having "its basis in the eternal self-communication within the triune life.... [This] ties together in the closest manner possible the self-revealing God (God-for-us in our history, or the *economic* Trinity) with the eternal God (God-in-eternity, or the *immanent* Trinity)."[19] Yahweh is "relational" in eternal essence since that it how the divine Self-reveals in voluntary relations with creatures. As Laurence Wood summarizes: "God the Father stresses the *ultimacy*.... Jesus Christ defines the *character* of God and of his Holy Spirit.... The Holy Spirit affirms the *intimacy* of omnipotent Power...."[20]

John Wesley understood well the critical paradox here. Yahweh has a dynamic constancy of character, seen best in Yeshua. It is not a de-

---

17. Kallistos Ware, *The Orthodox Way* (St. Vladimir's Seminary Press, 1999), 27.

18. Jürgen Moltmann, *The Crucified God* (N.Y.: Harper and Row, 1974); Abraham Heschel, *The Prophets* (N.Y.: Harper and Row, 1962).

19. Stanley J. Grenz, *Rediscovering the Triune God* (Minneapolis: Fortress Press, 2004), 217.

20. Laurence W. Wood, *Truly Ourselves, Truly the Spirit's* (Zondervan, Francis Asbury Press, 1989), 175-176.

tached divine immutability, not a raw omnipotence, but a living sovereignty of amazing and interacting love. Therefore, our spiritual lives as God's chosen people are not wholly predetermined and manipulated. As Israel knew long ago, she was to function in a covenant partnership with God. God's creative action is "always appropriate to the environment in which God acts, a world of creaturely causes and consequences.... By creating this world and not another, by creating things interconnected with one another with purposes that often conflict, and by creating moral persons whose intentions and actions express their own choices, God is self-determined to be God in relation to creatures, not God in the abstract."[21]

So much truth about God is learned first in the Foundational Testament. Here is a case where the Christian should not rush beneath the textual surface of the "Old" Testament to find Jesus Christ nearly everywhere—well in advance of his actual birth. We would say with various perceptive Christians that there is more to the triune God than the second member of the Trinity incarnate in Jesus—central and critical as that is. To say "all we know or will ever need to know about God we learn in Jesus Christ" is both a commendable comment and an inaccurate one that undercuts much of the Bible. The divine Self-identification present in the Foundational Testament is informative and essential to the larger theological picture completed in Yeshua. To insist otherwise is to demonstrate a disregard "for God's work in Israel, in Torah, in prophet, in proverb and psalm...."[22]

The doctrine of the Trinity, rather than contradicting Jewish monotheism, actually deepens and enriches it. The "persons" of the Trinity, Father, Son, and Spirit, indicate *agencies of relation* of the one God rather than separate entities. Confessing Yahweh as Trinity is to say that the one God (Yahweh) is a loving, reaching God who stoops to humans in order to save and sustain them. We perceive Yahewh in this way because of the nature of his relating with Israel and then also and especially coming in Yeshua (the *economic* Trinity). Thus, we come to understand that God's very essence involves a rich and relational inte-

---

21. Thomas D. Parker, in David L. Bartlett and Barbara Brown Taylor, eds., *Feasting on the Word: Preaching the Revised Common Lectionary*, Year B, vol. 4 (Louisville: Westminster John Knox, 2009), 298, 300.

22. Brent A. Strawn, "And These Three Are One: A Trinitarian Critique of Christological Approaches to the Old Testament," in *Perspectives in Religious Studies*, vol. 31:2 (Summer 2004), 209.

rior life (the *immanent* Trinity). Both biblical Testaments join to affirm this: All praise to the one God who *reigns above* and also *responds below*!

Psalm 114: A Contemporary Paraphrase

The Foundational Testament is rich in revelation about the nature and ways of Yahweh. One key revelation is about divine providence. Following is my modest attempt at a contemporary paraphrase of Psalm 114, a good way to appreciate the rich meanings of providence as known in ancient Israel—and as should be known by contemporary Christians.

We might think of this psalm as an ancient, prayerful reflection setting forth a perennial question. In the end, is it human *politics* or divine *providence* that carries the day. Given the perspective of the entire Foundational Testament, one could anticipate the bottom line. God is open and relational with his people, so that, at least in the short term, their decisions matter. However, in the longer term divine actions are more determinative of how things finally go than the selfish political scheming of humans. There always is at work a subtle synergism.

Speaking politically, at first God's people was a collection of tribes that on occasions of crisis would unite into a temporary federation for mutual benefit. Yahweh was their King. In time, there emerged a more "standard" organizational model patterned after other west Asiatic kingships. Swept along by the currents of international politics, "Israel's history became inextricably bound up with that of other peoples and increasingly took on their way and ideologies."[23] Political expediency became a primary concern, often at the cost of covenant faithfulness to Yahweh.

The Foundational Testament presents numerous scenes where a prophet of Yahweh must confront an Israelite king concerning who really rules in this world. Hosea, for instance, announces judgment on anyone who forgets that there is a higher sovereignty who rules over all kings of this earth—"Hear this, O priests! Give heed, O house of Israel! Listen, O house of the king! For the judgment pertains to you..." (5:1). Indeed, it pertains to many from that day to this. Yahweh is open to covenant partners. But when the use of their freedom is self-destructive and God-denying, judgment eventually comes. With divine judgment, however, there remains the loving faithfulness of God. In

---

23. James Muilenburg, *The Way of Israel*, 78.

the end, the result of the decisions and processes of the creation will come more from Yahweh's *providence* and less from the *politics* of humans—although the sinful decisions of humans will have their continuing negative results.

*Given these introductory comments, here is
my paraphrase of Psalm 114.*

Dear Lord, since confession is good for the soul, I'm prepared right now to do my soul a big favor! I confess that I, and humans generally, seem to see what is only on the surface of things. We remember only what we choose to remember. I finally recognize and readily admit how easily this subtle process of seeing so little and selecting our memories can serve very selfish ends. Please forgive my own inability to perceive and focus on what is most real. I want to go *beneath the surface* and locate the foundation of all things. I want You, Yahweh! I want Your will and Your ways and Your future!

Here are the big questions as I now understand them. What is really worth perceiving and then remembering? What escapes mere self-service and lies beyond the prejudice of my private bias and immediate circumstances? What pinpoints actual reality rather than being infected by how we humans are fond of identifying and naming it? What has happened on the human scene that is so important, so intentional on Your part that it should *shape us* rather than we shaping it? What lies *beneath the surface*? If you, O Creator, God of Abraham, Lord of the nations, were to show us the real truth and focus our blurred memories on the really important things, what would we be seeing and remembering most of all? This question is my most profound prayer.

Actually, since I am a student of the Foundational Testament, I already know something that would be emphasized. You, Yahweh, the gracious and revealing God, would teach that our human history, all those events, generations, battles, questions, sufferings, and joys have not been a random and empty process. What has happened, ultimately, has or still can have meaning because You, the creator and ruler of nature and nations, have put a God-shaped plot into the drama of history, making it *His-story*. It is Your story of a good creation made right and then gone wrong, and of Your choice to be deeply involved in it, whatever the cost, even to Yourself. We humans are obligated, therefore, to do more than just sing, "This is my Father's world." We must remember and act like it really is!

Let's get specific. When the Jewish people, Your people, escaped that Egyptian bondage long ago, it wasn't really an escape, was it? It wasn't just one of those numerous and annoying slave revolts, one that happened to work because of some quirk of nature at the water's edge. It wasn't an escape; it was a *deliverance*. The Egyptians were baffled, the mountains trembled, and the sea had to get out of the way as You, O God, made for Yourself a people. Moses may have been up front, but You always were the leader. The Egyptians may have seen nothing divine about it, but their blindness doesn't alter reality. Surface observations may have concentrated on human determination and a timely event of nature that drowned some and saved others. An adequate, beneath-the-surface understanding, however, brings us back to You, Yahweh God.

What really has happened? Where is all the "wisdom" in the deluge of data in our time? What is the right perspective in the pluralistic maze that now prevails in the twenty-first century? It always has been You, Yahweh, hasn't it? Now I'm remembering rightly. You lie beneath the surface of things, working out Your providential plan. Beyond the sound and fury of world events, somewhere in the shadows of time, there stands the One who created the world and remains Lord over its people and events. Even though You are anything but a cold manipulator of Your beloved people, You nonetheless are the chief architect of time and eternity. In the final analysis, Your *providence* is more potent than our *politics*. Your sovereign will supersedes our fragile and often foolish human ways.

How I wish that Your people could comprehend their divine birthright and the potential always latent in Your creating and leading. Let the mountains dance again! May the rivers that still obstruct and the captors who still enslave bow before the design that is deepest in things. And when it happens, may I and all others recognize Your hand beneath it and gladly join the trail of Your destiny. You, my God, are still making history, not only by establishing a special people, but by ministering through that people to the whole world. The future is open because You are open and keep tomorrow full of fresh possibilities.

It is the most wonderful of all realities. There is an open God, an open future, and openness for all of us to join in the divine work. How amazing it is that You are graciously open to our participation in this future-making. Praise to Yahweh! Seeing, knowing, and being transformed so that we choose to join in Your history-making brings hope and life at its best. What a realization! What a memory! What a responsibility and privilege! My heart is full of song.

Let all things their Creator bless,
and worship Him in humbleness;
O praise him, Alleluia!

Lead on, O King Eternal, the day of march has come,
Henceforth in fields of conquest,
Thy tents shall be our home.[24]

---

24. Verse one is from "All Creatures of Our God and King" by Francis of Assisi. Verse two is from the hymn "Lead On, O King Eternal" by Ernest Shurtleff.

Truth Stream #1

THE DIVINE CHOICE OF A PEOPLE

O Lord, our Sovereign, how majestic is your name in all the earth!... What are human beings that you are mindful of them, mortals that you care for them? (Ps. 8: 1, 4). This is the covenant that I will make with the house of Israel after those days, says the Lord: I will put my law within them and I will write it on their hearts; and I will be their God, and they shall be my people (Jer. 31:33).

The study of the Old Testament is an opportunity to rethink, from the ground up, the most demanding issues before us, and particularly before the younger generation that must live with our crisis into the coming years.... We will have to ask how chosenness is maintained without idolatrous hardening...."[1]

The two biblical quotations above show understandable amazement. God is so immense and wonderful, so absolutely everything ultimate. By contrast, we mortals seem to be so nothing! And yet, God loves, calls, chooses, partners, and blesses. But, as the other quote asks, how can the chosen of God avoid violating their select status by deteriorat-

---

1. Walter Brueggemann, *An Unsettling God*, xvi.

ing into an idolatrous hardening that arrogantly turns against others in God's name?

My undergraduate college years were spent at Geneva College in Pennsylvania. There I first was put in touch with the Scottish "covenanter" tradition and a conservative Presbyterian body that respects highly the direct, even comprehensive providence of God in human affairs. This faith tradition is rooted in the ancient Israelite concept of being a chosen covenant community, chosen by none other than Yahweh through his gracious initiative that is wholly undeserved. We humans were created by God to live in a chosen community, one formed and filled by the presence and guidance of God.[2]

One way of understanding the providence of God raises a concern for today's Christians: "The self-created individual is inclined to think mainly of himself and his own salvation. But one who stands humbly in the fear of the Lord understands also our corporate responsibility before God.... It is unfortunate that the idea of the covenant has so little place in the Christian thinking of our time. We have forgotten that the very titles of the two portions of our Bible are 'Old Covenant' and 'New Covenant.' In the last tragic hours of his life, Yeshua fastened on Jeremiah's ideal [Jer. 31:31] and spoke of 'the new covenant in my blood'...."[3] To be with Yahweh is to be one with Yahweh's chosen people.

Election and Covenant

I once was sitting in a restaurant along the shore of the Sea of Galilee. I was talking with an American Messianic Jew, a conservative Christian with deep respect for the Jewish roots of Christianity and the current relevance of those roots. The conversation turned to the relation between the modern State of Israel, where we were, and the prophecies of the Bible about the future of the Jews. His intensely pro-Israel comments led me to make an unwise comment of my own, one that shocked the young man. I said something like, "I'm not sure that the biblical prophecies have much to do with today's political entity called Israel."

I saw the blood drain from his face. I probably shouldn't have opened my mouth in the first place, at least not so abruptly and on so

---

2. See Stanley J. Grenz, *Theology for the Community of God* (Grand Rapids: Wm. Eerdmans, 2000).

3. G. Ernest Wright, *The Challenge of Israel's Faith*, 80.

sensitive a subject. The exchange that followed, however, helped to clarify for both of us that there are many complex issues involved when identifying God's chosen people across the centuries, and when trying to understand what that chosenness means today. Complex issues or not, there are basic biblical truths here. God did choose and call and covenant with a particular people. The Foundational Testament presents God as a personal agent who creates, acts, plans, and loves all people, particularly his own covenant partner called for an important purpose in the world. And there is more, more that seems so relevant to right where we now are living.

The big idea of the Foundational Testament is that we are to know, worship, and partner with the God "who is ready and able to make commitments and who is impinged upon by a variety of 'partners' who make a difference in the life of God. This suggests that the defining category for faith in the Old Testament is *dialogue*, whereby all parties—including God—are engaged in a dialogue exchange that is potentially transformative for all parties...including God."[4] The faith model of ancient Israel, and later that of Yeshua, is far from the individualism common in today's "entitlement" culture and meet-my-needs congregations.

God chooses and is faithful to a people, a people expected to return that love by worshipping, loving, serving, and witnessing in specific ways established by God. Before we explore this in some detail, more theological groundwork needs to be laid. The historical narrative of the Foundational Testament starts with Terah, his son Abraham, and the rest of the family. Some scholars think this family was an element of ancient Mesopotamian society called *Habiru* (Hebrew?). Whatever the case, by crossing the Euphrates River and heading far away in response to a call from God, this family group became the biblical *Ivriim*, the people who crossed over in faith to the other side of the river and marched with God toward a destiny that still blesses us all.

A large block of material in the Foundational Testament (Genesis through 2 Kings) apparently was compiled and edited by a group of Jewish theologians and historians, perhaps during the Babylonian Exile of the Jews. This compilation of materials was intended to preserve the memory of Israel's long tradition during a time of the people's tragic loss of their freedom and homeland. It also sought to interpret Yahweh's will and ways with his people so that whatever future they still had after the Exile could be reestablished on the proper basis. Un-

---

4. Walter Brueggemann, *An Unsettling God*, xi–xii.

fortunately, later Christian readers of this highly-influential material often have read *from its surface only* and have come to a prematurely negative conclusion.

Something important often is missed when reading only on the surface of the biblical text. What appears on the surface suggests that God automatically rewards those who follow his commands meticulously, and that God punishes all who do not (e.g., Judges 3:7-8 and 1 Kings 8:44-51). What is missed is what lies *below the surface* throughout this "deuteronomic" history. The theology that lies below is not some "works righteousness" where God automatically rewards good deeds, allowing people to work their way into God's favor and covenant community. The heart of the bedrock theology that actually lies below is found in Deuteronomy 7:7-8 immediately following the great *Shema* in Deuteronomy 6:4-5, teaching so loved by Yeshua and every faithful Jew. It reads:

> It was not because you were more numerous than any other people that the Lord set his heart on you and chose you—for you were the fewest of all peoples. It was because the Lord loved you and kept the oath that he swore to your ancestors, that the Lord has brought you out with a mighty hand, and redeemed you from the house of slavery, from the hand of Pharaoh king of Egypt.

Religious life should be based first and foremost on remembrance that God loves and freely chooses out of love, not because of the inherent value or "good works" of the ones chosen. The Foundational Testament presents a "by faith because of love" tradition of believing.

We are to love because Yahweh is God and graciously chose to love us before any response on our part. The loving Yahweh is faithful to his promises, unless his loved ones refuse the divine love and choose to flaunt his commandments. In that case, the covenant itself comes into question and there will be negative consequences. The covenant is voluntary partnership, a *love relationship* more than a cold courtroom filled with daily legal judgments. Yahweh is a loving Father who expects obedience in the family. Yahweh also is a Father creating and nurturing, and very patient in the process.

The concept of Yahweh choosing Israel to be his special possession is called "election," with the subsequent "covenant" the understanding that Yahweh established to define Israel's intended relationship with him, among themselves, and with their neighbors. It goes back to the original call of Abraham (Gen. 12:1-3; 15:1-6) where we find God's promise extending to Abraham's future descendents. The covenant again appears in God's voice to Moses (Ex. 3:6), certainly in the Law given at Sinai, and pervasively in the book of Deuteronomy. The ideal of a God-initiated covenant community, at least in principle, shaped the very character of Israel. The Foundational Testament celebrates this community and laments its sometimes failed attempts to weld its vision of the character and will of Yahweh onto all aspects of its life.

Something needs to be clear on the negative side. God did not call one nation *over against* all others, but called and formed a new nation *on behalf* of all others. The act of God's choosing tends to have two consequences when received by faith. One is a gracious wonderment on the part of the blessed humans; the other is a raising of some hard questions that faith does not automatically answer (see chapter nine). One question is in an old saying, "How odd of God to choose the Jews!" Why them? They had been no people and brought to the covenant relationship no outstanding worth in themselves. Yahweh threatened Israel with the same judgments brought on others; Yahweh also made clear that he was graciously at work with others (Amos 9:7). The few who were chosen were chosen *for all people*. How could it be otherwise? Yahweh is *one God for all*.

On the positive side, the divine choice was made out of an undeserved love and motivated by a graciously redemptive purpose. Yahweh's intent was that through his chosen people "all the families of the earth will be blessed" (Gen. 12:3). Much later, and personally embodying the suffering-servant image presented so vividly in Isaiah 53, Yeshua envisioned the carrying of the witness of the chosen to all nations, blessing them through the giving of his own life. Many of the Jews across the centuries, however, did not understand this breadth of vision. They guarded the truth involved in their divine election and even persecuted other peoples who did not share or seemed to threaten their divine privilege (see chapter eleven). Thus, the negative side of election is seen in various places in the Foundational Testament. The prophets of Israel regularly found themselves having to protest "in God's name against the perversion of the word of God in the interests of sectarianism, nationalism, power, and politics."[5] God's people at times thought and acted too much "like the nations."

Yahweh's choice of electing a people may have had the goal of blessing all people, but some of the decisions of Israel, implemented at the expense of others, suggest anything but patience, tolerance, and divine love. Given the polytheistic and often highly immoral settings

---

5. Thomas Merton, *Opening the Bible*, 18. See, for instance, Jeremiah 23:23-40.

in which the covenant people usually lived, one can understand Israel's instinct to protect the truth before sharing it. Aggressive competitors to God's truth had to be resisted for the sake of the truth's survival.

For instance, as Israel first entered the Canaan land that it was sure Yahweh had given it, she assumed that intermarriage with these alien peoples dare not be allowed. Yahweh surely wanted all symbols of Canaan's pagan worship destroyed, with no mercy shown to those who would readily *corrupt* rather than *carry* Yahweh's good news to the world (see the section on "holy war" in chapter eleven). One basic truth must be clear. Yahweh's jealously for Israel does not stem from indifference to other peoples; rather, it arises from Yahweh's concern that Israel transmit the truth to other peoples.

There was great fear in ancient Israel about contamination of the faith, something seen throughout the prophetic writings of the Foundational Testament. Sometimes this fear came into conflict with the mission of the faith itself. On occasion, Israel read Yahweh's concern for truth's purity as justifying and even encouraging the chosen to brutalize as necessary any who threatened the truth or the chosen ones. Looking at such occasions from the perspective of Yeshua and the Final Testament, it is likely that Israel did its share of over-reading of Yahweh's assumed will. For instance, Christians reading Numbers 31—about God's war of vengeance against the Midianites--must get below the text's surface to identify God's enduring revelation more than be mired in the bloody brutality reported on the surface of the text. The divine intent (election for mission) does not justify any human means for implementing the intent (e.g., mass murder). See the section on vengeance in chapter eleven.

Let us be clear. We are not suggesting that contemporary Christian readers should avoid hearing exactly what a text is saying on the surface. What we are saying is that below the text's surface lies the larger *theological* reason for that text's appearance in the first place. It often is that reason that is more pervasive and enduring, more "biblical" in current authoritative meaning that the text's surface words and their time-bound and culture-bound details.

Conditionality and Circumcision

God's gracious electing of a people was intended to create a vehicle for carrying the good news of God's love to all nations and peoples. This vehicle, this chosenness, however, can be compromised both by the chosen people themselves and by those who do not accept God's news and might infiltrate and pervert its carriers. Further, fear of such compromise, or just self-defensive arrogance on the part of the chosen, can lead the chosen to justify the destruction of the non-believers (see the commentary on Deuteronomy 7 and Psalm 137 in chapter eleven). This tragic possibility raises an urgent question. Can the chosen ever become *unchosen* by God because of their failure to function properly as the chosen? Is God's election conditional or unconditional?

The Foundational and later Final Testaments each respond in a similar way to this important question. The answer is "conditional"; God is always faithful, but unfaithful covenant partners can render themselves punishable and even unchosen. Those once elected who choose against who they are intended to be under God can also be rejected as the continuing chosen. God's promise prevails, even if the chosen must be replaced. Near the end of his eventful life, Moses addressed the people who had just into covenant relationship with Yahweh. A lengthy portion of Deuteronomy 28 details the negatives that will follow a breaking of the covenant with Yahweh. The privileges of being chosen are considerable; so are the responsibilities and consequences of deliberate defiance of Yahweh's expectations.

Yahweh is "jealous" for the faithfulness and well being of the elect people, and is strongly opposed to idolatry. After all, imaging and worshipping gods who are no gods is a dead-end business. Even so, there was ample provision of symbols to encourage Israel to covenant faithfulness. For instance, we are told in Genesis 17 that God initiates an everlasting covenant and assigns *circumcision* for all males in the community (not females as in some other faith communities). This was to be a symbol with a double meaning. (1) Those who bear this symbol agree to abide by the stipulations of the covenant relationship (2) Those who bear the symbol can rely on God to be faithful to his everlasting promises.

On the surface, the practice of circumcision hardly seems to apply to the Christian community, although it is practiced widely today for medical reasons, and without any religious meaning. As is often the case, one must go deeper than the mere surface of the text of the Foundational Testament on this subject. Does a convert to Christianity today have to be circumcised to be a full believer properly sensitive to the Jewish roots of the faith? No, at least not in the physical sense. Without necessarily downplaying the physical side of the practice, the Foundational Testament already was referring to circumcision in a figurative way (Deut.30:6; Jer. 4:1-4, 9:25-26). This symbolic sense would appear again and be emphasized in the Final Testament.

There is a circumcision that dramatizes repentance and obedience. Paul says that real circumcision is a matter of the heart (Rom. 2:29). Yahweh blessed the Jewish people with a sign to mark them as his and encourage them to covenant faithfulness. In the Christian setting, signs with such purposes remain crucial. If not actual circumcision, then what? Baptism often plays this role for Christians. It should be public and dramatic, marking the new believer as one of God's own who has consciously accepted covenant partnership with all its great privileges and related responsibilities.

The key issue is community, being in and living out the distinctive covenant community being called into being by God. The Hebrew word is *Shalom*. It is a picture of God's community, of life with relationships as they are supposed to be. *Shalom* envisions humans living in harmony with each other and their environment through expressions of love, actions of justice, and constant faithfulness to God. The Greek word *ekklesia* in the Final Testament suggests a people who have been called together into such an usual community formed by God.

The Foundational Testament presents both Yahweh and humans as *dialogic*. All of us have "the irascible yearning for *freedom in community*."[6] The lack of a healthy humanness within a wholesome divine community represents an urgent need in today's broken world. God has created us for such covenant community, has called us to it, and remains ready to enable it. Christians call it the "church." It is to be anything but a random collection of individuals who relate only when it seems convenient for their private ends.

The divinely ordained path to spiritual growth and world service is through a covenant people. To speak rightly about the Holy Spirit is to recognize that God is at work in the world and especially in the church, the community of faith. God remains present "as the Spirit of Christ for the purpose of transforming the world into Christ-likeness. The church is the concrete and visible, although obviously provisional and partial presence of the new creation promised by the Hebrew prophets and launched through the life, death, and resurrection of Jesus."[7] Unfortunately, much of Western Christianity, especially many branches of Protestantism, has been tempted by individualism and maintained a relatively weak doctrine of the church—something so unlike the covenant ideal of the Jewish tradition. The lives of believers

---

6. Walter Brueggemann, *An Unsettling God*, xiv. Emphasis added.
7. Barry L. Callen, *Authentic Spirituality*, 127.

are to be intertwined with the lives of all the others in the community of faith.

The Gift of Land

The relatively little piece of land lying on the eastern end of the Mediterranean Sea is arguably the most contested in world history. It forms a natural corridor connecting Africa, Europe, and Asia and has been a clashing point for numerous empires marching one way or the other over the centuries. This is one reason why this tiny piece of land has been so strategic. But there is another reason why the situation has been even more intense than mere geographic centrality. In the past and very much today, there is the added factor that two peoples simultaneously lay claim to this land by *divine right*. Thus, there are religious, social, political, economic, and military dimensions to this awkward and very dangerous standoff of land claims. Today it is Israel, the Palestinians, Jews and Arabs, oil interests, Iraq wars, disturbing memories of the Holocaust, and nuclear weapons. The complexity and danger of the circumstance can hardly be overstated.

International politics following the end of the World War II lead to the founding of the present nation-state of Israel. It now constitutes a place of identity and gives some sense of pride and security to the worldwide Jewish community that has suffered so much persecution. It is seen by many Christians as the fulfillment of biblical prophecy, a supposed pivotal event at the beginning of the end of times and the Lord's final return. The State of Israel also is viewed by millions of others in the Middle East as a rogue intruder in the area, outsiders enforcing mass injustice on the Palestinian peoples belonging on this land, some of whom are Christian Arabs. However one views this place on the eastern shore of the Mediterranean, it remains in on the world's center stage.

The Foundational Testament is appealed to by both Jews and Moslems as the divine source of justification for their claim to this land. Christians from the West join in this to a degree, typically calling the area the "Holy Land." The original promise to Abraham was that Yahweh would establish a covenant with him and his descendants so that the whole land of Canaan would be "an everlasting possession" (Gen. 17:7-8). This land was occupied by descendants of Abraham, especially after the Exodus from Egyptian slavery. Later it was largely evacuated when an Exile was forced on Jews by the Babylonians. God then promised through the prophets (Isa.35:1, 10; Jer. 33:7, 13) that there would be a return to the land, a restoration of the people now chastened after their earlier unfaithfulness to the covenant. The story of this return is one of renewed hope, additional unfaithfulness, and future domination of this promised land by later empires, right down to the Roman occupation seen at the time of the birth of Yeshua.

However one views today's nation of Israel and its relation to the ancient covenant among Yahweh, the elect people, and biblical prophecy, the Foundational Testament appears clear that the covenant issue is and always has been about more than mere land rights. Holding land in the ancient Near East was vital for survival itself. For most people it was a place of subsistence farming or animal herding. Often it was assumed by people of that area that particular gods were tied to given pieces of land. Therefore, it is not surprising that Yahweh promised land as a gift to his people—a necessary means of survival.

It is crucial to recall, however, that Yahweh was an exception among the "gods," not being limited to any land boundaries. Also to be noted carefully is that the land gift was *provisional*. Israel could never claim it as an absolute possession. Yahweh had made the real circumstance clear: "The land shall not be sold in perpetuity, for the land is mine; with me you are but aliens and tenants" (Lev. 25:23).

Recalling this provisional status of the land, Marvin Wilson is proper when he speaks with caution about "real estate theology," calling it at best "precarious theology."[8] Surrounding God's promise of land was always an assumption about expected *righteousness* and *justice*—how could it be otherwise or the gift of land would not reflect the very nature of Yahweh himself? The original conquest of this land after the Exodus from Egypt was not accomplished because of Israel's superior military might or righteousness, but because of the excessive wickedness of the Canaanite inhabitants being removed (Deut. 9:4-6) and Yahweh's gracious provision for his chosen people.

In fact, God's covenant always has been contingent on the faithfulness and righteousness of the human partner. The twin expectations of Israel always were *holiness* and *justice*, both rooted in Yahweh's nature and ways. Those graciously invited into covenant with God are to reflect the cleansing presence and healing intentions of God in the world. Something was made clear to the ancient Jews. Yahweh's goal of universal justice is especially sensitive to the needs of marginalized people, meaning that God's chosen people are to show the same sensitivity. God "loves strangers" (Deut. 10:17-18). Therefore, "you shall

---

8. Marvin Wilson, *Our Father Abraham*, 268.

also love the stranger, for you were strangers in the land of Egypt" (vs. 19).

Who God is and what God expects of the chosen people are spiritual realities not always easy to apply to real life without doubt or distortion. In the Foundational Testament, the book of Judges is a good example. It presents itself as a dramatic set of the early and troubled adventures of God's people now free of Egypt and actively occupying the Canaan land promised by God. Even if facing evil opponents, one wonders about the cruelty and oppression employed by God's people in God's name. This naturally troubles followers of Yeshua the Messiah when we read of Yahweh supposedly authorizing and enabling violence against "strangers."

Setting the book of Judges alongside Isaiah 53, for instance, creates quite the contrast and raises several critical questions. See the sections on "holy war" and "vengeance" in chapter eleven. This contrast within the Bible itself, both inside the Foundational Testament and between the Testaments, is intensified when one gazes at Yeshua hanging willingly on a Roman cross for all of us "strangers." Such a contrast encourages a reader of Judges to keep several things in mind. They include the social setting of that time, the potential of mixed motives or imperfect understandings of God's will by Joshua and his colleagues, the fact of "developmental" or "progressive" revelation (see chapter thirteen), and the need to distinguish the surface of the text and the theology that lies below it.

In the contemporary setting, Elias Chacour certainly struck a biblical note with his book *Blood Brothers*.[9] This Palestinian Melkite Christian's family, living in a small village in the upper Galilee, had been victimized in 1951 by Israeli soldiers who bulldozed all the homes in the village and allowed none of the residents to return. Elias was a boy of twelve at the time. Following his father's non-retaliatory response, this boy grew to be an aggressive peacemaker (an unusual pairing of words). He points out that Abraham lived as a nomad in the land and felt called by God to do justice to its inhabitants, including foreigners or any others present and in need (Isa. 56:1-8). He deplores any simple assumption that Jews returning to this land today automatically means the fulfillment of biblical prophecy, especially if such an assumption is accompanied by injustice in the land.

Many of today's Christians use a version of "premillennial eschatology" to predict current and soon-coming events in relation to end

---

9. Elias Chacour, *Blood Brothers* (Chosen Books, Revell Co., 1984).

times. They give much attention to contemporary Israel as the direct work of God. Often there is a high level of confidence in supposed knowledge of detail about God's future work. This work is thought to be assured in advance by "prophecy" so that whatever Israel does is justified as being God's will, even if its nature appears morally repulsive to others. Such thinking can easily deteriorate into a social irresponsibility that appears in conflict with the main covenant thrust of the Foundational Testament.

That covenant thrust links the continuing status of "election" with covenant faithfulness to God's love and justice in this world. After all, "if every action is preordained, then there is no need to measure one's actions by moral law, since the decision to obey or disobey the standard has already been made. If Israel is the elect, and Jewish history is predetermined by God and foretold by prophecy, then ordinary rules of international law (morality) do not apply to God's chosen people; and there is no absolute standard by which they can be judged."[10]

The Jewish prophets consistently announced this: Yahweh insists that his people live in the land with *justice for all* (Isa. 56:6-8; Jer. 7:6-7; Lev. 19:18). One biblical model of proper behavior is Isaac who lived peaceably with those who confiscated his wells (Gen. 26:12-24). He moved on until God "made room for him." Vengeance belongs only to Yahweh (see chapter eleven for commentary on psalm 137). Righteous living and justice dealing are always the obligations of God's covenant people. It may be that today "God will only allow the Jews to 'have room' in Israel if they 'make room' for their Palestinian Arab neighbors within their borders."[11] Making room, however, is very hard to do when the land in question is small, seen as the land that is one's own as a gift from God, and appears necessary for one's own safety.

This principle of "making room" is seen clearly in the ancient Israelite practice of "jubilee." The jubilee year was the one at the end of seven cycles of sabbatical years, the sabbath of sabbaths when the ownership and management of land was newly apportioned. While the regulations for the jubilee year have not been observed for many centuries, its original justification remains significant. The Foundational Testament argues that the jubilee existed because the land was the possession of Yahweh, and thus its current occupiers were merely ten-

---

10. Dwight Wilson, *Armageddon Now!* (Grand Rapids: Baker Book House, 1977), 143.

11. James R. Leaman, *Faith Roots: Learning from and Sharing Witness with Jewish People* (Nappanee, IN: Evangel Press, 1993), 108.

ants and stewards. Therefore, rather than the land being possessed permanently, encouraging injustice, there should be periodic times of new beginning.

On a rare occasion, even contemporary Christians informed by this tradition have employed the jubilee concept. For instance, Pope John Paul II announced a Great Jubilee for the year 2000. He judged the onset of the third millennium an excellent time for new beginnings in the Roman Catholic Church and hopefully beyond. He called for a three-year preparation period. The first year, 1997, was to be dedicated to meditation on Yeshua, the next year on the Holy Spirit, and the third on God the Father. As was typical of the Foundational Testament, a new beginning necessarily returns to the basis of all, the God of past, present, and future. But the question remains. What of the land in the present?

The message and sheer imagery of the Foundational Testament places strong emphasis on the importance of land that had been created by and always belongs to God. Life began in a garden, a lovely place to be treasured and cared for. However, the humans placed there by Yahweh failed in their stewardship and were driven out. The loss of this precious space has been virtually intolerable for all of us ever since. Land in the ancient Near East was essential for life; it was tied to one's family identity and defended at all costs. No text is more telling than 1 Kings 21. Naboth refused to sell or trade his ancestral land to the king. The king was determined to get it anyway. Naboth's continuing resistance cost him his life. To him, the land and his family were inseparable and worth the risk.

The sense of place is strong, very strong in Jewish history. Abraham was promised many descendents and land on which they could live and flourish. That promise, however, came with a condition. What those descendants learned the hard way was that the land is always *in the process* of being given by God. That is, it is never a one-time and forever gift apart from *its proper stewardship*, just as with that original garden given to Adam and Eve. The land that God gives still belongs to God. It is extended graciously, but only *in trust*. While enjoying its fruits, the land must be cared for, and that caring always is to include practicing justice and seeing to the needs of the poor and the stranger (see Deut. 8). Such is the heart of Yahweh; doing anything other is to violate Yahweh and his gift of land.

Isaiah 5:1-7 is a dramatic picture of God's gift of land and his promise to care for it wonderfully on behalf of the well being of his people. It also is a picture of what can and did go wrong. It is a song of God's personally chosen vineyard planted on a fertile hill. God did all possible to make it a perfect place for his beloved. Later, he came and looked for its intended fruit, and what he saw were wild grapes very distasteful to him. He threatened to destroy the vineyard and take it back because "he expected justice, but saw bloodshed; righteousness, but heard a cry!" Yeshua much later did much the same thing with a fig tree (Matt. 21:18-22).

It is not immediately clear, of course, how all of this should relate to today's much-changed circumstances in the Middle East. What is clear is that God's heart and intent involve gifts given to his people in trust, not because they are deserved or will be forever given if not used properly. We all have a stake in the goodness and preservation of this creation. Christians see in the coming of Yeshua a re-establishing of the original garden, a replanting of the devoured vineyard, a resurrection launching, almost the re-beginning of creation filled with new life from the very heart of God. It again is a gift *for all people*, including the outsiders that in a sense we all are.

The "Holy Land" is God's land. Yeshua announces the day of consummation "when what the prophets had promised stands ready at hand, breaking in upon the world in power. Zion is indeed the place of refuge for all.... Life is being transformed, the goods of earth do belong equally to all, and none dare be denied what God purposes that they have."[12] "Zionism" is a contemporary term referring to this theme of the Bible about the relationship of Jews and the gift of their ancient homeland—transferred now, in the view of many, to the State of Israel and God's enablement of the return of Jews to it from all over the world. Whether or not this transfer of meaning to current politics is appropriate biblical application, there is something that is clear. God's people are to be practicing righteousness and justice for all.

It is hard indeed to sort out the relationship between the "city of God" and the "cities of men." My former colleague George Rable wrote a masterful book exploring the influence of the Christian faith on the dynamics of the American Civil War.[13] In his second inaugural address delivered in March, 1865, Abraham Lincoln pained over the terrible costs of the ongoing carnage in the war-torn nation. He said, "Both [North and South] read the same Bible, and pray to the same God; and each invokes His aid against the other." Similarly, Jews, Christians,

---

12. Walter Harrelson, in Clark M. Williamson, ed., *The Church and the Jewish People* (St. Louis: Christian Board of Publication, 1994), 62.

13. George C. Rable, *God's Almost Chosen Peoples* (The University of North Carolina Press, 2010).

and Moslems have Abraham as their common father of faith, and they read the same Foundational Testament. Even so, often they confidently invoke their various readings against each other. And they struggle over competing claims to the same land in the Middle East.

In relation to today's State of Israel, should Christians suppose that they have replaced the Jews in God's work, or that Israel is God's continuing providential people and therefore is justified both in its being and in whatever it has to do to survive? Affirmative and negative answers have their weaknesses, and clearly their social, political, and military dangers. The best approach appears to be one that is cautious, humble, and morally sensitive in line with the related emphases of Foundational Testament. It relies on a sense of justice more than on a unilateral claim to the "divine right" of possession.

The Jewish people have suffered much, including at the hands of Christians (see chapter two). They deserve justice, whatever their failures. A secure homeland of their own is a reasonable alternative for Christians to support—but on *moral* grounds rather than on any simplistic claim that it is inevitable and "fulfills prophecy." People other than Jews have suffered as well, and justice is done only when God's love, righteousness, and land fruitfulness are also directed their way with a graciousness reflective of Yahweh himself.

There is an inherent family tie between Judaism, Christianity, and Islam, but the future of none of these faith communities in God's economy is completely clear. The future of the contested land is also not clear. What is clear is Yahweh's character of loving righteousness and justice, things intended for the land and expected of Yahweh's covenant people in relation to all who live in it—and elsewhere as well. For contemporary Christians, the same message prevails. All land is "holy" and deserves respect. It is to be used only in trust and for the good of all.

Truth Stream #2

WALKING THE WAY OF HOLINESS

Both the Torah and the Spirit at Mt. Sinai forged the ransomed Israelites into a holy nation of priests. The giving of the Spirit at Mt. Zion fashioned the redeemed disciples of Yeshua into a covenant community later called the Church.... Both the Torah and the Spirit are holy and they call forth holiness in the people of God.... This connection between the Torah, the Spirit, and holiness seems entirely natural to the Hebraic mind, but alien and obscure to the classic Christian mindset that prejudicially views the Law and the Spirit in opposition.[1]

God evaluated Noah as "a righteous man of integrity" (Heb. *tamim*). I take "integrity" here as denoting Noah's holiness.... God instructed Abram, on the occasion of changing his name to Abraham, "Walk before me, and be [a man of] integrity" (Gen. 17:1). To be a person of integrity is to be "one," i.e., to be wholly dedicated, without division of loyalties, to one person, one cause, one way of life. That is the essence of the holiness to which God also calls us. This call to "adventure ourselves with God" permeates the Old Testament every bit as thoroughly as it does the New, will we but see it.[2]

---

1. Karen H. Pryor, ed., *A Continuing Quest*, 7-8.
2. Joseph E. Coleson, "How Ever Shall We Preach Genesis 1-11?!" in Richard P. Thompson and Thomas Jay Oord, eds., *The Bible Tells Me So: Reading the Bible as Scripture* (Nampa, ID: SacraSage Press, 2011), 204.

We will explore in chapter eleven the concept of sacrifice in worship. We will identify and affirm "sacramental" worship, communion with a holy God through holy meetings filled with historical remembering, leading to transformation into holiness of heart and life. This process and goal lies at the heart of the Foundational Testament.

As the first quote above makes clear, God's teaching (Torah) is holy. Life in line with Torah and in the Spirit belong together. The centrality of holiness to faithful covenant living is captured in the memorable words of Leviticus 19:2. God is holy; his people are to be likewise. To draw near to the Holy One of Israel in covenant relationship is necessarily to become increasingly reflective of Yahweh's very nature—or the drawing near is false.

Moving to the Final Testament, we see much the same teaching. Rabbi Yeshua filled a common meal with such holiness meanings and potential. There are three critical dimensions to this "Lord's Supper" that form a virtual definition of what it means to worship rightly and become holy in the process.[3] These three dimensions are:

1. It is a *sanctifying* meal: To be holy is to benefit from Yeshua's sacrificial life by becoming like him in his servant life. To sit at the table with Yeshua is to be set apart from preoccupation with self and shaped by a preoccupation with the cross, empty grave, and present reign and mission of the Christ (Gal. 2:20).

2. It is a *social* meal: To be holy in a Christian sense necessarily involves the social implications of Christ-likeness.... Salvation involves more than the forgiveness of past sins. It includes the righting of relationships and the forming of a new community—the body of Christ on earth. To sit at the table with Yeshua is to be one with all who sit at the table and, as possible, with all for whom Yeshua died.

3. It is a *seditious* meal: To be "in Christ" and part of the Christ community is to participate in a new creation that is the radical antithesis of the values, structures, and dynamics of this world. Taking the meal of the Lord is subversive since it is

---

3. This three-point definition of the Lord's Supper is from Barry L. Callen, *Authentic Spirituality: Moving Beyond Mere Religion* (Lexington, KY: Emeth Press, 2006), 216.

joining a spiritual force working within the fallen world to renew it.

The path to holiness involves eating and then living with the Lord in a sanctifying, social, and seditious way. It is a call to obedience, but only after the receiving of divine grace. The "only after" is an important part of understanding biblical holiness.

Liberation Before Obedience

Many Christians assume that Judaism teaches salvation "by works of the Law," whereas Christianity is the way of divine grace. The supposed contrast is largely a fiction. There is no question about the biblical call to know the holy God and then walk obediently in the way of God's holiness. This special walking, however, is hardly some mindless path of rote marching to a set of rigid and grace-less rules, nor is it a way of life working to get divine "credit" for good practice. To the contrary, God's loving grace precedes and permeates all aspects of the life of faith.

We sinful humans must bring our sinfulness to God's altar. Only then can we rise and walk away cleansed by God's grace. There is to be no bragging about the worth of our faith performance, only rejoicing in the great love and sheer grace of God. Anything else is biblical faith gone wrong. Unfortunately, many modern readers of the Foundational Testament refer to the first five books, Genesis through Deuteronomy, as "the law." That "law" word makes many contemporary people think of courtrooms, causes for punishment, rigid guidelines, now-outmoded restrictions, all the opposite of grace. But "torah," the Hebrew word, can mean much more than regulations. It is teaching, wise instruction, the wholesome path to life (Ps. 78:1).

Deuteronomy opens with Moses expounding on *torah* in a series of speeches to Israel. His first speech contains no regulations at all, only a recitation on Israel's history or, more properly, on Yahweh's gracious acts on Israel's behalf and their responses to those acts. Accordingly, "one of the most common mistakes that people make is thinking of the law as a set of demands that Israel must keep in order to be in relationship with God; they see Israel's relationship with God as a matter of *works* and not *grace*. They couldn't be more wrong."[4] See chapters six

---

4. Andrew Sloane, *At Home in a Strange Land*, 38-39. Emphasis added.

and eleven for the importance of relationship in the nature of Yahweh and in why Israel was to worship Yahweh through sacrifice.

The Foundational Testament is clear on the fateful choice of humans to live life against God's intention—turning "live" backwards into "evil." In fact, immediately after the creation story (Gen. 1 and 2) comes the sad tale of creation's corruption (Gen. 3 and 4). God chose to enter and interact redemptively with this gone-wrong creation, naturally doing so in a manner consistent with his own nature. The resulting view of the Foundational Testament is neither that of *kismet*, the fatalism of Islam, nor *karma*, the deterministic cause-and-effect of Hinduism and Buddhism. The "open" God relates interactively with women and men who are freed to make real choices and be really responsible for them.

Here is the core principle. There is divine grace *before* legal obligation; there is freedom granted to choose to obey or not; there is enabling divine grace to make possible a freely-chosen and joyful obedience. The Jews recognized this clearly. In Exodus 20 the sequence is clear—it is Exodus *before* the Ten Commandments. First, God acted to free an enslaved people; only then came the commandments, the rules for right living for those previously freed by God's powerful and gentle grace. John Wesley called it "prevenient grace." We are a fallen people raised by God's wholly unmerited grace to a level where faith and obedience at least become possibilities again.

There is a right way to live, a walking of the holy way that is reflective of the holy God who establishes the way and lights it for our successful walking. The overarching theological paradigm is very evident here—*because I am your holy God, therefore, be ye holy!* (Lev. 11:45). For Israel, there was Torah, a description of the proper life with God and each other. It was presented primarily through the story of God's relationship to his people. Torah is about one's whole life—no distinction made between the *sacred* and *secular*. It speaks about one's identity in community, one's personal relationships, faith, health, and ethical precepts. Being *holy* has to do with the *whole* of things.

Thinking in contemporary terms, I live next to a university campus where the Indianapolis Colts do their pre-season football training. The rookies and free agents, newcomers to the team each year, are handed the team's secret playbook. It contains all of the team's offensive and defensive plays, including how each should work perfectly and lead to an immediate touchdown. The challenge in every instance is for each player on the field at the time to be in the right position and execute effectively the proper thing called for by the given play. The book is the team's "torah." Memorizing it is one important thing; an equally important thing is to live it out as designed when game-day comes.

The way of holiness in the Foundational Testament is the priestly way. However, much of the detailed work of the priests in the Temple in ancient Jerusalem appears unpromising for today's Christians to think of as relevant. The book of Leviticus, a central one for the work of the priests, would seem to have almost no enduring value. For instance, it contains details on how to carry out animal sacrifices—hardly a part of Christian or Jewish worship today. Beneath the surface of all this, however, is the grand theological theme of God's reality and presence among his people. As one reads, one must be prepared to go below the text's surface.

Following is an excellent statement of the general priestly viewpoint that lies beneath the surface of these texts about sacrifice and worship. The prevailing viewpoint is clearly more significant for today than some of the passing particulars in the upper text:

> According to Israel's central story, God had manifested his presence with his people to save them. Further, God continued to be present in their midst. This was experienced in the sanctuary, eventually identified with the Temple. God's presence there created a center of holy *space*, just as the Sabbath and the great festivals constituted holy *time*. To live as God's people is consequently seen, at least from the priestly perspective, as living in constant awareness and recognition of God's hallowing presence.[5]

In the sanctuary's set-apart (holy) space, and in its symbolic practices, the people of God constantly got fresh glimpses of God's holiness, and thus were inspired anew to go out and practice holy living in their everyday lives. The priests were asking the right question. How can people be holy in the midst of a decidedly unholy world? Their answer was clear. It is through a regular awareness of God's gracious presence with them, making possible the conforming of their thoughts and actions to his shared holiness.

The priestly keynote is always this: "Because I am God, therefore you should...." Many of the particulars that follow the "therefore" are on the surface of the text and heavily influenced by the needs of given times and settings. Even so, it is not proper to caricature the priestly ministry as one that assumes an earning of God's love by the proper washing of hands and sacrificing of animals. What is beneath the sur-

---

5. Waldemar Janzen, *Old Testament Ethics: A Paradigmatic Approach* (Louisville: Westminster/John Knox, 1994), 106-107. Emphasis added.

face of these texts is as valid for our time and setting as it was for theirs. Since God is holy, so must we be in our time and place and culturally appropriate ways. God's gracious presence, when regularly realized in the remembering and worshipping community of faith, makes possible a conforming of the lives of the people to the timely way of God's holiness in an unholy world.

I remember vividly the old holiness campgrounds in Ohio where I spent part of every summer of my growing-up years. There was a big wooden tabernacle surrounded by a circle of little cottages. This arrangement reflects the plan described in Numbers 2:1-34. The liberated Jews were traveling through the hostile wilderness on their way to their promised land. When they made camp, they were instructed to do it in a particular way. They were to put the tent of meeting in the middle of the camp and surround it symmetrically with three tribes encamping on each side. The community of God's people dwells more secure in the threatening wilderness with such an arrangement, especially with the centralized awareness that God tabernacles in their midst. As everywhere in the Foundational Testament, Yahweh is in the midst of things or they will go very wrong.

Christian congregations today can learn from this ancient text of Numbers 2. They must ask themselves how they ought to focus and conduct their worship so that their people can be regularly made aware of a critical fact. God tabernacles *in the midst of his people*, and thus enables them to be a holy people together in the wilderness of their journeys toward God's final promised land. How sad that Christians have tended to sanctify their denominations, camping almost alone with institutionalized fences between them and the rest of God's people. To be God's holy people is to have God in the center of the camp and to maintain an intentional relatedness with each other as well as with God.

As God's people called "Christian" learn to camp together around the central tent of meeting, they now must decide where the Jews fit into the camp. The negative impression of pre-Christian Judaism is found readily in the Final Testament. It is both right and wrong, as impressions usually are. The Judaism of Yeshua's time certainly was marked by a considerable amount of the formalism and legalism of scribes, by the false piety of some Pharisees, and by an arrogant priestly oligarchy represented by Annas and Caiaphas. But worldliness, hypocrisy, and mere ritualism did *not* represent the best of Judaism or Pharisaism at the beginning of the Christian era.

False piety was denounced by the Final Testament to be sure, and with good reason, but it also was being denounced at the same time by

Jews in the *Talmud-Torah*. And who could properly deny that plenty of such denouncing would be justified in relation to many Christian churches today! God's tent of meeting invites all of the chosen people to gather around in order to teach and learn from each other, not to stereotype or judge prematurely. Only when the people gather around with God in their midst will they learn, worship, and relate properly.

Yahweh, Measure of All Things

Families, religious communities, and entire cultures have their differing moral and ethical norms by which they measure behavior and administer people's accountability to set definitions of what is good, just, legal, and holy. Where do these norms come from? On what are they based? Or are they merely what the group has decided it will use? Are the norms written into the very fabric of nature and then, once identified, built into legal codes, or are they essentially arbitrary standards that function for social convenience by a community's choice? The stance of the Foundational Testament is clear:

> One of the radical differences between the Hebraic [Jewish] worldview and our Western worldview is that the latter is fundamentally *egocentric*. Everything is related to "me" or "I." Jesus in his thinking was instinctively and without exception *theocentric*. Everything is about God.[6]

Ancient Israel, as it tended to do on most subjects, went to its central theological root. Yahweh, its overarching paradigm, for determined for it what is good and beautiful and just. Accordingly, "this inner sense of 'ought' that resides in every human breast has its basis in the nature of Yahweh."[7] Why were believers instructed to do this and not that? It is because one action was understood to be reflective of the character and will of Yahweh and the other not (see chapter nine). Yahweh had created a universe of love, beauty, and order. To "sin" was to defy the holy, to be out of tune with the ultimate essence and order of things, to act offensively to the Creator, to do as Yahweh would not do, to act in self-destructive ways.

Yahweh alone is holy, purely, eternally, and essentially so. Anyone or anything else can share in that holiness only derivatively and partially. The holiness standard and possibility for us is all from and of Yahweh. We should not think of holiness as the achievement of spiritual or ethical perfection. Its primary meaning is not rooted in our

---

6. Dwight A. Pryor, in Karen H. Pryor, ed., *A Continuing Quest*, 73.
7. Dennis Kinlaw, *Lectures in Old Testament Theology*, 111.

achievement of anything by any means. The meaning of holiness (Hebrew *kadosh*) comes from the verb meaning to demarcate, separate, set apart. Holiness becomes a reality when God sets us off from all that is ungodly and places us in a covenant community in relationship to the holy God. In that community we are granted the privilege of receiving and learning and growing into what God has created and chosen us to be. Honoring our special status and obeying Yahweh's gracious commandments "sanctifies" us. We walk in divine ways in God's chosen community and thus become reflective of God's loving nature.

To be "righteous" in ancient Israel was to be faithful to a special set-apartness. It was to walk in God's ways and be judged by God's standards. That applied to everyone, even King David. On one occasion he had taken another man's wife and had that man killed in battle to cover the sordid act. This celebrated king had violated everyone involved, and yet later confessed, as any sensitive Israelite would: "Against *you* [Yahweh], you only, have I sinned" (Ps. 51:4). To violate a human relationship is to give offense to the God of all relationships. By contrast, to live in a way that honors the holiness of God is to reflect in our living this fundamental truth: "The true desire of YHWH is for neighborliness of a radical kind."[8]

God's people are not the source of their own standards of behavior. They live in the world of a holy God, and their ways are to be God's ways. Abraham is the great model, choosing to walk with Yahweh by faith, not knowing the journey's end, knowing only that Yahweh had called and was the source and definer of whatever the future was to be. He believed that Yahweh was wholly good, always right, and would be his constant walking companion into the future. Knowing all of that and living accordingly is to be "holy."

Here is the essence of what it meant for Abraham to be the faith model of Christians yet today: "It is not intellectual, it is not moral and ethical, it is not institutional.... No, the essence of it all is that absolute reliance on, that personal relationship with the God whom he says has spoken to him. Without the externals that you and I have, Abraham staked everything on this One."[9] The commitment and courage of that staking risk is what constitutes real belief.

---

8. Walter Brueggemann, *An Unsettling God*, 69. See Christine D. Pohl, *Making Room: Recovering Hospitality as a Christian Tradition* (Eerdmans, 1999) for an excellent study of "hospitality" as a key element of Jewish and Christian spirituality and holiness.

9. Dennis Kinlaw, *Lectures in Old Testament Theology*, 124.

The questions come and must be addressed in our contemporary settings. Memberships are declining in "establishment" Christian denominations. The news blares out about pastoral and priestly scandals. There is a new breed of atheists on the philosophic scene. The church of Yeshua is both human and holy. The human part is clearly obvious to everyone inside and out—as it was of the chosen people of the Foundational Testament. The church "is holy because the Holy Trinity present in and to the church is holy.... If the pure word of God is proclaimed and the sacraments duly administered, then it is not because the priest or the pastor is homiletically sound or because he or she flawlessly pronounces the words over the Eucharist.... [It is] because the Holy Spirit is present and at work in the church's liturgical services, bearing witness to Jesus Christ crucified, resurrected, and exalted over all the earth."[10]

Palaces in Time

Christianity, especially much of Protestantism, continues to have much to learn from the Jewish practice of annual religious festivals. The issue is the holiness of time and the remembering and celebrating of Yahweh's pivotal interactions with the real history of the chosen people. Annual festivals created for the Jews a rhythm for life tuned and timed by Yahweh. They gave shape to each year with a periodic set of graphic links between Yahweh and his people. They made history continually present and thus filled it with potential for generating new holiness for each new day. The festivals were divine palaces in ordinary time.

The classic seven Jewish festivals combined into a comprehensive pattern of remembering that issued in the proper perspectives for living. Through symbolic actions they taught Yahweh's provisions and faithfulness, and kept life's focus on Yahweh. Here is the annual Jewish cycle in brief:

> The God of Israel set apart festal seasons for His people to reflect upon the important things of life. In the Spring, we are reminded of His great Redemption wrought in the Passover (*Pesach*). Fifty days later, at Pentecost (*Shavu'ot*) we are reminded of the great Revelation given by the Holy Spirit, first at Mt. Sinai and then on Mt. Zion. And then in

---

10. Jason E. Vickers, *Minding the Good Ground: A Theology for Church Renewal* (Waco: TX: Baylor University Press, 2011), 37.

the autumn, we are enjoined to rejoice in the goodness of the Creation by celebrating our Creator during the Feast of Tabernacles (*Sukkot*).[11]

God's people must never forget that there was that amazing time when Yahweh delivered them from Egyptian bondage and made them into a people. Several of the festivals recall and celebrate aspects of that deliverance. Many of the festivals had agricultural backgrounds common to Israel's neighbors, and Israel always had to be careful not to infuse these celebrations with pagan religious assumptions. They were not to worship the rhythms of nature, but the God who created nature and enters its time-life in concrete ways.

The most wonderful of these ways was celebrated on *Yom Kippur*, the "day of covering" (atonement), the most holy day of the year. On this day in ancient Israel, the sins of the nation were laid on a scapegoat that was then driven into the wilderness. The high priest went into the most holy place of the Jerusalem temple to make an atonement for sin. Upon recalling this, Christians naturally think of that fateful day when Yeshua died and the curtain of the Temple tore and fell away (Matt. 27:51)—the atonement of atonements had been made by the holiest of the holy!

Beyond sin's resolution was the need to participate again in the experience of God's people being commissioned for a purpose—holiness is both purity from sin and participation with God in the divine mission in this world. Seven weeks after the *Firstfruits* festival came *Shavout* ("weeks") or, in Greek, *Pentecost* ("fifty days"). The freed Israelites had reached Mount Sinai fifty days after being liberated from Egypt. God had come down, given Moses the Ten Commandments to seal and give practical substance to the covenant, and marked the moment by the mountain itself seeming to be consumed by fire. The people needed to be freed, forgiven, cleansed, instructed, and commissioned. The Holy God intended a holy people in order for the covenant to be a workable partnership. They were to be holy people in real time and in real places.

Final Testament believers were instructed to be *Shavout* people. Yeshua's disciples learned from their Lord that they were not to rush into the world, into their "promised land," without first having a Mount Sinai experience. For Christians, the Pentecost season became the fifty days after the resurrection of Yeshua when God's Spirit fell like fire on the disciples (Acts 2:2-3), purifying and equipping them for their mission as God's people in the world. It was a Jewish remembering, a Jew-

---

11. Dwight A. Pryor, in Karen Pryor, ed., *A Continuing Quest*, 115.

ish re-experiencing, a Yeshua commissioning. A growth in holiness is enhanced by participation in annual festivals focused on the person and work of God. They break the routines of life and highlight for renewed attention the gracious acts of Yahweh on behalf of the chosen people.

Annual, however, was not the only unit of time prominent in the Jewish mind. God had created in six days and rested on the seventh. Throughout the year there was (should be) a weekly rhythm of work and rest, activity and reflection, six days on and one off for holy purposes. From each Friday evening through the following day was *Shabbat* (Sabbath, "to cease"). To keep one's focus on God throughout life requires a weekly ceasing, a brief breaking of life's demanding routines. Which day is not the really important question; the important thing is that there is a day set aside.

Many religions sanctify *places*, supposed holy places. The Jews were oriented to the Yahweh of all places and active in the ongoing activities of history. So they judged it proper, even mandatory in Yahweh's eyes, to sanctify *time*. Time was set aside weekly to stop manipulating the things of this world and focus on God who is the creator of all these things. The phrase "palaces in time" is a good way to picture the annual festivals and the weekly Shabbat.

Jerusalem was built on a small mountain overlooking a deep ravine. Some of the festivals required a "going up" to Jerusalem, although God was there and everywhere else at the same time. The regular practice of Shabbat observance allows the worshipper to get away, to ascend into God's presence where quiet increases and the divine view of things increases in one's consciousness. Holiness requires regular renewal. The temple in Jerusalem may be gone, but these appointed palaces in time remain.

Has something important been lost by Christians who have abandoned the practice of the Jewish Sabbath, whether observed on Saturday or Sunday? Is there not a need to rest from the seven-day-a-week whirlwind of contemporary society? Is there not a need to periodically hold still as the world hurries by in its frantic and relentless pursuit of money, pleasure, fashion, sport, etc.? Is there not an urgent need to counter our human tendencies toward self-centeredness and idolatry? Habits of holiness must be practiced so that their rich spiritual potential can be experienced.

The Jews at the time of Yeshua may have gone too far in legalizing many things in order to protect the integrity of the Sabbath. There were so many "don'ts" to avoid on that sacred day. But does their accumulated excess eliminate the basic need? The Foundational Testament tells us that the Earth is the Lord's (Ex. 9:29). Therefore:

> On Sabbath we acknowledge the Creator as King, and we set apart [sanctify, make holy] the day unto Him and His sovereignty. Only under His reign do we experience the fullness of peace. In Shabbat we find *shalom*.... We invite God by His Spirit to lead us by the "waters of rest" (Psalm 23:2) and restore our souls. We build a sanctuary in time and the Holy Spirit comes and fills it with the *shalom* of God.[12]

What did Rabbi Yeshua say? The Sabbath should indeed be holy, but holiness is not defined narrowly by the absence of all reasonable actions. For example, the disciples of Yeshua were hungry on a Sabbath day and plucked heads of grain while walking with him through a field. The Pharisees challenged them with the unlawfulness of such a work action. Yeshua responded, referring back to an earlier incident involving King David. God desires "mercy and not sacrifice," said Yeshua (Matt. 12:7). He even dared to say, "the Son of Man is lord of the sabbath" (Matt. 12:8). On another Sabbath day, Yeshua healed a man with a withered hand. He had not set up this timing; it had just happened that way. As usual, he was challenged for functioning unlawfully. His response was a question: "I ask you, it is lawful to do good or to do harm on the sabbath, to save life or to destroy it?" (Lk. 6:9).

So, all technicalities of action or inaction aside, believers need periodic days of rest and reflection, worship instead of work, remembering God's work in the world instead of more running after the routines of life that easily consume attention and finally one's very being. As did the Jews of old, so Christians of today require palaces of time in order to be whole, holy, God's people in the world.

---

12. Dwight A. Pryor, in Karen Pryor, ed., *A Continuing Quest*, 118-119.

Truth Stream #3

DEALING WITH THE DISORDER OF THINGS

O Lord, how long shall I cry for help, and you will not listen? Or cry to you "Violence!" and you will not save? (Hab.1:2). The end of the matter; all has been heard. Fear God, and keep his commandments; for this is the whole duty of everyone. For God will bring every deed into judgment, including every secret thing, whether good or evil (Eccl. 12:13-14).

Wisdom and discernment are an antidote to unbridled technical knowledge in a can-do society that seems bent on damaging the earth for immediate private gain.... Wisdom is an invitation to be present in the world in ways that resist both abdicating obedience and unrestrained technical freedom, by putting the inscrutable insistencies and generosities of YHWH at the core of the decision-making process.[1]

We already have established that Yahweh created all things and then granted to the creation a meaningful independence within the larger established order. This independence included the freedom to choose

---

1. Walter Brueggemann, *An Unsettling God*, 73-74.

for or against Yahweh's desired will. The divine love was so great that it would risk rejection by granting real dignity to creatures—and a genuine loving potential.

The Genesis story of the "fall" in the original garden tells of the negative choice of humans and the disastrous results. It happened with the reluctant allowance of Yahweh. The initial freedom granted by Yahweh was an aspect of the creation itself. It had been bestowed with love, but with limits. Yahweh had said of the tree of the knowledge of good and evil, "you shall not eat, for in the day that you eat of it you shall die" (Gen. 2:17). There are boundaries planted in the very order of things beyond which it is not good for humans to go.

Life's Painful Questions

We humans were not created to live in separation from or defiance of the limits established by Yahweh. Unfortunately, we chose to do so. Yahweh has allowed this choice and remained faithful to his original loving purposes, remaining redeemingly engaged with a fallen world and committed to the chosen people. That divine engagement gives hope as we deal with the present disorder of things. The disorder now exhibits itself in several ways, including:

1. People resisting authority, from parents to teachers to police to God.
2. Nation states acting like ultimate power centers answerable to nothing except another nation that happens to have more money or bigger weapons.
3. Our planet's own environment being plundered and crying out for respect and sustainability.

Life in the world as it now is cannot be glossed over as a delightful fairy tale that always has a happy ending. Jews of old, and more recent thinkers like Karl Marx and Sigmund Freud, ask openly about whether religious traditions function like opiates that numb people to the harsh realities of life. Do we live in comforting illusions about reality, with God being only a projection of our wishful thinking? Psalm 1 is a gentle and confident presentation of how things ideally should be. It is the first in the book of 150 psalms, with many of the others being quite different in tone and substance. Some sound much more like Freud that the writer of Psalm 1. The Foundational Testament is open and honest, even when it really hurts.

The life of faith in this fallen world certainly has many dimensions, and the Foundational Testament tends to address them all quite openly. Yes, there is the bedrock of all belief, Yahweh. Yes, there is Torah that tells of Yahweh's gracious choice of a people and explains how that people should walk the holy way in this life. But that is not all that there now is. Since God left room for creatures to defy the divine will and way, and since we have done just that, there also is evil, injustice, suffering, and unanswered questions on every hand. One truth stream flowing from the being of Yahweh involves how the negatives and nagging questions are to be faced.

Do you remember Gideon's very direct question (Judges 6:12-13)? An angel of the Lord had spoken this to Gideon: "The Lord is with you, you mighty warrior." Knowing the apparent desperation of his situation, Gideon's response was a penetrating question: "But sir, if the Lord is with us, why then has all this happened to us? And where are all his wonderful deeds that our ancestors recounted to us...?" Why do bad things happen to truly good people? Why the apparent silence when one pleads for an answer from God? Such questions have appeared many times in the lives of God's people.

This seeming disconnect between how it is and how it should be is often the case even for those seeking to be faithful followers of the Most High. Jews and Christians need more than the *ought* of faith. Yes, we ought to believe, but we also need a clear view of the *actual* of faith's full and often fragile life in this broken world. One great merit of the Foundational Testament is this. It was developed over a much longer span of time than the Final Testament. It knows and frankly shares both the glowing and the glaring aspects of the life of Yahweh's people. Here is the helpful confession of Philip Yancey:

> From initial resistance, I moved to a reluctant sense that I *ought* to read the neglected three-quarters of the Bible [the "Old" part]. As I worked past some of the barriers (much like learning to read Shakespeare), I came to feel a *need* to read, because of what it was teaching me. Eventually I found myself *wanting* to read those thirty-nine books, which were satisfying in me some hunger that nothing else had—not even, I must say, the New Testament. They taught me about Life with God: not how it is supposed to work, but how it actually does work.[2]

Many Christians shy from the Foundational Testament because it reports so many of Israel's failings over the centuries. But look on the

---

2. Philip Yancey, *The Bible Jesus Read* (Grand Rapids: Zondervan, 1999), 20-21 (his emphasis).

positive side of this amazing record of faith and faithlessness. Why do today's Christians know about all these failings? It is because Jews were brutally honest and recorded them for the learning of later generations. The Final Testament covers a relatively short period of time when the new faith in Yeshua the Messiah was proclaimed and initially lived out. One can see in its books the problems and compromises already arising and being dealt with in preliminary ways. But the Foundational Testament covers a much longer period of time and reveals how lives of faith played out across generations and centuries of shifting empires and cultures. A special wisdom lies in the wholeness and frankness of this longer view of things.

The Foundational Testament recognizes that people must deal with things as they now are. One way of facing life gone wrong is to protest, to dare to ask God hard questions. Doubt, protest, and stiff questioning are at home in the Jewish tradition, and thus they need not be foreigners to the Christian life of faith. Things just do not always work out properly, at least as far as we can see, and despite the assurance of Romans 8:28.[3] So, we can argue with God. Job did and R. B. Y. Scott says of him: "Here speaks a free religious spirit, untrammeled ether by orthodox belief or by dogmatic atheism.... He challenges the very world order of which he is a part.... [This] is the profoundest kind of religious faith...a sublime confidence that to ask ultimate questions of God is not to turn away from him but to draw nearer to him."[4]

There is a humorous but not altogether meaningless comment: "If there are three Jews vigorously discussing something in one room, there could be as many as five opinions in that room—two of the Jews may not agree with themselves!" Back to the theme of paradox in the Foundational Testament, it well may be that a searching and self-critical faith reflects a more genuine engagement with God than a faith that refuses to allow itself to be tested by doubt and questions.

---

3. The King James Version renders this verse, "And we know that all things work together for good to them that love God...." But the New International Version renders Rom. 8:28 this way: "And we know that in all things God works for the good of those who love him...." In one, things do work together for good; in the other, God works in all things for good. These are not quite the same meanings. Our faith is that God is lovingly at work in all circumstances, not that all things—especially bad things—somehow are being orchestrated to bring happy endings in this life.

4. R. B. Y. Scott, *The Way of Wisdom in the Old Testament* (NY: Macmillan, 1971), 141.

Job learned a key lesson. At one point at least, his protesting to God wandered into self-justification that he based on his own good performance of covenant guidelines. Then Job learned quickly that Yahweh patiently entertains honest questions *and* is prepared to ask his own questions when humans slide into self-destructive ways that set divine grace aside in favor of their own "works" (Job 40:7-8). Questioning God is acceptable. But be ready for an answer, and not always the one you might want!

In the Christian context, the word "doubt" has gotten more than its share of bad press. If faith is the victory that overcomes the world, then doubt appears to be faith's chief enemy. All who seek to believe have a stake in this ancient prayer: "I believe; help my unbelief!" (Mk. 9:24). Christians must learn from their Foundational Testament, moving beyond feeling guilty for merely doubting and questioning God. Indeed, "there may be more genuine faith in honest doubt than in a blind acceptance of some conventional creed. Faith involves risk, a calculated risk that always leaves room for mystery and some uncertainty. If there is never any doubt, it is questionable if there is ever any faith."[5]

For those affirming the great *Shema* (Deut. 6:4), the hallmark of Jewish faith, all that exists has come from God's creative and gracious hand. Everything somehow can be revealing of an aspect of God's will and ways. Surely, "the fear of Yahweh is the beginning of wisdom" (Prov. 1:7). God has set a pattern of order into the very fabric of creation. Therefore, the good and right life is the one lived in accord with that order. That is what the Torah is all about. It teaches how to live in light of God's created order. But, unfortunately, life as actually experienced is not always that simple.

How do we explain the discordant parts of life's experiences? The body of material in the Foundational Testament often called the "Writings" faces such a hard question directly. No problems are covered over; no questions are disallowed. True faith, it is assumed, can proceed only when honest confusion and doubt are looked right in the eye and Yahweh is called upon to answer. Be warned that "a proper wrestling with the First [Foundational] Testament may at times be a bruising match, one from which we may emerge with a decided theological limp."[6]

---

5. Barry L. Callen, *Authentic Spirituality*, 144.
6. Ronald Allen and John Holbert, *Holy Root, Holy Branches*, 53.

That, of course, was Jacob's experience, a wrestling with God that brought its price (Gen. 32:21-32). In April, 2002, Pastor Ron Thomas of Rogers Baptist Church in Garland, Texas, used this ancient story in a very modern context. He directed his congregation to today's world of professional wrestling with its bizarre stunts and superstars. He noted that over the years this extremely popular form of "entertainment" has grown darker and ever more violent. Then he went back to Genesis 32 and announced that we all have ringside seats to witness the wrestling match of all time. It was staged in an open-air arena beside the Jabbok River. In one corner was Jacob. In the other corner was Yahweh himself. The match had been advertised as "Big Jake Versus Jehovah!" The Foundational Testament records a blow-by-blow account. The amazing thing is not so much who "won." It is that God so respected his "opponent" and the nature of the occasion that he showed up and participated at all!

Abraham may be the ideal faith model, but the eyes of his faith were not always clear and pure. He and his elderly wife foolishly laughed at what seemed an outlandish promise of Yehweh about the possibility of their having a future son (Gen. 17:7, 18:2). He also once questioned the wisdom of Yahweh (Gen. 18:22-33). Many of the Psalms reflect similar things. They are laments, cries to Yahweh calling for him to overcome his apparent reluctance to finally act as God should. "How long?" is the common complaint against Yahweh's apparent inaction. Psalm 73 devotes the first sixteen verses to the perceived meaninglessness of life when the wicked have the upper hand and seem to get away with it.

Job makes a remarkable speech that calls into question the basic teachings of the Foundational Testament (Job 9:22-24). The amazing thing is that the Foundational Testament dares to record his speech! There is no ducking the dark downsides of present reality. It was done in part because it was believed that darkness is not all that there is. Even when things are at their worst, even when Yahweh seems wholly absent, the divine being is still recognized as the key character with whom one must deal. In fact, "it is the central conviction of Israel that human persons in the Pit may turn to this One who is powerfully sovereign and may find that sovereign One *passionately attentive*."[7]

In the book of Ecclesiastes, Koheleth (the Teacher) recounts his life observations and concludes that they add up to only emptiness and weariness. One may assume that this reporter of life's enigmas deliber-

---

7. Walter Brueggemann, *An Unsettling God*, 97.

ately uses the phrase "under the sun" since this unusual phrase appears several times in the book (2:17, etc.). It means looking at life apart from the assumption of God's existence and ordering of creation. When looking at things in that limited way, this world typically appears quite erratic and eventually empty. This pessimistic view is given its voice in the Foundational Testament, although eventually it is not allowed the last word (Ecc. 12:13-14).

What the "Wisdom" literature of the Foundational Testament seeks is the guidance for life that is to be found right in the tangled reality of this world as it is experienced. It seeks to discover truth by analyzing the world without being guided by any supposed "revelation" available from outside the immediacy of human experience. Biblical materials like Job, Ecclesiastes, and some of the Psalms look life square in the face and try to judge how faith does or does not correspond with claims about Yahweh, covenant, righteousness, Torah, and those prophets speaking words "from above." What about this world when it is viewed only from its own narrow point of view? It is a sad tale finally signifying nothing, even if full of sound and fury along the way.

A basic conclusion of the Foundational Testament is that, in the end, creation is not self-fulfilling. Nor is it self-explanatory, whatever the partial truths of "evolutionary" theories. Judging only from creation's present functioning, initial observations usually bring negative results. What the reader of the Foundational Testament is encouraged to do is recognize and accept the original divine ordering of things. We are to believe that things were designed well and lovingly, but went wrong very early. Yahweh had told Adam (humankind) the one thing not appropriate for him to do, and that is one thing that he and Eve decided to do. When caught, Adam blamed his action on his wife and she blamed a snake. The results of such disobedience and blame-passing were swift and tragic (Gen. 3:17-19), stretching all the way to today.

A college student living in our home for a summer suddenly announced to me that I was "the most unpretentious intellectual I can imagine." I took this as an unusual compliment. I try to use my intellect to its fullest capacity, but I do so humbly, being quite aware of my limits and the great difficulty of finding a pattern of "wisdom" in the piles of supposed and very unsorted "facts" that now bombard us constantly through multi-media. I am not blind to the good and the bad, the right and the wrong, or to my limited ability to always distinguish between them.

A little passing pleasure can be had in life "under the sun" and most of us can find some modest insights for living each day reasonably well. But is that all? Is that enough? The book of Proverbs is filled with lessons for life learned over time. But what about life in general? There is so much disorder and irrationality! The wisdom writers of the Foundational Testament saw it all, admitted it all, and found no obvious way to make ultimate sense of it all—*unless*, of course, one finally goes "above the sun." The biblical writers sensed that somehow, somewhere, beyond the tangle and contradictions, there was "a hidden order, and that hidden order would rob chaos of the last word in human existence."[8]

This "above the sun" perspective is precisely where the final editors decided that the Foundational Testament should begin. When the original creation was yet "a formless void" with no apparent order or meaning (Gen. 1:2), it was Yahweh who said, "Let there be light," order and meaning (Gen. 1:3). And there was light—the light of divine order and the potential of understanding and living in accord with that order under the guidance of Yahweh. And that is where the editor of the book of Ecclesiastes decided that all of the searching should find resolution: "The end of the matter; all has been heard. Fear God, and keep his commandments; for that is the whole duty of everyone" (12:13). In other words, "natural revelation," wisdom to be gained through the creation itself, however real, is seriously limited "under the sun."

Finally, the God *above* must shine the light of revelation to uncover the fullest meaning of the creation *below*. Finally, sense is made of this life only as it is lived in accord with the order that is built into its very fabric by the Creator. Knowing this by faith, however, does not end the questions. The faithful often ask "when" and "how" the meaning will emerge or the end will arrive (see chapter ten). Many supposed answers come to the table, most claiming to be well informed from teachings or at least hints from the Bible itself. Usually the answers are still wrapped in some mystery and sometimes even appear in conflict with each other. Mark 13:14-27 lists the supposed signs of the coming future and then undercuts our arrogance with the warning in 13:32: "no one knows the day or the hour, neither angels, nor the son." If that very special crowd is not sure, maybe the channel should be changed on some television preachers whose knowledge apparently exceeds that of the angels themselves!

---

8. Gerhard von Rad, *Old Testament Theology*, vol. 2 (Edinburgh: Oliver and Boyd, 1961), 420.

There is a set order to things, but we humans look through a frosted glass, particularly as we seek to understand the exact nature, timing, and meaning of the creation's final destiny. Yeshua made it clear that speculating about the future is a poor use of the time of his disciples; instead, they have important jobs to do and are to be *faithful in the meantime*.[9] Knowing the future in detail may be beyond us, but the Jewish heritage of Yeshua does keep the door open to raising hard questions about life as it now is. Such is a natural byproduct of who Yahweh is and how Yahweh chooses to work.

The views of both God and humanness seen in the Foundational Testament are very relational and interactive in nature. There is to be both self-abandonment to Yahweh and, on occasion, self-assertion toward Yahweh. We are to ask our questions, face our doubts, and hide from nothing. Since questions are part of a loving relationship, a covenant partnership which Yahweh has established, we are to

> ...ask God whatever you will. Be warned, however. If you want to manipulate God for your own agenda, forget it. God is God! But if you are crying out in repentance and love, seeking the highest good of others, and wanting to be made more like Christ and better able to serve, then God says to you, "Bring on your questions!"[10]

Our question is obvious. Why, since this is Yahweh's world, are things as bad as they are? As people in covenant with God, Israel assumed the God-given right and dignity to experience well-being and get answers to their obvious questions.

God's covenant partners are to be humble and obedient, of course. That, however, does not mean that they are to be docile and silent in the face of persistent evil. Jewish prophets often cried out, calling God to accountability. Knowing Yahweh, they were sure that chaos and injustice are not how things are supposed to be. Somehow, someday, things would be different. Yahweh would see to it! As an example, see the commentary on psalm 137 in chapter eleven. Meanwhile, there is love to be had and life to be celebrated.

---

9. Barry L. Callen, *Faithful in the Meantime* (Nappanee, IN: Evangel Publishing House, 1997).

10. Barry L. Callen, "Dare We Ask God Anything?" in David Liverett, ed., *Questions for God* (Anderson, IN: Chinaberry House, 2009), 17.

Love Poetry and Christian Theology

More than asking hard questions is allowed for people of faith. So are the simple joys of physical life in this world. There are points at which the Foundational Testament is anything but prudish. In fact, the assumption of God's being and presence in the midst of the divinely-created order is so pervasive in the Foundational Testament that considerable theological guidance can be gained even from one of its books that never mentions theology.

The Song of Songs, or *Song of Solomon*, is poetry about human love, sometimes rather graphic poetry. Many interpreters have tried to make it into theology because of discomfort with its being in the Bible otherwise. Some have said that this book is about God's love expressed in human terms. Some have said that it is about the church and Christ's great love for it. Some, offended by its explicitness, have just looked the other way. Asking questions of Yahweh is one thing; but is it not quite another thing for humans to engage in unbridled romantic love right in front of the open eyes of Yahweh?

Many Christian preachers avoid this biblical book (as they do some others in the Fundamental Testament). In this case, the avoidance is because the material appears not appropriate for "polite" church company—although in most homes and movie houses and on mobile devises what is viewed by many of the same church people is not only more graphic, but perverted and sold as "mature entertainment." Where, if not in church and straight from the Bible, are young people to receive wholesome instruction on matters of love, sex, and family? The Foundational Testament does not hesitate to raise these subjects and instruct.

As made clear in chapter three, a responsible approach to the Bible insists that we first determine the plain meaning of a text. We are to allow that plain meaning its full voice before we decide to move on to a more symbolic, allegorical, or mystical interpretation. The plain meaning that the Song of Songs presents straightforwardly is a description of a romantic relationship between a young woman and her beloved, and the language used is both beautiful and unabashedly arousing. Whatever else this biblical material might evoke in terms of theological insight or spiritual application, it must first be allowed to exercise its sensuality. We must face it. This book is a celebration of conjugal love. It elevates the rightness and value of human sexuality when it is not twisted away from its God-given meaning and context. It is part of the natural order of things as Yahweh created them.

The synagogues and churches today need the witness of this love song to help recover an attitude of wholesome celebration regarding sexual love. People have many questions, and many perverted answers being thrown their way. When the world has abused the beautiful, making it truly ugly, biblical believers should not hide the original fact that, apart from the abuse, the beautiful was and still can be beautiful. Yahweh made sexual love to be a natural and lovely thing!

There are various ways to go beneath a biblical text that appears unacceptable on the surface. The problem for some biblical readers, especially in this case, is the seeming glorification of romantic love (4:5-6). Sometimes the problem is just awkward language. For instance, the King James Version renders some of the intense romantic words in the Song of Songs in a way almost revolting to the modern ear—for instance, "My beloved put in his hand by the hole of the door, and my bowels were moved for him" (5:4). But apart from such surface things as outdated language, what is there about the graphic poetry of the Song of Songs that holds important implications for Jewish and Christian theology and contemporary life?

The words of Davie Napier are wise: "If the theological perspective has any depth at all, then erotic love will always have its sacramental overtone: this love is born of God's love, is a reflection of that love, and may be in a real sense participation in that love."[11] As we will see in chapter eleven about sacrifice, we say here in a similar way about sex. It is at its best when viewed and practiced *sacramentally*. An opening to the presence of the divine is experienced through participation in a loving act upon which God smiles and through which comes an intensified awareness of God.

Yeshua picked up the many Jewish marriage and family metaphors, even beginning his public ministry with a miracle at a wedding celebration in Cana of Galilee. The last pages of the Final Testament are filled with Christ the Bridegroom, the church the Bride, and the culmination of creation's history pictured as a huge marriage supper of the Lamb. Is the Song of Songs about human love? Yes, unashamedly, it is. Is that all it is about? Surely not, not when one also goes beneath the surface of the text to its larger theological base. Is there a natural transfer from the Foundational to the Final Testament when this subject is featured? Yes, there is.

People learn to love by first being loved (1 Jn. 4:10). Therefore, it is very wrong to suggest that the content of the Song of Songs, sensual

---

11. Davie Napier, *Song of the Vineyard*, 303.

love, is not "spiritual." To the contrary, sexual love, in the proper context as originally created by Yahweh, is deeply spiritual, leading to a cluster of images from both Testaments that are love-covenant-family oriented. Biblical theology at its best flows from these images. God called, established the covenant, and loved his people dearly. In turn, they are to live in loving community with each other and practice a healing justice in this troubled world. Christians obviously look at Yeshua on the cross and see divine love in its most dramatic form.

The Foundational Testament highlights a loving, divine-human covenant, an interactive partnership. God wonderfully relates to his people with sheer grace and tender mercy. Dennis Kinlaw recognizes that the division between the Testaments is artificial at best. He slips beneath the text's surface and suggests a "nuptial" theology for Christians. The Song of Songs is in the Bible "because there is a profound correspondence between human love and the meaning of life. It is there because human love is a metaphor for the way God wants to relate to his creatures."[12] He goes on to identify four metaphors or paradigms in biblical theology, transfers of key meaning from one Testament to the other. Since we humans are forced to resort to metaphors when thinking of God's presence and work among us, it is important to see the critical ones used widely first in the Foundational and then in the Final Testament.

Naturally, each of these biblical metaphors assumes God, the persistently overarching paradigm of all biblical revelation. God is expressed through differing literary devices, each meaningful and none fully adequate. There is: (1) the *King* and his kingdom, a political metaphor; (2) the *Judge* and his courtroom, a juridical metaphor; (3) the *Father*, a family metaphor; and finally (4) the *Groom* in his wedding chamber, a marriage metaphor.

We humans draw on what we already know to picture what we are only coming to understand about God. When taken together, we learn much from these four metaphors. The one and only God reigns supremely, executes justice, and births and loves a people called to be his own. As the Song of Songs would have it, love, sex, birth, and death are all natural parts of human life—and they also are indications of even greater realities.

These biblical metaphors are emphasized differently by Jews and Christians in different times and places. Much of the variation appears to be culturally based. Early Christian theology, for instance, often

---

12. Dennis Kinlaw, *Lectures in Old Testament Theology*, 445.

drew on the world of Roman law. The Bible, however, is an Eastern book. Christians in the Eastern Orthodox tradition have tended more toward the family and marriage metaphors. Whichever of them is being emphasized in a given time or place, all of them are meaningful, and each is limited when isolated from the others. All are Jewish; all are Christian; each seeks to probe in its distinctive way the multiple meanings of "One God for All."

In the process of honest probing, there emerges an effective dealing with the present disorder of things in this world. Questions for God are allowable.[13] The fullness of life is encouraged. Even in the worst of circumstances, hope need never die.

---

13. See David Liverett, ed., *Questions for God*.

Truth Stream #4

LIVING WITH PERSISTENT HOPE

Lead me in your truth, and teach me, for you are the God of my salvation; for you I wait all day long (Ps. 25:5). And now, O Lord, what do I wait for? My hope is in you (Ps. 39:7).

The Old [Foundational] Testament can only be read as a book of ever increasing anticipation.... This continuous reinterpretation to which...the old stories about Yahweh were submitted [by the Final Testament] did not do violence to them. Rather, they were predisposed to it from the very start. Their intrinsic openness to a future actually needed such fresh interpretations on the part of later ages; and for the latter it was essential to their life to take up tradition in this way and give it a new meaning.[1]

There always is hope. It is rooted in a belief in Yahweh, God of the distant past and eternal future. The hope grew over time for the Jews; then the time finally came when the disciples of Yeshua read in a fresh way their Foundational Testament and found a wonderful fulfillment of its hope. This fresh reading was natural in light of the Christ event

---

1. Gerhard von Rad, *Old Testament Theology*, vol. 2 (Edinburgh: Oliver and Boyd, 1965), 319, 361.

happening in their very midst. Such freshness is an example of the "surplus of meaning" explained in chapter thirteen.

Since creation originated with Yahweh and the ultimate destiny of the creation also lies solely in Yahweh's hands, there always is hope for the faithful people of God. Unlike most religious communities surrounding ancient Israel, and many yet today, the Jews did not embrace a circular view of history that often is tied closely to the cycles of nature. The flow of time and events, seemingly circular on occasion and appearing to go nowhere, often does seem confusing. Nonetheless, the Foundational Testament is based on the assumption that all of history came from the hand of God and eventually is going somewhere that God intends. Meanwhile, the life of faith is not to be one of trying to escape history, as though this world and all its realities have no present meaning that can be enhanced by people who have a future hope. The life of faith is not to be one of despair, a quiet yielding to some inevitable fate, not for Jews or the Christians who emerged from among them.

The Hebrew view of time and history was "essentially linear, durative, and progressive. In short, it was going somewhere; it was en route to a goal, a glorious climax at the end of this age."[2] Even in the apparently worst of times, God still is known to *be*, and to *be moving* human history toward something yet beyond our ability to see. Something sacred is at stake in each moment. It can be a God-directed small step toward a better tomorrow. Hence, we must never *kill* time, but seek a way to *redeem* it (Eph. 5:16).

In the Foundational Testament, the ideal and surely coming future is referred to variously as the "day of the Lord," the "remnant," and the "messianic age." The Jewish prophets, in all their varying situations and emphases, were agreed on at least a few things. They "did not attempt to analyze the exact process by which the new age was to come…. While striving with might and main with their present, they threw all their hope upon God. He would intervene, they believed, and transform all things."[3] Christians later would look back on the "suffering servant" passages in Isaiah, especially chapter 53, and see a clear image of Yeshua the Christ, the apparent fulfillment of the long hope of the Jewish covenant community. Yeshua was the natural linking of the two Testaments. He was Yahweh with us humans, a major step on the way to the final future.

2. Marvin Wilson, *Our Father Abraham*, 161.
3. G. Ernest Wright, *The Challenge of Israel's Faith*, 97.

God Is Not Done Yet!

The Foundational Testament is full of joy, agony, questions, and persistent hope. Even so, it ends with failures, prophetic judgments, and unfulfilled anticipations. Here are sobering words:

> If judgment is the last word which God's prophets have to speak in Israel's history, then the story of the Old Testament is a meaningless tragedy.... If judgment is God's final act in Israel's history, then the Old Testament is a witness to God's weakness.... God started something in history...which he could not finish. He uttered a promise which he could not fulfill. He created a human race over which he could not rule. His lordship was shattered against the unbreachable barrier of Israel's rebellion, and his word was ineffective against the stone shell of Israel's heart.[4]

But those dismal judgments were not the end! Israel was much more than failure. God's final actions were still to come. Yahweh had not given up in partnering with a chosen people. Much harsh judgment and unfulfilled hope is obvious in the late portions of the Foundational Testament. Still, that would not be the end of the matter. God was not done yet. The story of God-with-us would go on.

The origin of Christianity was keynoted by the bold announcement that the long-expected Jewish Messiah had finally arrived in Yeshua. The Jewish tradition was one of hope in the God who is never done yet! It is the record of a people of God on pilgrimage with Yahweh through our ongoing and sordid human history. The ancient Jews were in covenant with the One who was willing to journey with his called people, despite their many failures. Yahweh had launched the story, and would keep it going no matter what. His faithfulness was unending even if the nature of its fulfillment would take dramatic new turns.

As the author of Hebrews 11 makes clear, the Foundational Testament is the record of the heroes of the faith who never fully entered into God's blessing, but who nonetheless were clearly on their way to its blessed fulfillment. As they had journeyed on, they always seemed to be inviting all us to go along. This hope of the continuing journey, one that finally is going somewhere important, can be seen in the very structure of the Foundational Testament. In fact, it is seen in the structure of the whole Bible.

---

4. Paul and Elizabeth Achtemeier, *The Old Testament Roots of Our Faith*, 115-116.

The Foundational Testament is comprised of three major parts, with the end of the Final Testament being the fourth biblical "ending" that even then anticipates another beginning. Note that each of these literary endings reflects both *persistent pain* and *undying hope*.

1. The Torah — ends with Deuteronomy 34:1-12. Moses, a giant in the Jewish tradition, died and was buried in a location known only to God. He saw the promised land from afar, but never managed to enter it. How sad. He had gone through so much in leading the people out of Egypt and through the wilderness, but he would not make it with them to the final goal, the promised land. And yet, this should not be viewed as a tragedy because the people of God would enter the land, with Moses always living on in their hearts and lives and writings. He was one with the people and, therefore, would go into the future with them. The Israelites learned that the life of faith is a life lived in light of God's promise, a promise that somehow, sometime will be fulfilled. The Lord said to Moses, "This is the land of which I swore to Abraham, to Isaac, and to Jacob, saying, 'I will give it to your descendants'; I have let you see it with your eyes, but you shall not cross over there" (Deut. 34:4). Thus ends the Torah, with one man's faith partly unfulfilled and the community of faith still journeying on into God's future.

2. The Writings — ends with 2 Chronicles 36:15-23. Jerusalem had fallen and the Exile had been very long indeed. Nonetheless, the promise was that there again would be liberty, even a new Jerusalem. After the disaster of the Exile, it turned out that God still lives—and so does his people! Hope refused to vanish despite everything, just as Jeremiah said it would not (Jer. 29). When the exile had run its course in the eyes of God, an amazing thing happened. The new King Cyrus of Persia declared: "The Lord, the God of heaven, has given me all the kingdoms of the earth, and he has charged me to build him a house at Jerusalem, which is in Judah. Whoever is among you of all his people, may the Lord his God be with him! Let him go up" (2 Chron. 36:23). There ends the Writings, with the Exile ending and a new future looming just over the horizon.

3. The Prophets — ends with Malachi 4:1-6. After all of the scoldings, warnings, and predictions of the several great Jewish prophets, the collection of their works ends with the promise of the return of Elijah. He will turn the hearts of parents to their children and the hearts of the children to their parents. The future is open, in other words, and the life of Israel awaits what God still has in store. Yahweh announces that he "will not come and strike the land with a curse" (Mal. 4:6). In fact, the Final Testament notes that Yeshua was thought by some to be Elijah returned (Matt. 16:14) and, at the transfiguration of Yeshua, Elijah appeared along with Moses (Matt. 17:3-4). The work and revelation of God continues from Testament to Testament, from the beginning of the creation until the will of God is fully complete. So ends the prophetic writings, with hope unfulfilled but still very much alive.

4. The Book of Revelation — ends with chapter 22:21. The Foundational Testament has three major sections, Torah, Writings, and Prophets. Each knows pain in the life of God's people; each finishes by projecting hope because of the God whose love persists despite everything. The second division of the Bible that Christians know finishes just as the earlier biblical sections, with hope like the earlier Jews, the life of the church of Yeshua is always in danger of compromise and often the victim of persecution. The Jewish experience over the centuries already was being mirrored in these Jews now joyously following Yeshua. Even so, faith in God's future persisted. The Final Testament finishes with this: "The one who testifies to these things says, 'Surely I am coming soon.' Amen. Come, Lord Jesus! The grace of the Lord Jesus be with all the saints. Amen" (Rev. 22:20-21).

The book of Revelation, as does the Foundational Testament, focuses finally on Yahweh, the faithful God of all times. Dennis Kinlaw says wisely: "Do you know what I think is primary in the book of Revelation? It is like the Old Testament; when the book of Revelation talks about the future it does not tell you the *what* in your future, but it tells you the *who*."[5] The who is none other than the eternal Yahweh, now known most fully in the exalted Yeshua. The fulfillment grows from the persistent hope of the Foundational Testament. In light of Yahweh's dramatic coming in Yeshua, he would remain with his people in Yeshua's Spirit as they continue to journey on.

In a world divided by rampant racism, the Final Testament echoes a major theme of the Foundational Testament— a chosen people that is to function as agents of God's work in history. It proclaims that God has created another race, a chosen race (1 Pet. 2:9-10). The chosen ones are to function very differently than those who divide on human bases. The new race is to be the united and re-creating people of God,

---

5. Dennis Kinlaw, *Lectures in Old Testament Theology*, 203.

the body of Christ. As the church, it is called to accept the Spirit's ministry and thus become first fruits of the coming new order (Rom. 8:23; 2 Cor. 1:22, 5:5; Eph. 1:13-14). The church is to live in the power of Christ's resurrection (Col. 3:3-4), which is the dynamic of the coming new day.

The future reign of God works in the world now by the power of the divine Spirit who already is introducing that reign and one day will bring it to fullness. When Yeshua spoke of God's kingdom, his emphasis was heavily Jewish—naturally. His question was much less "What can you expect to happen eventually?" and much more "What shall you do now in history to evidence the current and growing presence of God's reign?" The foci are "in history" and "now." The reality of God's reign was already arriving for those who would repent and receive it. Yeshua's clear implication was that, in his own presence, something extraordinary was happening. The Kingdom of God was drawing near; the King himself had arrived with loving redemption to launch a new creation! (Lk. 11:20).

Accordingly, a central concern of the church of Yeshua should be to avoid distracting speculations about details of the future. Instead, in the meantime prior to that future's full arrival, the church should focus on two things. Those things are the God of the future and faithfulness to God's agenda in this present world. The church is to know God as present and active, a loving sovereignty that calls for the real partnership of responsible disciples. All is in continuity with the story of Israel. The Final Testament insists that Yeshua was everything that God intended his chosen Israel to be. In fact, "in him and him alone, God's lordship was perfectly made manifest. In him and only him, God's rule was clearly seen, God's kingdom was come on earth, even as it is in heaven. Jesus Christ perfectly exercised the obedience which Israel owed to its Lord.... Who, then, is Jesus Christ? He is the fulfillment of the Old Testament story. He is the new Israel...."[6]

Culminating in a Song of Praise

A major message from the Foundational Testament surely is this: "Yahweh can be depended upon to be passionately loyal to His people, even if they do not deserve it. The Hebrew word for this characteristic of Yahweh is *hesed*. If two parties are in covenant with each other, they

---

6. Paul and Elizabeth Achtemeier, *The Old Testament Roots of Our Faith*, 128, 132.

are obligated to do *hesed* with each other, to be passionately loyal to one another, come what may. The life of God's people, however, often came to involve faithlessness, struggle, and suffering. Given this, the faith community revealed in the Foundational Testament was so ready for and in need of the arrival of the Final Testament. It would spawn a wonderful move from struggle and suffering to the wonder of renewed communion, surprising joy, and persisting hope.

A sturdy faith in God's *hesed*, divine faithfulness in the midst of all failure, evil, and loss, permitted Israel "to make the move from the obedience of Psalm 1 to the doxology of Psalm 150.... The way from torah obedience to self-abandoning doxology is by way of *candor about suffering* and *gratitude about hope*.... The move is from *willing duty* to *utter delight*...." It is crucial to be aware that "the requirements of Psalm 1 are not scuttled; they are assumed. But they are superseded in the delight the community knows about God."[7] Again, Yahweh is the overarching paradigm of all the basic beliefs of Israel; Yahweh's will and ways are the backbone of the creation's order and known to be the right way to live; and Yahweh's faithfulness comes to be accepted as certain, allowing hope for the unseen divine future yet ahead.

The book of Psalms incorporates the full range of this complex life of faith. Psalm 1 is safe, ordered, reflecting almost the simplistic expression of a perfect faith in a world that seems everywhere to affirm and fulfill it. The covenantal faithfulness of God appears to guarantee moral coherence in how things are and how they go. Those "who delight in the law of the Lord are like trees planted by streams of water which yield their fruit in its season..." (vss. 2-3). There is God and God's way; walk in that way and all will be well. But then it happened. This rather simple premise of Psalm 1 faced the horrors of divided kingdoms, wayward kings, and a humiliating exile among unbelieving foreigners.

The resulting psalms of lament understandably call into question even God's fidelity. This brings a stressful transition indeed, such as is seen in the pivotal Psalm 73. Here we hear God's people crying out and questioning, almost in despair. Even so, eventually they manage to mature through the suffering toward the awe and communion that shines through in Psalm 150. The same positive move is seen between two decisive speeches of Job reported in 31:35-37 and 42:1-6. The hard issues addressed in the first speech are not fully resolved in the second,

---

7. Walter Brueggemann, *Psalms and the Life of Faith*, ed. Patrick D. Miller (Minneapolis: Fortress Press, 1995), 202, 196.

as they rarely are in this life. But somehow the hardest of issues are absorbed and accommodated by the wonder and beauty of a now-enriched communion in fellowship with God that finally is found beyond the questions.

That move between the speeches of Job represents well the three-part journey of faith that finally bursts forth from the long travail of Israel's story. From an almost ideal orientation to God and creation (Psalm 1), through the disorientations of life with God in this world (Psalms 73), God's people manage to move on. They are refined in fire and mature, neither abandoning the orientation of the beginning nor being crippled by the disorientations of the long historical path. They are prepared through it all for a transcending, holy communion and praise of God (Psalm 150). Psalm 73 starts by reporting that the initial orientation—"truly God is good to the upright, to those who are pure in heart" (vs. 1); then it transitions to a sharp awareness that things are not always well with God and his people in this world—"my feet had almost stumbled.... I saw the prosperity of the wicked.... All in vain, I have kept my heart clean and washed my hands in innocence" (vss. 2-3, 13).

The speaker in Psalm 73 is tempted to give up on the supposed moral structure of all traditional religious piety, even to yield to an arrogance and self-indulgence born of despair. Then it happens, another move, the final one (although, unfortunately, the cycle can circle around and begin all over again). This additional turn is one "of perception, no longer fixed on conduct and 'payoffs.' The rhetoric of verses 73:23-26 moves from calculating conduct to trustful communion with God as the speaker discerns that *face-to-face engagement with God is finally what matters*.... The old troublesome issues of 'conduct and consequence' established in the categories of Psalm 1 are not resolved. Those issues are rather left behind for a greater good.... It is enough that the God of long-term fidelity is present, caring, powerful, and attentive."[8] The psalmist now sings, "Nevertheless, I am continually *with you*; you hold my right hand.... Whom have I in heaven but you? And there is nothing on earth that I desire other than you.... But for me it is good to be *near God*; I have made the Lord God my refuge, to tell of all your works" (vss. 23, 25, 28, emphasis added).

The journey of faith is from uncomplicated obedience through stressful experiences to the maturity of praise even in the face of unre-

---

8. Walter Brueggemann, *Psalms and the Life of Faith*, 208-209. Emphasis added.

solved questions. Israel found herself, in all her doubt, suffering, and even alienation, with nowhere else to go than to God's presence and wonderful love. The irony, maybe the amazement, is that the arena of questions and suffering turns out to be the birthplace of enduring hope. Being in God's presence may not answer all questions in this life, but it tends to remove the need to have all the answers.

The center of all future expectations regarding David was the divine promise found in II Samuel 7. David's throne in some way would be established forever. Jeremiah added that there might have to be a new covenant (Jer. 31:31-34). The kingdom of God would come on earth one day and God's law would be written in the hearts of his people. The destiny of God's people would be secure; her destiny lay in God's promises, not in her perfect performance. The "Servant of the Lord" would play a large role. Israel should have been that servant, a light to the nations, God shining through to all peoples. At times Israel had been what she was called to be, but only partially and never dependably. The election of Israel "is not a mark of exclusivism and national pride but of responsibility to the nations. She is her truest self, most faithful to her heritage of election and covenant, when she issues the universal invitation, 'Ho, every one who thirsts, come to the waters' (Isa. 55:1a)."[9]

The witness to the world, God's intention to save the world, would require suffering, as pictured graphically in Isaiah 53. How natural it was to see the death and resurrection of Yeshua as the fulfillment of all God's promises. Isaiah sang in anticipation of what Yahweh one day would surely do: "Sing, O heavens, for the Lord has done it...for the Lord has redeemed Jacob, and will be glorified in Israel" (Isaiah 44:23). The Gospel writers of the Final Testament finally would announce what some lowly Jewish shepherds suddenly heard: "Glory to God in the highest heaven, and on earth peace among those whom he favors!" (Lk. 2:14). Yeshua had come. Promises found fulfillment. The divine Kingdom had dawned and one day would arrive in its fullness.

---

9. James Muilenburg, *The Way of Israel*, 147.

SECTION THREE

FACING SOME OF THE HARDEST ISSUES

Four Inter-Testament Studies

Not by might, nor by power, but by my Spirit, says the Lord of Hosts. (Zech. 4:6).

One of the traits of the Old Testament story, sometimes linked with bloody battles but also sometimes notably free of violence, is the identification of YHWH as the God who saves his people *without their needing to act*.... Thus, even when Israel uses the sword, in a fearful and most destructive way, the victory is credited not to the prowess of the swordsmen or the wisdom of the generals, but *to the help of YHWH*. This remains the main point of the accounts throughout Joshua and Judges.[1]

The introduction to this book calls Christians back to their Jewish foundations. It announces that such a going back soon gets caught *between* truths. There emerges an awkwardness in dealing with some of the biblical material. With that awkwardness comes an awareness that the Bible is not *flat* nor *dormant*. It is a living, growing revelation from God that is only partial at its beginning. Even so, the beginning is essential for the ending to be understood and appreciated. Therefore, regardless of occasional awkwardness, the Foundational and Final Testaments necessarily belong together and significantly inform each other.

1. John Howard Yoder, *The Politics of Jesus*, 2nd ed. (Eerdmans and Paternoster Press, 1994), 76-78. Emphasis added.

Some of the material in the Foundational Testament stands in sharp contrast with what is found later in the Final Testament. We mentioned above that an early Christian named Marcion rejected the entire Foundational Testament because the contrast was just too much for him. Even so, all of the earlier biblical material is believed by Christians to be authoritative in some manner still today. In order to clarify how this can be, we have proceeded through the first ten chapters of this book looking for a path through the contrasts and questions, identifying the enduring truth streams, seeking the way for Christians to find instruction and inspiration from all of the Foundational Testament, even from its most awkward parts.

We have affirmed that the way is there. It leads to and from the very being of Yahweh, the one and only Holy God known by the ancient Jews as the Fountainhead, the Water Source of all eternal truth. Yahweh's being and will came to be known progressively, not all at once and not expressed culturally in ways fixed forever. The increasing knowledge of the divine came to flow through four central truth streams, each originating from the single Water Source. They now underlie all biblical materials in both Testaments. The challenge for Christian readers is to encounter all biblical texts in their original settings and then, when necessary, to go *beneath* given texts to discover the supporting truth stream(s) that gives them their enduring truth value and current authority for Christians.

We attempt in this chapter to engage in such in-depth discovery in four instances. In three of them, the surface of the text of the Foundational Testament is particularly troubling to Christians and in varying ways involves what is said to be divinely-sanctioned violence. In the fourth, we observe Christians adapting an ancient text and giving it fresh meaning in the Final Testament, something troubling to Jews who see their text being violated by its adaptation. The story of the two Testaments is a continuous one, each necessarily informing the other. Tensions rise, however, in the transition from one Testament to the other. The following four case studies seek to address the tensions constructively.

1. Holy War and Vengeance?... Deuteronomy 7 and Leviticus 24

Jihad is the Arabic word for what can be translated "to struggle" or "to fight," depending on the context. In the West today, with the great problem of terrorism and suicide bombers who often identify themselves with an extreme form of Islam, the word is generally understood to mean "holy war." Giving the word exclusively military connotations, however, is inaccurate and unfair. The *Quran* does call for "jihad" as a military struggle on behalf of Islam, but it also relates this word to an individual spiritual struggle toward self-improvement and moral cleansing. Muhammad is said to have considered the armed-struggle version of holy war "the little jihad," with the spiritual version of holy war--the war within oneself--"the great jihad."

Giving a military meaning to the concept of jihad certainly has a long tradition. We spoke earlier of Nazis attempting Jewish genocide and Christians carrying out "crusades" against "infidels." In the Middle East, and not exclusively in Islam, holy war often has appeared. This includes it appearing among the ancient Jews. For example, there are instances in the Foundational Testament of commands to violence said to have come to the Jews from Yahweh. Deuteronomy 7 appears to issue an order from Yahweh for the Jews to carry out genocide against the Canaanites. "And when the Lord your God gives them over to you and you defeat them, then you must utterly destroy them" (Deut. 7:2).

Such a passage brings shudders today as the world suffers from religious extremists and hears cries for "holy war" that have clear genocidal overtones. For Christians who believe that all Scripture, including all of the Foundational Testament, is useful for "training in righteousness" (2 Tim. 3:16), the question is obvious. How can Deuteronomy 7 possibly be part of a contemporary Christian curriculum in righteousness? One must go beneath the text to find an answer.

The Hebrew word *kherem* typically means to destroy totally. It might seem to those viewing Yahweh as "one God for all" and as the Father pictured by Yeshua that such a command could not have come from Yahweh in reference to any peoples. Even so, in the ancient setting of the Deuteronomy 7 reference, it might not have seemed so unimaginable. We all interpret our faith and its demands in some context. Whether or not the ancient Israelites over-read the will of Yahweh as recorded in Deuteronomy is an open question. It clearly is a possibility in light of the further revelation of Yeshua in the Final Testament. The hard fact is that those ancient Jews understood Yahweh to be commanding them to "utterly destroy," unless one accepts the view of some scholars that the term should be translated "utterly renounce" and used in reference to the religious perversions of Canaan that immediately threatened the integrity of the Israelite faith.

Even if one accepts the reading of *kherem* as "renounce" instead of "destroy," and much in the Fundamental Testament certainly does call for renouncing idolatries, the violence of the Deuteronomy 7 text remains. As the Israelites first entered the Canaan land, there was great concern for the safety and continuing integrity of the distinctive faith of the people of God. They would have to maintain the purity of their faith in settings that sought to destroy it with various forms of syncretism—being willing to combine the worship of Yahweh with local, idolatrous alternatives. Should they stoop to violence when apparently required to do so by extreme circumstances?

Andrew Sloane's words are of some help here: "Deuteronomy is not, in the first instance, about the genocidal slaughter of the Canaanites; rather, it is about the danger that future generations of Israelites will turn away from following Yahweh and thus fall under the same sentence as the Canaanites.... The primary concern is what the Israelites are to do about the removal of idolatry from the land—in part as a defensive measure to ensure that Israel is not corrupted...."[2] Defensiveness against encroaching idolatry is the priority. But does defensiveness sometimes justify in Yahweh's eyes a violent offense against the idolators?

Even if Sloane is right, the violence command is still there. Deuteronomy 7 is an instance where it is crucial for Christians to go *beneath the text* of the Foundational Testament to locate the informing theology and thus the authoritative meaning for contemporary Christian faith. What is said on the surface of the text seems utterly unacceptable. The theology below, however, brings us back to the one God, Yahweh, the singular Water Source of truth, and to the responsibility of God's chosen people to be faithful to God alone, even in the most extreme of circumstances. Israel was being called to enter a new land and live there as the people *of God*.

Now, as then, God's people are called to live faithfully by an intentional religious *non-conformity*. God's people are to be "resident aliens, an adventurous colony in a society of unbelief.... The church knows that its most credible form of witness (and the most 'effective' thing it can do for the world) is the actual creation of a living, breathing, visible community of faith."[3] Therefore, living as God's chosen and holy people is the theological base, authoritative for all times. The question is *how* to do this.

---

2. Andrew Sloane, *At Home in a Strange Land: Using the Old Testament in Christian Ethics* (Hendrickson Publishers, 2008), 132.
3. Stanley Hauerwas and William Willimon, *Resident Aliens* (Nashville: Abingdon Press, 1989), 49, 47.

The surface of Deuteronomy 7 offers one answer, seeming to be timely and appropriate long ago. A more enduring option, however, one certainly championed in the Final Testament, is being a credible witness to Yahweh by being "a living, breathing, visible community of faith." One does the best for others by first being the best for oneself. The example of Yeshua does not include violence toward others. It receives, as necessary, violence to oneself as a witness to who God revealed himself to be in Yeshua; it chooses to function self-sacrificially for the peaceful healing of a broken creation.

In the time and setting of this Deuteronomy text, everything seemed to depend on such an intentional non-conformity. The Israelites had to be on guard and utterly reject for themselves the ways of the Canaanites. What will be said below about violence in Psalm 137 bears repeating here. The psalmist would long for God's intervention, but envisioned inadequately *the means* of God's coming intervention. The ultimate returning and redeeming presence of God with his people after the Exile would not be the reclaiming of Jerusalem by violence, but by the sacrifice of the Son on an ugly cross planted in a hill outside Jerusalem's gates. Protecting the faith of Yahweh from idolatrous alternatives in the environment of one's living cannot be accomplished by violence toward others without violating the faith itself—at least as taught and exemplified by Yeshua.

Chapters five and six of this book describe the increasing revelation of the nature of Yahweh as the Jews came to know him. Yahweh risks partnership with a people who are in process and understand God's will and ways only partially and in their own cultural contexts. But, to be fair, that limitation of the Jews is not to their total discredit—limitations exist for all of us in our own times and places. Christians should learn from the fragile faith applications of their Jewish past and thus be helped to avoid their own in the ongoing present.

The lowly Bethlehem manger was the unlikely scene of the eventual coming of the full presence of God. This fullness had not yet been seen by the Jews as they were first entering Canaan. The full presence of Yahweh would not come in any destruction of Canaanites or anyone else, but in the much-later birth of a little baby, a miracle child named Yeshua. When he was born, almost immediately the ruling power of the time was threatened and tried to dispose of the boy. It would be another violent setting. Matthew tells the story, pointing out that Yeshua was the son of David, the son of Abraham" (1:1) and that Herod ordered a massacre of the new-born boys in Bethlehem. His henchmen, however, missed Yeshua whom God sent off to Egypt with Joseph and Mary for his safety. What irony this is in the Jewish tradition, Egypt the place of former slavery now become the place of safety for their Messiah!

Here is additional irony. The price to be paid for violating God's will and spoiling his people would be paid by violence. However, it would not be violence against the enemies of the Jews carried on by God's people. Instead, it would be violence against *one Jew*. Yeshua also would live under foreign domination, but would reject calls to violence that he certainly knew from Deuteronomy 7 and were echoed on occasion from his own disciples. By contrast, he taught forgiving love, *even of one's enemies* (Matt. 5:39, 41, 44). He understood Yahweh's will and the related prophecies in the Foundational Testament as his call to be the "suffering servant" of Yahweh as described so well in Isaiah 53.

Followers of this Jewish Messiah, therefore, are called to endure, hope, wait, and always be one with Yeshua in his serving and suffering ways in the world. What is it like to be in and of Yeshua? It is "to have this mind among yourselves, which is yours in Christ Jesus who, though he was in the form of God, did not count equality with God a thing to be grasped, but emptied himself, taking the form of a *servant*" (Phil. 2:5-11).

The Foundational Testament, in Deuteronomy 7 and elsewhere, lays valuable groundwork for this later revelation in Yeshua. It reports the early stages of God's people coming into being and trying to find their way in a very troubled world. Their journey, with all of its limitations, brings valuable lessons to later generations of believers. It highlights enduring theological themes that, however inadequately understood and applied at first, projected forward to what turned out to be Yeshua and his humble way in the world. The Final Testament refines the themes, clarifies the exact *means* of God's intention, and announces the Person who would be God-with-us, the final fulfillment.

To be more precise about what happened in Yeshua, violence against God's will was accepted *by God himself* through the suffering of his Son. Finally, God would absorb into himself the pain of the Jews and the sin of the whole world. Rather than act *against* sinners, God would choose, out of an amazing love, to act *on their behalf*! It would be a very different kind of justice, the kind that comes only because the focus is on God—and the character of Yeshua finally designates best *who God really is*, and *how* God's people are to be in this violent world.

Human justice typically is understood to mean that each gives to others what is rightfully theirs, and receives the same in return. By sharp contrast, as seen through Yeshua, God's mercy and grace mean that we humans are given what is clearly only God's and is wholly undeserved by us, with nothing asked by God in return except gratitude, faithfulness, and our showing *a similar loving mercy to others*. Rather than leading with "an eye for an eye," Yeshua turns the tables and instructs that his disciples are to "turn the other cheek," renounce violence against enemies however wrong they may be. Returning to the concern of the ancient Israelites to protect the faith, Yeshua teaches protection of the faith *by an active revealing of the loving fruit of the faith*.

Surprising to some, this renouncing of violence is not out of character with the Foundational Testament. It had been said from early times that Yahweh would "guard the feet of his faithful ones; *for not by might shall a man prevail*" (1 Sam. 2:9). The Jewish prophets often echoed this principle: "Not by might, nor by power, but by my Spirit, says the Lord of Hosts" (Zech. 4:6). Therefore, when Jesus "used the language of liberation and revolution...without predicting or authorizing particular violent techniques for achieving his good ends, he need not have seemed to his [Jewish] listeners to be a dreamer; he could very easily have been understood as updating the [Jewish] faith...whereby a believing people would be saved *despite their weakness*, on condition that they 'be still and wait to see the salvation of the Lord'."[4]

On this sensitive subject of violence, neither biblical Testament is well understood apart from the other. The Final Testament explains that severe punishment would come not by God's people punishing or even destroying Canaanites or Babylonians or Romans. Yahweh reserves the sole right to determine the manner and timing of judgment and punishment. These would come, but so surprisingly, not by a divinely led army, but by the humble sacrifice of one Jewish man for the sins of the whole world, including those of God's own people. When Christians identify the man Yeshua with God's sacrificial presence with us humans, the clear meaning is that God chose to take all justified punishment *into himself*, suffering the pain, acting in love and not violence. This surely is a model for the disciples of Yeshua to follow today.

The most recent years of military intervention by the United States in Iraq and Afghanistan, and also the tragedy of "9-11" in the United States itself, have made an important lesson newly clear. There are definite limits to what violence can get accomplished, whether the cause is good or bad, and no matter how large the weapons available or how well trained and equipped the combatants may be. Jews have felt justified at times over the centuries in the use of violence—as have so many

---

4. John Howard Yoder, *The Politics of Jesus*, 84. Emphasis added.

other peoples and nations. Christians generally support at least the concept of participating in "just" wars, although defining "just" in a given circumstance is extremely difficult. The current State of Israel judges its military strength and threat of its use as a necessary and appropriate element of national defense. The issue of violence does not go away.

The challenge for God's people remains. What is the best way to represent God in this world, a sinful world that runs largely on greed, balance of power, and the use of violence? The answers are never easy. Yeshua was caught in this very dilemma and was unjustly crucified. From that event, understood by Christians as a voluntary act of self-sacrifice, believers are challenged to learn a divine way of being in this world. It is extraordinary, dangerous, counter-cultural, apparently Yahweh's preferred way. The person of Yeshua stands as the enduring biblical model and message from God, one lying beneath every biblical text, including Deuteronomy 7. Put down the sword! Unless a seed is placed in the ground and dies, it will not grow and bear fruit. According to Yeshua, only the humble ones who are willing to yield their lives in this world are going to keep them eternally (Jn. 12:24-25).

Chaos, injustice, and suffering remain very much with our world. The temptation to violence in God's name remains strong. The persistent question is how believers in Yahweh God, known best in Yeshua, should respond. In the 1940s, Mahatma Gandhi said something of significance in the context of his opposition to British rule in India. A few years later, Martin Luther King, Jr., said the same thing in his struggle for the proper civil rights of African-American citizens in the United States. They both said: "The old law of an eye for an eye leaves everyone blind." Yeshua once said that, when the blind lead the blind, all would likely wind up falling into a pit (Matt. 15:14).

The eye-for-an-eye concept is found in the Foundational Testament (Ex. 21:24; Lev. 24:20; Deut 19:21). Having just given the Ten Commandments to Moses, Yahweh instructed him in many things regarding how this newly-freed people should conduct their lives. Several instructions were given about how to handle violence, so common in the daily lives of those times. The eye-for-an-eye principle is there. Harsh by contemporary ethical standards? Yes, at least in many places. Yes, although in the Bible there are some compassionate and moderating elements that should not be overlooked.

Many have observed that a command against all violence or retaliation for injustice would have been incomprehensible and suicidal when the Israelites were first in that wilderness. The effective ordering of this new nomadic people, traveling through lands of numerous violent opponents, seemed to require the use of force, although within some controlling moral guidelines. Numerous aspects of Yahweh's law moved his newly-freed people *away from* the cruelty of surrounding cultures and toward justice *with increased compassion*. One scholar calls this a "redemptive movement," urging that contemporary readers not fix attention on the wrong thing. Instead of judging certain laws in the Foundational Testament in isolation from their time and cultural context, we should go beneath the text and focus on the movement, the divinely-intended "trajectory," the moral maturing that finds its fuller maturation in the Final Testament.[5]

Yeshua and his disciples were faced with persecution and cruelty. His teaching recalled the old rule of an eye-for-an-eye and a tooth-for-a-tooth, but he intensified the original intent of limited response from only equaling the offense to no violent response at all: "But I say to you, Do not resist an evildoer. But if anyone strikes you on the right cheek, turn the other also" (Matt. 5:39). Paul soon would call for believers in Yahweh God to imitate the humility of Yeshua. They are "to be of the same mind, having the same love" (Phil. 2:2). They are to recall that dramatic moment when soldiers were arriving to arrest Yeshua. One disciple asked, "Lord, should we strike with the sword?" (Lk. 22:49). One actually did, cutting off the ear of a slave of the high priest. Yeshua responded with, "No more of this!" (Lk. 22:51). He healed that severed ear and submitted to the injustice rushing upon him. Having the mind of Yeshua, then, is to give up the right to "get even" as God's way of gaining justice.

Note Paul's instruction to a Christian slave owner whose runaway slave was being sent home, now himself a believer in Yeshua. Paul makes his appeal to the slave owner out of love and as "a prisoner of Christ Jesus" (Philemon 9). He says: "Perhaps this is the reason he was separated from you for a while, so that you might have him back forever, no longer as a slave, but more than a slave, a beloved brother..." (Philemon 15-16). Granted, the very idea of slavery is disgusting to a contemporary Christian, as in fact it was for the most part to the ancient Jews (they themselves had been freed from a hated slavery in Egypt). Its wrongness would be recognized and challenged only over time—an example of "progressive revelation."

Therefore, given the progressiveness of divine revelation, or at least the stages of its human understanding, the eye-for-an-eye principle

---

5. See, for example, William Webb, *Slaves, Women, and Homosexuals* (Downers Grove, ILL: InterVarsity Press, 2001), 31-33.

appears to have been given at first as a *limit* to retaliation, not a license to strike back at will. Such wisdom becomes clarified only over time, one reason why biblical passages like Deuteronomy 7 and Leviticus 24 remain valuable for Christians today. They are beginning baselines that highlight well the initial trajectory toward compassion and its greater understanding and application that would come only later. Those older baselines caution us today not to arrogantly assume that we have gained even yet a full understanding of God and God's ways among us humans.

2. Sacrifice As Worship?... Hebrews 9

Religious traditions always express themselves in set patterns of worship. There are typical outward acts that reflect the group's inward convictions. Regular re-enactment of these convictions through the set patterns helps to maintain the community of faith. Ancient Israel was no different. Its early worship patterns were worthy of Yahweh in many ways, but also included an element of violence that tends to confuse and embarrass contemporary Christians—and some Jews as well.

In order to understand the earliest "system" of worship seen in the Foundational Testament, one must come to appreciate the distinctive faith that informed this unusual covenant community. Since we find little direct attention to the underlying "theology" of worship—the Jews spent more time *doing* it than trying to *explain* it to others, we will have to read carefully, go beneath the text, listen in, and even join the set patterns of holy celebration.

The first worship patterns of Christians, since they were Jews, naturally were very reflective of Jewish Temple and synagogue worship. Jews affirming Yeshua as their Messiah were still Jews worshipping Yahweh, but now in light of Yeshua. It was a rich worship tradition, with the practice of sacrifice an important element. To locate the distinctiveness and continuing significance of such ancient Jewish worship for today's Christians, we must introduce the concept of "sacrament." This word is defined as *the sacred being experienced through engagement with some aspect of the material world*. God comes to us and Self-reveals through the concrete history of the people of God and through the concrete elements of worship when they are properly considered and used for the proper reasons.[6]

The long worship tradition of Israel had many dimensions, some troubling to itself at times, and also troubling to later Jewish believers in Yeshua. Admittedly, some Jewish worship practices, at least their outward forms, were much like those of their neighbors, the Canaanites, Egyptians, and Babylonians. Even so, one must keep in mind an important point. Two people appearing to do much the same thing may, in fact, be doing two quite different things—intent sometimes is more important than mechanics. For instance, one obvious concern for contemporary Christians is the subject of sacrifice. Here is the critical point. We must distinguish between sacrifice practiced as "sacrament" and sacrifice carried on as selfish and manipulative indulgence. This distinction will take some explaining, but its importance is worth the time.

As always in the Jewish tradition, we must begin with the overarching paradigm, the one source of living water, the foundation of all beliefs, Yahweh God. It is reasonable to suppose that beginning with the Person and presence of Yahweh is the proper path to characterizing the inner meaning of the worship of the Jewish people, at least as it was supposed to be if not always actually was. The difference between Israelite worship and that of her neighbors, even with all the outward similarities, were real. They rooted more in *who* Israelites were worshipping and less in the language or forms of the worship itself. That brings us to the troubling subject of sacrifice.

Some concept and practice of sacrifice is common in religious communities worldwide. Regardless of the commonality, the critical questions are: *Why* sacrifice? Sacrifice *to whom*? Sacrifice *what*? The answers range widely, and often were troubling to ancient Israel, and likewise to contemporary Christians. For instance, sacrifice sometimes is understood by people outside the Judeo-Christian tradition as an act of feeding the gods, caring for divine needs. Sometimes gifts are given to the gods to keep them from being angry, supposedly bringing safety to the worshipping community. The gifts can range from money to animals or even human lives.

---

6. In the Eastern Christian tradition, icons are frequently used as aids to worship. They are pieces of art through which perceptions of the divine become available. They are not idols, thought to be sacred in themselves. They are recognized as having the potential of conveying the presence of the divine.

Usually, whatever the exact practice, there sometimes is the prominent element of influencing the gods on behalf of human agendas. At other times, probably less frequently but much more related to the worship of ancient Israel, the intent of the faith community when it sacrifices is *to deepen the relationship between the worshipper and the divine*. It is here that we introduce the concept of "sacrament" and see the distinctive worship of Israel. When one begins with Yahweh instead of the wants, needs, and selfish agendas of the worshipper or the "god" in question, the end result changes significantly.

Feed the deity? But Yahweh has no dietary needs. Manipulate the divine with calculated bribes (sacrifices)? But Yahweh is Lord of all and beyond being paid off. God is self-sufficient, fully content in and of himself. The last thing needed by Yahweh is some kind of ego boost from mere humans. Nor does Yahweh seek our praise because he is in short supply of it or anything else. The truth could not be put more plainly than this: "We can set aside the false accusation that God is a divine, pompous windbag seeking to have his ego stroked by human flattery. That's the argument of village atheists, not those who have seriously examined the Scriptures."[7] God seeks our praise not because he lacks it, but because we need to give it for our own spiritual well being. God does not need more praise from us; we are the ones needing to be praising God.

The biblical account of creation makes clear that Yahweh was without need prior to the creation, and remains without need of sustenance of any kind from the creation. When slipping beneath the surface of the biblical text, we see that the book of Leviticus is about much more than the messy and morbid business of bloody animal sacrifices. The covenant partnership that Yahweh established with Israel created the unusual setting in which worship was to be an expression of gratitude, self-surrender, and personal transformation through increased identification with God's nature, presence, will, and ways. Viewing sacrifice in this sacramental way allowed it to be readily reaffirmed in the Final Testament, enabling both traditional Jews and Jews now following Yeshua to continue this worship tradition. This was the case even after the Temple in Jerusalem was destroyed by the Romans and animal sacrifices were ended altogether. Animal sacrifices as such never had been the central point of worship.

Worship sometimes went wrong, even in Israel, as it does among Christians and all others. In Genesis 28, Jacob promises that he will be

---

7. Paul Copan, *Is God a Moral Monster?*, 33.

generous with his giving to God *if* God will keep his promises to him—worship as selfish bargaining. How easy it is to worship *ex opere operato*, assuming that the act of worship is itself enough to guarantee the desired result. Many of Yahweh's ancient people had been pagans and polytheists and always were surrounded by such people. They struggled to focus their worship on Yahweh and their relationship to Yahweh, and not revert to a lesser focus and compromised motivations for worshipping. Sometimes they failed.

The prophets of the Foundational Testament repeatedly cried out against all compromises. Some of the chosen people made worship a mere formality, honoring God with their lips while their hearts were far away (Isa. 29:13). The ringing message of the Jewish prophets is that Yahweh does not want animal sacrifices or ornate rituals. Yahweh never did. He wants the willing gift *of the human heart* (Ps. 51:16-17). No sacrifice can be a substitute for repentance, submission, and justice. The word from Yahweh was never clearer than through the mouth of the prophet Amos (5:21-24):

> I hate, I despise your festivals,
> I take no delight in your solemn assemblies.
> Even though you offer me your burnt offerings,
> I will not accept them;...
> Take away from me the noise of your songs;...
> But let justice roll down like waters,
> and righteousness like an ever-flowing stream.

In other words, Yahweh was saying: "Don't try to placate or use me. Don't just play at some religious game. *Relate* to me humbly with all your heart. Dare to be transformed *in relationship with me* and then live out of the richness of that transformation. That is the sacramental worship I want!"

Later, the question would come to Rabbi Yeshua from a woman of Samaria. Where is the right place to worship, on this mountain or in Jerusalem? Yeshua ignored the question of *location* as not the really important one. He moved the issue to the proper *manner* of worship – "true worshippers will worship the Father in spirit and in truth.... God is spirit, and those who worship him must worship in spirit and truth" (Jn. 4:23-24). As to Jerusalem, Yeshua would find himself disrupting the chaos of commerce in the Temple—"Take these things out of here! Stop making my Father's house a marketplace!" (Jn. 2:16). Worship should be a matter of relating humbly to God, being changed by an intensified divine-human relationship, and experiencing the "sacrament" of prayer and praise. Worship is not to be the occasion for selling and buying, bargaining and using.

According to the Foundational Testament, worship is intended to be "sacramental," an actual experiencing of the presence of the divine through the concrete objects and actions of worship. This experiencing changes the worshipper into a child of God and an agent of God's good news and justice in this world. There is no better picture of proper worship than the experience of Isaiah in the temple. There, in the year that King Uzziah died, "I saw the Lord sitting on a throne, high and lofty.... And one [seraph] called to another and said: 'Holy, holy, holy is the Lord of hosts; the whole earth is full of his glory.'... And I said: 'Woe is me! I am lost, for I am a man of unclean lips, and I live among a people of unclean lips; yet my eyes have seen the King, the Lord of hosts!'" (Isa. 6:1, 3, 5). Once a cleansing coal of fire from the altar had touched Isaiah's mouth, God asked who was ready to represent God in the world. Isaiah responded as a completion of his transforming worship experience, "Here am I; send me!" (6:8).

In the Final Testament, Yeshua is pictured as the high priest who can sympathize with our human weaknesses because "in every respect [he] has been tested as we are, yet without sin" (Heb. 4:15). Under this high priest's administration of all things holy, the ancient theme of sacrifice emerges again. Believers are told to "present your bodies as a living sacrifice, holy and acceptable to God, which is your spiritual worship" (Rom. 12:1). Believers are to let themselves "be built into a spiritual house, to be a holy priesthood, to offer spiritual sacrifices acceptable to God through Jesus Christ" (1 Pet. 2:5).

There is a stewardship theme. To sacrifice to God is to acknowledge that all is God's in the first place. Nothing is *ours*. But there is more than stewardship. Given the very nature of Yahweh (see especially chapter six), there is *relationship*. In good Jewish fashion, the Final Testament puts it this way: "If we walk in the light, as he [Yeshua] is in the light, we have fellowship with one another [and with him], and the blood of Jesus, his Son, purifies us from all sin" (1 Jn. 1:17). There are to be no bribes, no attempts to manipulate the divine on behalf of human agendas. There is only to be a basking in the purifying beauty of the holy God, a basking that cleanses and intensifies communion with God and leads to a commissioning by God. From holy precincts should come sounds of joyous praise of Yahweh: "How lovely is your dwelling place, O Lord of hosts! My soul longs, indeed it faints for the courts of the Lord; my heart and my flesh sing for joy to the living God" (Ps. 84:1).

True worship is meant to be a "holy meeting," a rich relating of the worshipper and God. Since Yahweh, the holy one of Israel, is not bound by time or space, this meeting can be at any time and anywhere. Since Yahweh is the one who reveals himself in the events of human history, the divine is never trapped in given places or reduced to concrete images easily turned into inert idols. We are not to localize, concretize, and therefore try to isolate and "manage" the Lord of both creation and history! However "holy" temples, synagogues, or churches may be, Yahweh is never confined to any sacred sanctuary (2 Sam. 7:5-7; Ezek. 10:18ff). The rich relating is wherever the holy meeting happens.

Since divine revelation comes "sacramentally," that is, in and through the concrete realities of creation and its history, *remembering* is central to worship in the Foundational and Final Testaments. Worshippers remember the holy past of God's goodness to the creation, and certainly God's particular acts of grace on behalf of the chosen people. Worshippers then are to seek to have that sacred past become an active present in their own lives and communities of faith. The "holy meeting" of God and worshipper yields a holy transformation. Worship "brings the ancient events into the present, and their present meaning is that Israel is *now* accountable for her historical life to the God who has created history and rules over it to realize his purpose in the creation of the universe."[8]

Yeshua, inheriting this Jewish worship tradition, and just before his betrayal to the Romans, took a loaf of bread and a cup of wine. He said the one was his body about to be broken and the other the new covenant in his blood. His disciples were to partake of it on a regular basis "in remembrance of me" (1 Cor. 11:25). In doing so they would "proclaim the Lord's death until he comes" (11:26). Yeshua was being "sacramental," investing in a concrete practice the conveyance to his disciples of divine presence and meaning and grace.

Soon the writer of the book of Hebrews was also being sacramental. No more would there need to be the blood of calves and goats. Why? Because in Yeshua the Eternal Spirit had offered himself without blemish, once for all time and all people. The result? This final sacrifice would "purify our conscience from dead works to worship the living God!" (Heb. 9:14). An ugly Roman cross had been transformed into a beautiful icon, something concrete through which we humans

---

8. James Muilenburg, *The Way of Israel: Biblical Faith and Ethics* (NY: Harper and Row, 1961), 112.

could see God with us, saving us, loving us, calling us to a new relationship, a new creation.

How Jewish this all is! The Psalter is the prayer-book of the Jews. It is filled with accounts of the memorable events of the past (Pss. 44:17, 74:20, 78:10, etc.). The world's evil fosters "numbness that tempts believers to live again as though the present is all there is, and things will have to stay the way they are. Returning to the biblical texts and worship themes encourages a new opening of one's self to God and a patient waiting in hope."[9] To remember rightly in God's presence all that God has done is to allow oneself to be *repositioned* in order to *re-enact* with God such goodness and justice in the present and future. That was the Jewish way; it is the biblical way, the sacrament of sacrifice, the way of remembering and living called for by Yeshua.

3. Vengeance?... Psalm 137

Frustration can breed violence. The long Jewish exile in Babylon raised questions that bred calls for vengeance against the Jewish enemies, and in their eyes also the enemies of God. Will God ever come? When will God's salvation finally arrive? What is the best way to keep waiting? Why do we have to wait so long? How should people of faith deal with the dark days before the expected dawn? Could something have happened to God, making him unable to come on time? Is it time to take things into our own hands? The Foundational Testament poses at points such urgent and painful questions.

Isaiah 64:3 relates the hoped-for coming to Yahweh to the remembered comings of Yahweh in the past: "When you [Yahweh] did awesome deeds that we did not expect, you came down, the mountains quaked at your presence." The verbal phrase "come down" echoes the formative memory of Israel's exodus from Egypt (Ex. 3:8), while the quaking mountains suggests the undying memory of the covenant-receiving experience at Mount Sinai (Ex. 19:16-18). Long ago, Yahweh had defeated evil, freed a people for the future, and granted them identity in covenant relationship with himself. The Jews were able to cling to hope in the present because they remembered a foundational past when Yahweh did come.

The constant danger of the faith community is forgetting the divine dimensions of yesterday, thus having no basis for hope in the tomorrows. But then it happens. After seven verses of admitting to sin

---

9. Barry Callen, *Authentic Spirituality*, 194.

and lamenting God's continuing silence, we encounter in Isaiah 64:8 the disjunctive "yet," "nevertheless!" It nearly leaps off the page. "Yet, O Lord, you are our Father; we are the clay, and you are our potter; we are all the work of your hand." We humans, even God's own chosen people, have become disfigured clay, so undeserving, over anxious, faithless raw material. *Nevertheless*, there is good news. God still is, loves, remains faithful, and will come again to reshape the precious, even if perverted clay.

For Final Testament believers, there are multiple divine comings or "advents." The pivotal ones in the past are found in the Foundational Testament and shared as a long and solid base of remembering. In addition, Yahweh has come in Yeshua as the Christ and has promised to come yet again at the end of the age. The life of faith is thus a journey in the interim between divine arrivals. The interim always is a time of tension marked by ambiguities and uncertainties. Paul, highly schooled in the Jewish tradition, instructed a young congregation of Yeshua's followers to pray for the divine gifts that are sufficient for the in-between times (1 Cor. 1:3-9).

When the ancient Jews or contemporary Christians were (are) near the end of their (our) individual or collective ropes, the hope remains the same. It is for the fresh advent of the God who remembers us, even in our forgetfulness of God. We hope that God is still prepared to graciously re-form us as we become willing to receive and become agents of the divine grace in the world. We believe despite the present. Yes, God will come; thus true community is possible after all. Yes, God will come; thus justice can be more than paternalistic language used by the rich and powerful. Yes, God will come; thus joy can be more than a cliché, and a "holy-day" like Christmas can be more than an annual economic binge.

There is a strange twist to Advent, that season of the Christian year preceding the celebration of the birth of Yeshua. The fact is that we are the ones invited to come. Instructed by the Foundational Testament, we are to "come and see what God has done: he is awesome in his deeds among mortals" (Ps. 66:5). As we come in response to God's coming, we have this promise given by Yeshua as he was going away: "And remember, I am with you always, to the end of the age" (Matt. 28:20). God has come and always will be coming to the remembering, grateful, and faithful ones who wait in faith.

A Christian hymn begins, "O come, O come, Emmanuel, and ransom captive Israel, that mourns in lonely exile here, until the Son of God appear." Another announces the news at the other end of the Advent journey: "Joy to the world! the Lord *is come*. Let earth receive her King." The appropriate prayer is:

> Renew my memories of what you, God, already have done in past comings.
> Be my Potter, reshaping my life according to your holy image.
> Lessen my anxieties by increasing my faith.
> Grace me with wisdom and strength for the interims now being faced.
> Change the church from a random crowd to a covenant community of faith.
> Let me be light and hope for the darkness of others.
> Holy God, come and make us a holy people!
>   In the name of the One who once blazed
>   on Mount Sinai and later illumined Bethlehem
>   on a dark night so long ago. AMEN!

Hope can be hard. Delayed and deeply frustrated hope can turn bitter. That brings us to Psalm 137. It begins as a communal complaint, continues like a hymn, and ends as a virtual curse. This can shock the modern reader of the Foundational Testament, especially when that reader is looking for important guidance in understanding the Final Testament. Here is another instance when getting beneath the text will be critical. As explained above, however, we begin by giving this text the integrity of its original setting.

Since Psalm 137 includes a specific historical reference, we can assume that it came from the Jewish community exiled in Babylon after Jerusalem's brutal destruction in 587 B.C.E. The surviving but again enslaved Jews were clinging to the memory of a glorious past and hoping passionately that Yahweh somehow would soon enable a Jewish homecoming in Jerusalem, the beloved city of God now lying in ruins at the hands of Yahweh's enemies.

With the deeply desired homecoming came the bitter wish that deserved judgment would fall on those responsible for such a horrible deed as destroying Jerusalem. This "lament" psalm is a crying complaint and a desperate hope. It begins with, "by the rivers of Babylon—there we sat down and there we wept when we remembered Zion" (vs. 1). There is a sense of irony since this psalm follows immediately two other psalms that celebrate Yahweh's great gift of the land to his people. Then comes the great reversal, the sad shock, the complaint of Psalm 137. It stares at the unthinkable thought of the great gift stolen and spoiled. Is Yahweh not God after all? How could this have happened? The later use of this psalm in Jewish worship and home instruction transmitted to each new generation of Jews the yearning and even the hate that was thought appropriate for every dislocated Jew.

The great danger for such exiled Jews, in Babylon and then elsewhere through the centuries, was this. Once their faith was torn from its historic and geographical moorings, would they be drowned in a sea of Babylonian culture, lost in the mire of pagan disbelief? In fact, could (should) Yahweh be worshipped in a strange land where other gods seemed to be in control? The answer was (is) affirmative, with insistence that the only real hope is in remembering stubbornly, in cherishing the memory of Yahweh's gift of land and the holy city, recalling Jerusalem "above my highest joy" (vs. 6). To forget is to be lost, leaving only the perverted identity that the Babylonians would choose to give the Jews.

Then comes the harshest part of all. Assuming that they would always remember, and that Yahweh could and should be worshipped in any foreign land, how should Yahweh's people think of those who had yelled out about Jerusalem, "Tear it down. Tear it down. Down to its foundations!" (vs. 7). Psalm 137 ends with the vindictive hope that brutal destruction would come to such awful enemies of Yahweh's people. "Happy shall they be who pay you back what you have done to us" (vs. 8). Here is the ugly a picture being projected: "Happy shall they be who take your little ones [Babylonian children] and dash them against a rock!" (vs. 9). These feelings and this image of violence are understandable, but hardly transferred easily into the setting of the Final Testament and its featuring of the "Prince of Peace" (although Christian "crusaders" would manage later to make such a transfer and slaughter thousands in attempts to recapture the "Holy Land").

The reader's need is again to go downward. When we go beneath the text of Psalm 137, we see the strong Temple tradition of the Jews supporting this psalm.[10] The Jews had focused on an assured place for encountering the holy presence of Yahweh. The struggle now had become how to assure the continuing presence of Yahweh among his covenant people when the architectural centerpiece of the traditional assurance was destroyed. Can faith in Yahweh survive dramatic dislocation of the people from the promised land and its destroyed Temple? Is one place more holy than another? Is Jerusalem not the possession of the Jews by "divine right"? Dare Yahweh's people express their real feelings, ugly as they were? Obviously, they assumed they could—

---

10. "Temple" is one of the four major themes found in the Synoptic Gospels of the Final Testament, a theme clearly shared with the Foundational Testament. See a development of this theme in Willard M. Swartley, *Israel's Scripture Traditions and the Synoptic Gospels* (Hendrickson, 1994).

Yahweh is not nearly as fragile as themselves or the Temple in Jerusalem. Should they seek revenge on Yahweh's enemies with their own hands?

Note that the prayer of defiant hope for vengeance is addressed to Yahweh—"remember, O Lord" (vs. 7). Those praying are not necessarily assuming that *they* should take action against the Babylonians. What we have in this psalm is violent *speech*, not violent *acts* (while easily connected, they are not the same). Yahweh can be trusted to judge justly on his own. Yahweh surely would not always remain in the background like some deposed hero of a now-dead faith tradition. Yahweh's faithfulness and infinite ability can be assumed—bedrock theology, but the divine ways and timing often lie beyond us humans (Isa. 55:8-9). Note also that the ancient Jews had no highly developed belief in justice being done after this life was over. Concepts of heaven and hell developed only later through "progressive revelation." Further, the Jews, in all of their frustration and fear, may have expected Yahweh's justice to come in ways not necessarily in accord with what God intended—thus the need for Yeshua and the Final Testament.

The composer of Psalm 137 "is claimed by God with a claim that will not let him go, yet he understands and responds to that claim from a pre-Christian perspective and in a not-yet-Christian spirit [as Christians sometimes do also!]"[11] The psalmist rightly longed for Yahweh's intervention, but envisioned inadequately the *means* of Yahweh's intervention. The ultimate returning and redeeming presence of Yahewh with his people would come, but it would not be the reclaiming of Jerusalem by violence, but by the sacrifice of the Son on an ugly cross planted in a hill outside Jerusalem's new gates.

Here, as elsewhere, Christians seek the right way to read their Foundational Testament. As is explained in chapter three, they should begin the reading by seeking the original intention of the writer (editor) and seeking to experience the text as the first hearers/readers would have heard/read the text's meaning. How would texts on violence and holy war have been intended/read originally? Hardly in the contemporary way that poses abstract ethical questions like, "What about the justice of war in the context of faith?" and "Is killing potentially a worthy act for the followers of Yahweh in particular circumstances?" There is ample evidence that beneath all texts is a pervasive theological bedrock, the basis of the text's intended enduring mean-

---

11. John Bright, *The Authority of the Old Testament*, 238.

ing. That bedrock is Yahweh from whom flows the four truth streams, one or more of which is beneath every biblical text.[12]

In brief, here is the enduring meaning that lies beneath Psalm 137. *God will preserve his people.* We know this because the very existence of Yahweh's people is the byproduct of Yahweh's past actions on their behalf. The future preservation of the people is certain regardless as how or when it happens, or who chooses to be part of the divinely chosen family. Yahweh's people are called to hear, believe, and obey, but never to act under the assumption that what Yahweh's people do in their own power and wisdom will make the difference in their success. Success is not the result of the merit or numbers or weapons or strategies of Yahweh's people. A classic example of what does bring success is the exile of the Jews from Egyptian bondage, the launching event of the beginning of the people as a covenant body sent on its way to the promised land. Moses said to the people,

> Do not be afraid, stand firm, and see the deliverance *that the Lord will accomplish for you today....* The Lord will fight for you, and you have only to keep still" (Ex. 14:13, emphasis added).

A difficult text like Psalm 137 carries beneath it elements of all four of the truth streams that flow from Yahweh and cover the full landscape of the Foundational Testament. Stream #1 affirms Yahweh's gracious choice of the people, and thus somehow their continuance. Stream #2 affirms their call to be holy people, even in dire circumstances like exile in Babylon. Stream #3 legitimates their questions and frustrations, even if not providing immediate answers. Stream #4 undergirds their ongoing faith journey with an undying hope.

4. A Virgin Birth?... Isaiah 7:14 and Matthew 1:23

The Jewish tradition certainly was open to signs and wonders—after all, it was none other than Yahweh, God in their midst. Many Jewish scholars, however, have been less than supportive of certain of their

---

12. Brent A. Strawn suggests several important truths that can be learned by Christians from Psalm 137 and other Foundational Testament materials like it. Strawn, "Imprecation" in *Dictionary of the Old Testament: Wisdom, Poetry, and Writings* (eds. Tremper Longman III and Peter Enns, Downers Grove: InterVarsity Press, 2008), 314-320.

sacred texts being "adapted" for Christian purposes. A key example found in the Final Testament is Matthew's use of Isaiah 7:14 in reference to the miraculous conception of Yeshua.

In the seventh chapter of Isaiah we read about a clash between apparent military/political interests and God's direction about how the king of Judah should proceed in a time of looming crisis. Yahweh sent the prophet Isaiah to King Ahaz with a message of encouragement about his unpopular policy. He had not chosen to join the Aram and Israel rebellion against Assyria, and now they were threatening him because of his choice. The prophet's message essentially was: "Be calm; do not be afraid; stay your course. In due time the rebellion against Assyria will fail and you'll be glad you weren't part of it. This is Yahweh's word to you."

To support this prophecy, a sign was given to the king. It was announced that soon a young woman would bear a son and call his name Immanuel, meaning God-with-us. By the time this child was old enough to make decisions, so the prophecy explained, the land of the two kings of the rebellion would be devastated. The Hebrew word *almah* typically is used to designate an age group, in this case the young woman, with no necessary relationship to her sexual status. In fact, this predicted devastation did occur in 733 B.C. when Tiglath-Pileser reduced the agitators of King Ahaz to the status of Assyrian provinces. The sign was fulfilled in a timely manner just as the prophet had said.

Much later, Matthew, another Jew, was recording the dramatic story of Yeshua and filling his story with numerous ties back to the earlier story of the Jewish people and their future expectations. He came to the verse in Isaiah 7:14 that speaks of the coming child of political promise. Matthew, however, saw in that text a heightened significance quite beyond its original historical setting. His claim for this verse and its relationship to the birth of Yeshua soon became a tension point in Jewish discussions. At issue was whether or not Yeshua should be accepted as the expected Messiah of the Jews, and how Yeshua-believing Jews should read their Foundational Testament.

What Matthew had done was follow the Jewish translators of the *Septuagint*, the Greek translation of the Foundational Testament. It translates *almah* with *parthenos*, meaning *virgin*. He then related the word directly to Mary, the mother of Yeshua, identifying specifically her sexual status at the time of his conception. This use of an ancient prophetic text, quite apart from its original historical setting, is often criticized by Jewish and even some Christian scholars. Even so, such "adapting" happens many times in the Final Testament and is supported by the assumption of "progressive" revelation. That is, material in the Foundational Testament sometimes has extended (new) meanings once the revelation of Yeshua in the Final Testament is taken into consideration.

The Isaiah sign about the young woman and the coming child certainly has the potential to illuminate the meaning of the birth of Yeshua. For instance, John D. W. Watts concludes: "Thus the announcement of God's sign to Ahaz in his hour of despair is a fitting reference to illuminate the birth of a lowly infant in stable straw whom God has destined to save the world, *not by force of arms* but by meek acceptance of humiliation and death [as is clearly pictured in Isaiah 53]. That God chooses to accomplish his primary goals in such ways is the message of Isaiah as it is of the Gospels."[13]

Likely more important than the exact physical manner of Yeshua's physical conception is the intended theological indication of God's saving presence among his people. John's Gospel speaks of believers in Yeshua being "born from above" or "born of the Spirit" (Jn. 3:31). Believers have the ability to be God's children because they have been born "not of blood or of the will of the flesh, or of the will of man, but of God" (Jn. 1:12-13). Stress falls less on the *how* and more on the *why* and the wonderful end result.

While the divine aspect of the conception of Yeshua, often called the "virgin birth," is reported as a literal occurrence by Matthew and Luke, it is not mentioned elsewhere in the Final Testament. Belief in biblical inspiration tends to lead one to accept as literal fact the miracle conception merely because it is so reported. However, no mention of it elsewhere, including in all the biblical reports of early Christian preaching or the theological writing of Paul and the others, discourages speculation about the theological implications of the exact *manner* of the conception of Yeshua. What is meant without question, and clearly of primary importance, is that the arrival of Yeshua was also the saving arrival of none other than the presence of God among his people.

In order to keep full faith with the original Isaiah text and the dramatic story of Yeshua as told by Matthew and the other Gospel writers, this much can be affirmed. The theological claim that comes from the report of the virgin birth of Yeshua is that, from its very beginning, the life of Yeshua came from the life of God. Eduard

---

13. John D. W. Watts, *Word Biblical Commentary*, vol. 4, Isaiah 1-33 (Waco, TX: Word Books, 1985), 104. Emphasis added.

Schweizer puts it well: "The focus of the [Matthew] story is not the physical, biological process, but the theological watershed.... What the text asks is therefore not whether we can consider a virgin birth physically possible, but...whether in this birth we can see God's own intervention for [our] salvation."[14]

We should not distract ourselves with questions that the Final Testament does not raise or answer, questions like: Was Yeshua's birth a scientific possibility? Was a miraculous birth necessary for Yeshua to be kept from sin like the rest of us? Is sin carried in the male's DNA? Did Mary also have to be immaculately conceived in order to protect her divine baby? Is a virgin birth more holy than normal marital relations and the resulting births? More biblical than such questions is the wisdom of Karl Barth: "When we look at the beginning of the existence of Yeshua, we are meant to be looking into the ultimate depth of the Godhead.... The male, as the specific agent of human action and history, must retire into the background as the powerless figure of Joseph."[15]

****

These four inter-testamental studies highlight several important things. If God's Word, all of it, remains truly authoritative for Christians today, a careful interpretation of the text will be crucial, especially "troubling" portions of the Foundational Testament. Sometimes a proper interpretation will lead the reader beneath the text in order to find the deeper meaning, the underlying theology, the longer view, the contemporary significance. One must recognize and accept the *partial*, the *paradoxical*, and the *progressive* nature of divine revelation as found in both Testaments.

The final two chapters of this book explore this complex biblical and theological terrain. The Word of God is fixed, unchanging; it also is alive, growing, and understood only in stages and applied variously in differing times and settings. This constantly shifting circumstance will not be adequately "clean" and comfortable for some interpreters. So be it. God is who God is. God's revelation is as we actually find it in the biblical record, all of it. The contemporary meaning of the revela-

---

14. Eduard Schweizer, *The Good News According to Matthew* (Atlanta: John Knox Press, 1975), 35.

15. Karl Barth, *Dogmatics in Outline* (Harper & Row, 1959), 99.

tion is rooted in the ancient text—and also dependent in part on the current ministry of God's Spirit.

SECTION FOUR

FURTHERING EVEN THE FINAL TESTAMENT

FOUNDATIONS ARE ALWAYS FOUNDATIONS

Christians have always been...a "people of the book." All Christian traditions value the Bible as Scripture. But the Reformation elevated Scripture as its special concern, and consequently Protestants...are cognizant of the foundational role of the Bible.... The elevation of Scripture in personal and community life is evident in the typical evangelical equation of the Bible with "God's Word."[1]

Both Martin Luther and John Calvin correctly insisted that the work of the Spirit was always checked and given guidance by the Word. The Spirit works in and through the Scripture but never contrary to it. His leadership is always within the parameters of the revelation of God in Jesus Christ.[2]

We have been referring to the two biblical Testaments as "Foundational" and "Final." Together, and *only together*, do they comprise what Christians call "the Bible." The concept of a "closed canon" means that not all religious writing from the past related to the Jewish-

---

1. Stanley J. Grenz, *Renewing the Center: Evangelical Theology in a Post-Theological Era* (Grand Rapids: Baker Academic, 2000), 54.
2. H. Ray Dunning, *Grace, Faith, and Holiness* (Kansas City: Beacon Hill Press of Kansas City, 1988), 93.

Christian heritage is "inspired" by God in a way so special that makes it basic, enduring, and unquestionably authoritative for the faithful in all generations. Some writing clearly belongs inside and some clearly outside the "fence" of the biblical canon.

The word "canon" in this context refers to an exclusive list of "books." In the case of the Final Testament, reference is to the books written during the formative period of the Judeo-Christian faith tradition. These books (Gospels, essays, letters, etc.) were believed to be divinely inspired and expressing the authoritative base for the tradition. Once this canon was closed, it was the intention that it remain closed. God had breathed into (inspired) certain writings his own special presence and truth in a way that assures their integrity and enduring significance. The Christian tradition believes that both the Foundational and Final Testaments are comprised of a set of interconnected memories that were so "inspired," and thus are dependable interpretations of God's creating and redeeming activity across the centuries. Therefore, they are basic, distinctive, and unchanging in importance for believers of all times.

That is the "closed" sense of the biblical canon. We will explore this here. But there also is belief in at least a limited "openness" related even to this closed canon. We will explore this openness in the chapter to follow. Of particular importance now is the awareness that closing the Final Testament did *not* ever mean sealing it away from its enduring base, the Foundational Testament.

Closing the Canon

It likely is the case that the decision to adopt a particular list of materials to comprise what we now know as the Bible is as significant as any choice ever made in church history. While the process of decision is much more complex than can be addressed here, the outcome involved *both* the "Old" and "New" Testaments. In making this choice, the church came to have a dependable yardstick (canon) by which to shape and continually evaluate its ongoing theology, life, and mission across all generations to come. Whatever the human dimension of the materials chosen and the process of their final selections, the materials finally chosen came to be regarded as the *Word of God*. As Clark Pinnock and I once put this:

> The "Scripture principle" is the assertion that the Bible is the primary and fully trustworthy canon of Christian revelation, the reliable medium for encountering and understanding the God who seeks to trans-

form all persons who read the sacred text into the image of Jesus Christ.[3]

Note with care our emphasis on "transform all persons."

The role of the Christian canon is not primarily to fully and finally define Christian doctrine, nor to provide a comprehensive body of theological information about the Christian faith like some religious encyclopedia that works with a master index. The canonical process had more to do with enabling the spiritual formation of a community of believers responding to God's call and covenant. The early Christian church turned repeatedly to particular texts because of the effective ways they were found to function within the Christian community. The Bible lives as sacred Scripture in the hands of God's Spirit for the primary purpose of transforming the lives of those who comprise the church.

Accepting this "Scripture principle" predisposes one to trust the Bible and expect it to teach truth. And it does teach truth, although it does so for transformational purposes. It does not answer all of our questions or clearly explain how we should view its perplexing textual features—an occasional contradiction of fact, a few improbable numbers, a confusion of dates, or a conflicting sequence of the same events from one biblical reporter to another. Since minor discrepancies like these have always appeared in the biblical text, apparently they are of no significant concern to God. The "truth" being conveyed does rely on any supposed perfection of textual mechanics or comprehensiveness of doctrinal presentation.

Without knowing or even needing answers to occasional perplexities of the biblical text, the followers of Yeshua are to be very clear about one thing—and it is the same thing that was clear to the ancient Jew. Following the model of the Foundational Testament that highlights Yahweh over all and for all, it is the goal of all holy Scripture to lead the reader to an encountering and understanding of the *only God*, the One-for-all God who speaks through these biblical materials in order to transform us humans back to God's original intent for creation. The Bible's emphasis tends to be on the saving truth of its core message and the profitability of that message for our renewed lives of faith and discipleship (2 Tim. 3:16). So, as we read, that is also where our focus should be.

Given our Western minds that are so steeped in a scientific rationality, it is so easy to use the biblical canon inappropriately. We want

---

3. Clark Pinnock and Barry Callen, *The Scripture Principle*, 11.

absolute truth, fixed standards of behavior, and systematic theologies that dependably tie everything together in a neat package. The Foundational and Final Testaments frustrate us at this point. They aren't exactly what we often want them to be—and as we often try to make them be. To be a truly biblical Christian is to accept gratefully the Bible *as it actually is*. We must not employ our rational minds to read the Bible as we think God should have made it be—and thus surely did ("inerrant" in every way).

Here is an important guideline for reading the Bible. Now that the biblical texts are set in a fixed canonical collection, each text should be read in light of the *whole canon*. Full meaning is not to be found in the Foundational *or* Final Testament, but *in them together*, not in any one verse, but in the available range of verses on a similar subject. Individual texts gain their full meaning in the midst of their canonical relationships. William Abraham says, "Canonical materials, practices, and structures are the outcome of the work of the Spirit, designed for pedagogical and pastoral purposes in the church."[4] In other words, the biblical materials are intended to guide us fallen humans toward an encounter with the one true God and then nurture us toward salvation with and through God. The Bible seeks to facilitate our transformation to a living holiness fashioned in God's very image.

Without devaluing the Foundational Testament in any way, Christians would add the following in light of our broadened canonical view. The Bible invites us to know Yahweh best in Yeshua the Christ. Then we will be guided into lives of effective discipleship in the service of this Christ. While closed, the biblical canon remains active in the dynamic among its many parts and in relation to the best of contemporary applications.

Prying Open the Canon

The chosen people of God always are called to live out and proclaim the good news of Yahweh, including Yahweh's amazing love now known best in Yeshua. The well-being and mission effectiveness of God's people lie, in significant part, in their having, trusting in, and reading wisely the Word of God in their hands. Since this is so, why would any church leader or scholar challenge the Bible as the assured Word of God? There have been many such challenges.

---

4. William J. Abraham, *Canon and Criterion in Christian Theology* (NY: Oxford University Press, 1998), 52.

Among the several possible answers, one appears most prominent. We must be careful when speaking of the motives of others, but we know from the past that personal agendas sometimes overwhelm theology—there are many examples of this in both of the biblical Testaments, and certainly in Jewish and Christian history since biblical times. Moving to a Christian setting in current times, there is one major cultural shift that has affected the church of the Western world in negative ways.

This fateful shift is now several centuries old. It usually is called "secular modernity." It began especially in the Renaissance and moved through the Enlightenment period and the "liberal" response to that among many Christian scholars. In short, the result has been that the modern mind dislikes traditional authorities such as a closed-canon Bible. Many scholars, even in the church, have been trained to submit everything to intense rational scrutiny. There sometimes is an outright apathy or even active opposition to speaking about God in "premodern" categories. The Bible lacks credibility in the judgment of those who are taught to prize human autonomy and self-sufficiency over all else. The Bible presents itself as God's book that challenges human self-sufficiency.

One result of this "modernist" shift has been the rise of "biblical criticism." The text of the Bible has come to be studied as a collection of religious literature that should be subjected to vigorous and "objective" examination by all of the available tools of literary, historical, comparative religions, and other academic disciplines. These many efforts have had genuinely beneficial results, of course. Since the biblical materials certainly have human dimensions to them, studying them in such multiple and supposedly "objective" ways is a legitimate enterprise. One important result on the positive side has been keeping in check any excessive claims of biblical believers that virtually deny the human aspects of the biblical materials.

Even so, and without devaluing their benefits, often "critical" studies have been conducted as though the biblical materials were *merely* human documents in search of God. This "objective" approach loses the dimension of God searching through the Scriptures for lost humanity. Scholars sometimes are not open to engaging the Bible for purposes of their own spiritual growth. Instead, they focus on employing professional and technical skills in relation to the biblical text for "academic" purposes, potentially missing the voice of God's Spirit.

Beyond the literary issues related to the biblical text, and they are many and very real, the grand fact is that Yahweh remains at work. He works in part through this inspired text, seeking to activate human transformation and bring into being a people after his own heart. Readers embracing this spiritual dimension of the two biblical Testaments allow the ancient text to move from being merely *biblical writings* to being *sacred Scripture*.

The Judeo-Christian community of faith now finds itself in a new environment of biblical interpretation that brings a sense of emergency. The general culture of the Western world appears to be in a time of transition from the "modernist" to a "post-modern" mindset. Leaving the highly scientific and rationalist focus of modernism, the new move is toward viewing truth more contextually, locally, and pluralistically.[5] We learn and believe in community; we learn from each other, including from people very different from ourselves; and we come to know by use of more than our capacity to reason. We increasingly are aware that we are experiencing and feeling beings who flourish in relationships. This opens new doors to transformational biblical reading, doors sometimes more related to the original world of the Bible's origin than to the rationalistic preoccupations of recent generations.

My purpose here is not to explore the contemporary cultural context in detail; it is only to note that the Judeo-Christian community of faith is facing a new challenge, or maybe the same challenge it has always faced, and some fresh opportunities. Believers are impacted by their cultural environments, sometimes more than they know. Any effective communication of the faith must be done in ways that connect with the prevailing culture. Biblical "criticism" is certainly not to be rejected wholesale. It is to be employed in a believing context where faith seeks to be purified in any legitimate manner while it seeks a transforming encounter with God.[6]

God gave his Word in an historically situated way and through the agency of many real and limited human beings. Therefore, any increased understanding of that history and agency is to be welcomed. But an effective reading of the biblical text, transformational reading, will move through and beyond rational, critical methods. Rather than prying open the canon with only the tools of critical study, thereby virtually defaulting in advance on the Bible as divine revelation, today's Christians and their congregations should read, analyze, and *experience* it. Consider this:

---

5. Walter Brueggemann, *Texts Under Negotiation: The Bible and Postmodern Imagination* (Minneapolis: Fortress Press, 1993).

6. Clark Pinnock and Barry Callen, *The Scripture Principle*, 164ff.

For some Christians, the Bible is irrelevant, boring, and disconnected from faith. This may be the result of the church's inability to educate and model for congregants that Scripture is less about *information* and more about *formation* and *transformation*. Christians who view Scripture in formative ways can newly experience Scripture. Congregations should develop practices of Bible reading, Bible study, preaching, and worship that promote Christian formation.[7]

This experiencing of the Bible's revealing and transforming power is never to be done blindly and irresponsibly. Wise faith never dispenses with the intellect, even while it sometimes moves beyond it. Experiencing the biblical revelation is to be done humbly, always with an open and inquiring mind, and yet also always with an openness to the voice of God that comes through the biblical materials.

Maintaining the "Scripture Principle"

Recent decades have witnessed various attempts to protect the integrity of biblical revelation from "unbelieving" scholarship, what we have called an inappropriate prying open of a closed canon. The "attack" on the Bible has been what one especially vigorous combatant called the "Battle for the Bible."[8] That combatant and some other "conservative" believers have determined to keep the "Scripture principle" intact. In the process, however, they have defined the principle in a way that is highly questionable. Wrote one conservative:

> The very nature of inspiration renders the Bible infallible, which means that it cannot deceive us. It is inerrant in that it is not false, mistaken, or defective. Inspiration extends to all parts of the written Word of God and it includes the guiding hand of the Holy Spirit even in the selection of the words of Scripture.[9]

The word "inerrancy" often has been used as the touchstone for true biblical believing. The irony is that this reactionary insistence on a mechanical, textual perfection is itself an expression of the "modernist" mind. It is, unintentionally, a "scientific," rational, systematic ap-

---

7. Mark A. Maddix and Richard P. Thompson, "The Role of Scripture in Christian Formation," in Richard Thompson and Thomas Oord, eds., *The Bible Tells Me So: Reading the Bible as Scripture* (Nampa, ID: SacraSage Press, 2011), 188.

8. Harold Lindsell, *The Battle for the Bible* (Grand Rapids: Zondervan, 1976).

9. Harold Lindsell, *The Battle for the Bible*, 31.

proach to the biblical text, an approach foreign to the "pre-critical" text itself. Observes one critic of this reactionary trend: "If being biblical means speaking about the Bible in a manner that is consistent with the Bible, then the doctrine of inerrancy is unbiblical."[10] A "modern" mindset must not be allowed to pull the Bible into a place where God never intended it to be, even if that place sounds comfortably conservative.

Being "biblical" is to place oneself in the text of both Testaments in a way that listens actively for the voice of God *from* yesterday and *for* today, and in the terms the Bible sets for itself. It is correct to assume that the biblical writers and final editors were human media for "inerrantly" expressing God's will for all matters relevant to our salvation as wayward humans. There is a sure Word of God. However, we have no reason to expect that the biblical prophets and apostles possessed or were given by God such an inerrancy of knowledge and judgment about matters unrelated to our salvation (geography, geology, science, etc).

In fact, the biblical text as we have it suggests strongly the very opposite. Yahweh is the relational One, the only Savior, not the One who makes his people unnatural and unreal in their times and places. Composers of biblical material did not have comprehensive knowledge related to some subjects they happened to touch upon marginally in their writings—nor did this disturb them since such was not the issue. The truths Yahweh has been conveying are limited. They come in the four truth streams that flow from Yahweh through Yeshua.

These streams have to do with (1) forming through a covenant a faith community, (2) being transformed into the holy likeness of the covenant-making Yahweh, (3) grappling honestly with the dilemmas and questions along the faith journey, and (4) maintaining hope in God's future no matter what intervenes in the meantime. However, all that being said, what about "assured truth" when it comes to the subject of the proper path to salvation?

The subject of salvation is something central to Yahweh's own heart and the direct intent of divine revelation. The cry of the prophets and apostles of God echoes some famous words of John Wesley: "I want to know one thing, the way to heaven—how to land safe on that happy shore. God himself has condescended to teach the way: for this very end he came from heaven. He hath written it down in a book. O

---

10. Delwin Brown, *What Does a Progressive Christian Believe?*, 17.

give me that book!" That book is the Bible, both Testaments together, the continuous story of God with Israel and in Yeshua.

The biblical story is all about the creation of a holy people who will reflect the divine life and share always in a restored relationship with the Creator, covenant partner, and eternal Friend. To be clear about the full intent of John Wesley, and certainly that of the biblical Testaments, the book of God leads dependably to restored eternal life with God *and* to the accompanying will to live in divine holiness and community, and to practice justice *in this present world.* "Salvation" is restored life now and hereafter.

There is a helpful aid in maintaining the critical concept of the "Scripture principle." It insists that there is a God-revealed Word that is authoritative--without denying the human dimension of the biblical text itself. Often called the "Wesleyan Quadrilateral,"[11] it is a plan for interfacing properly the various influences on our human truth perceptions. The revealing and interpreting Spirit of God reigns supreme in the whole process. The full biblical record of Yahweh in Israel and then in Yeshua is the basic medium through which God's truth reaches us. But to achieve an adequate understanding of this record that is historically correct, currently relevant, and more from God than from the reader, one must profit from three means of careful biblical interpretation. Failing to profit from these means encourages readers to "open" the canon with the tools that usually come to involve their own ignorance and prejudices.

A series of factors should always be at work. They are church tradition, spiritual experience, and human reason. Believers are blessed with "a written witness to divine revelation (the Bible), a remembering and reading community (the church traditions), a process of existential appropriation (spiritual experience), and a way to test for internal consistency (human reason)."[12] Reading the Bible appropriately is a complex process. We are caught among these interpretive factors and are challenged to keep them active and in good balance.

We must celebrate the grand truths that God is and has spoken to our human circumstances. We also must be aware of our own limitations as Bible readers, and then be patient with the humanness of the

---

11. The word "quadrilateral" is not John Wesley's, but it captures the dynamics of his nuanced thought. See Don Thorsen, *The Wesleyan Quadrilateral: A Model of Evangelical Theology* (Lexington, KY: Emeth Press, 2005).

12. Barry L. Callen, *Caught Between Truths: The Central Paradoxes of Christian Faith* (Lexington, KY: Emeth Press, 2007), 45-46.

biblical text, not demanding of it what it was never intended to be. The Bible is a closed canon—not just anything goes for the faithful of the Judeo-Christian tradition! Foundations remain foundations. The Bible is a sure place for experiencing God's presence and gaining God's provision for our salvation. Even so, the Bible is not a computer-generated document designed by the latest in flawless scientific/literary software—the stuff of Hollywood. It is the long and complex narrative of a divine story within which God's Spirit forever lurks, waiting for us to read, listen, and be transformed!

13

GOD'S SPIRIT AND A SURPLUS OF MEANING

The Old Testament's laws exhibit a redemptive movement within Scripture. It's easy to get stuck on this or that isolated verse—all the while failing to see the underlying redemptive spirit and movement of Scripture that unfold and progress.[1]

Sound theology is theology that is faithful to the biblically narrated story and articulates its meaning and significance in a way that respects its original integrity.... Unsound theology would be theology that strays away from the canonical narrative, operates out of another story, and inhabits a different universe of meaning.[2]

As was made clear in the previous chapter, the Bible, including both Testaments, is believed by Christians to be authoritative for the believer's search for truth, life, and mission. What is foundational must remain foundational in all times. We spoke above about inappropriate attempts to pry open what is intended to be a closed canon, exposing the biblical text to numerous corrosions from the outside, and thus

---

1. Paul Copan, *Is God a Moral Monster?*, 62.
2. Clark H. Pinnock, *Tracking the Maze* (San Francisco, Harper & Row, 1990), 190.

stealing the text's integrity as a vehicle for the voice of God. We also noted a reactionary response, also inappropriate regardless of how understandable and noble its intent may be.

Now we will look at the other side of the coin. The biblical canon is forever closed; in a sense it also is forever open. The Spirit of God hovers over the biblical canon and keeps it fresh and looking forward. While fixed, it also must remain a pliable vehicle for God's voice to be heard progressively and relevantly in circumstances and times far removed from those of the Bible's original composition and canon closure. As is made clear in the second quote above, freshness and forwardness, while very important, must respect "the original integrity" of the biblical text and must not "inhabit a different universe of meaning."

Yahweh, known best in the coming of Yeshua, is unchanging in being, character, and intentions. However, our full understanding of all of this and its specific relevance to our own times is always a work in progress. Accordingly, disciples of Yeshua must be committed to the ongoing work of the Spirit of Yeshua in nurturing our growing understanding of divine revelation and its specific relevance for our times.

The Text Is Always Alive

Religious belief can harden and turn in on itself, compromising that which is most basic. Having affirmed strongly the Scripture principle as critical for the ongoing communities of authentic Christian faith, we face a danger. The canon of Scripture, and our church doctrines that we are certain have been drawn Scripture, can be both entirely correct and yet held too tightly. We can so "protect" the Bible truth we are sure we know that we paralyze it from being the *living* Word of God in our times. We insist that the Bible means exactly what it says, no matter the changed culture or apparent growth in the church's understanding, and regardless of any new information that is claimed to have become available. Likely, we are right some of the time, at least in general. But there are times when "orthodoxy," straight thinking and believing, builds such a high wall around itself that it

> ... silences God from speaking today—locking the divine in a book—and creates a petrified and rigid style of faith that is false to the dynamic transcendence of the Bible. It closes us off from appropriating fresh truth and creates a whole set of oppressive attitudes

and dogmas. Surely *religious experience* is the heart of Christianity, and although this gives rise to dogmas in time, such are the work of human beings, not the declarations of God.[3]

The above statement makes a strong point that is fully in accord with the overarching paradigm of the Foundational Testament. Yahweh alone is God; Yahweh is a dynamic transcendence; Yahweh works in the creation and among his people as he chooses; the heart of faith is not perfect cultic practice or a highly developed and rationally perfect systematic theology; the heart of faith as Yahweh desires it is encountering, yielding with the whole heart, and being willingly transformed by direct encounter with the divine. The center of the faith is Yahweh, not any set of abstract biblical or theological statements, accurate as they may be.

The many texts of the Foundational Testament are rich with continuing meaning. Some of the enduring meaning is on the surface of the writing and some is seen only beneath the textual surface and made clear only over time. Some of the meaning lies with the text's original setting and with the direct awareness of the intention of the writer. Some of it lies beyond the mere words, original historical context, and the author's conscious intention. Otherwise, there would be no Final Testament that expands, refines, and sometimes even refocuses assertions of the Foundational Testament. Nor would there be need to study the biblical materials freshly in today's life context if fresh meaning were not a possibility.

Apparently, the God who stands behind the fixed revelation in the unchanging, closed biblical canon remains free to reveal fresh understandings and new applications of sacred biblical texts. In other words, as we have said before, the Bible is neither flat nor dormant. It is a living Word in the hands of the ever-living God. It has a set meaning that is basic, and a surplus of meaning that is fluid. This paradox is delicate and demanding, but no less true. The past biblical revelation of God was inspired, inbreathed by God. While that wonderful truth will always be the fixed baseline, God must act again on behalf of contemporary readers of the biblical text.

God now must *illuminate* what was first *inspired*. Both of these divine actions, past inspiration and present illumination, remain con-

---

3. Clark Pinnock and Barry Callen, *The Scripture Principle*, 17. Emphasis added.

sistent with Yahweh's unchanging nature and will as known fully in the coming of Yeshua. Seven of the early Christian congregations were warned that their integrity lay in their hearing and obeying the fresh word of the Spirit coming to them in their individual circumstances. "Let anyone who has an ear listen to what the Spirit is saying to the churches" (Rev. 2:7). Times were changing. God's voice was speaking. What was being said was both fresh and yet consistent with Yeshua since the Spirit speaking was and always is the Spirit of Yeshua.

Yahweh, the measure of all things and the giver of all life, is both unchanging and open to adapting to altered circumstances in his creation. He applies fresh strategies and calls new prophets with divine messages adapted to current needs. The messages, of course, are always consistent with the unchanging nature of Yahweh, but their exact content can change in differing circumstances. Reading the two biblical Testaments provides numerous examples of this divine flexibility at work within the biblical canon itself. That creative divine work continues beyond but not contrary to what is found in the canon.

Paradoxes are present and important. They must not be feared or aborted. One cannot explain adequately the richness of the biblical text, its amazing ability to be a vital source of spiritual life for many peoples in many times, apart from the divine Spirit who spans all peoples and all times. Beneath all of the biblical text, with its diversity and progressions, and sometimes even seeming contradictions, there broods the Spirit of Yahweh who brings order out of chaos, light in the darkness, new creations (Gen. 1-2). The biblical text is ever alive because the One who breathed it into existence breathes on, keeping it alive and relevant and ready to change each new reader.

Dynamic Within the Closed

There is a significant contrast between the "Roman" view of biblical authority and the more "Hebrew" (ancient Jewish) view which originally spawned the Bible itself. The first focuses on an objective measure to which believers must conform. As the ancient Romans tended to say, "the law is the law." A clear teaching is established and remains binding on all coming generations of believers. The second view of authority is a more complex and dynamic one. In the Jewish tradition "each generation treated its authoritative past with respect, *and with creativity!*... Creativity rather than conformity was at work. Tradition was authoritative, but not as a fixed and singular past that must be replicated."[4]

New circumstances bring to God's faith community new challenges, opportunities, and sometimes fresh readings of the past. We understand this freshness in part from seeing such developmental activity inside the Foundational Testament and between the two biblical Testaments. For instance, Jewish teachers appear at one point to have reversed the tradition of having the story of the conquest of Canaan as part of the Pentateuch (the first five books). Why did they decide to end the "books of Moses" with Deuteronomy instead of Joshua? It appears to be because emphasizing the taking of the "promised land" no longer seemed the right priority for Jews languishing in Babylonian captivity, now far from that now-devastated land of promise.[5] Changed circumstances brought shifting perceptions and priorities.

The Jewish prophets sometimes interpreted the Mosaic materials in fresh ways and then applied the new ways to new situations. They obviously did not consider the text absolutely closed to new readings and applications. The impression given is that "from the promise to Abraham to bless all the nations through the prophetic anticipation of a new covenant and changes in the people's relationship with God in the messianic era, we have a forward-looking and revisable trajectory, one open to the future. It is not a closed text, complete and forever sufficient in itself."[6]

A similar developmental process is seen inside the Final Testament. We discussed earlier how Matthew 1:23 places a fresh interpretation on Isaiah 7:14, one that Isaiah would not have recognized, although that does not make wrong what Matthew did. There are many such instances of "fresh" interpretations of older biblical texts. Yeshua himself did exactly this several times. For him, the good news from his Father was more than a legalistic code to be followed strictly and mindlessly. He would dare to heal on the Sabbath, for instance, despite many Jewish leaders of the time insisting that such an act was breaking God's sanctioned code of conduct. For Yeshua, doing the loving thing superseded the legalism of codes of conduct—which sometimes were based on a wrong understanding of the Foundational Testament.

---

4. Delwin Brown, *What Does a Progressive Christian Believe?* (NY: Seabury Books, 2008), 21-22. Emphasis added.
5. See James A. Sanders, *Torah and Canon* (Philadelphia: Fortress Press, 1972).
6. Clark Pinnock and Barry Callen, *The Scripture Principle*, 58-59.

Yeshua's quotations from the Foundational Testament reveal no concern for a mechanical duplication of the original text. For him, what was most important was the message, the divine intent, not the precise textual wording or earlier understanding. Yeshua was so excited about what Yahweh was doing in the present that once he even said that anyone in God's kingdom today was greater than the greatest of the previous prophets (Matt. 11:11). There was in such a comment no disrespect for the past, which Yeshua honored and deeply loved; there was only an emphasis on the significance of his Father's continuing work in the world that sometimes sheds fresh light on God's past work. The conclusion is clear. To read the Bible biblically, and to remain relevant in new circumstances, today's believer must be open to God's guidance in fresh readings of the sacred text.

The writings of the Final Testament cite the Foundational Testament often, calling on it for support or illustration of the fresh new teaching about Yeshua, the now-come Jewish Messiah. This was wholly natural for these Jewish writers. They were steeped in the thought and language of the Foundational Testament and turned to it to express the gospel of Christ in traditional Jewish terms. They demonstrated a "dialectical" attitude, accepting the Foundational Testament both as sacred text from God's hand and incomplete revelation now understood most fully by the dramatic divine work in their own time—the life, death, and resurrection of Yeshua, the Christ.

Yeshua himself summarized this well: "Do not think that I have come to abolish the law or the prophets; I have come not to abolish but to fulfill" (Matt. 5:17). In other words, the Foundational Testament, while the authoritative, written Word of God, is intended to be read in light of Yeshua. The fact is that Yeshua and the Final Testament writers "respected the Old Testament text enormously as God's written Word and qualified it only in view of the new messianic situation."[7]

There are six statements of Yeshua recorded in Matthew 5 that say, "You have heard...but I say...." These contrasts should not be understood as reversing previous teaching. Instead, given the heavy overlay of traditional interpretations, Yeshua was telling his Jewish listeners, "Here's what you have heard, but here was and is the true intent of the Father." Yeshua was not abolishing core teachings of the Foundational Testament; he was announcing what he understood to be their true meaning and present significance.

7. Ibid., 63.

Instead of nullifying Torah, Yeshua radicalized it and supported the conclusions with his own authority. For instance, "do not commit adultery" he intensified to "but I say to you that everyone who looks at a woman with lust has already committed adultery with her in his heart" (Matt. 5:28). He confronted the mentality of those who were interpreting Scripture too narrowly or literally to justify conduct that in reality dishonored God. See the discussion on the Sabbath in chapter eight. Beyond direct actions, prevailing attitudes and intentions are also morally weighted.

Yeshua gave a more radical and expansive interpretation of some teachings of the Foundational Testament, a fresh interpretation that he said revealed more accurately the heart of the Father. It is the loving and gracious heart of Yahweh that should infuse disciples and direct their actions. This is the inspired authority for contemporary Christians who must focus on the Father's heart and rethink stances claimed to be "biblical." Some such claims, in fact, are too narrow or literal or are based more on a particular church tradition than on true biblical revelation from Yahweh through Yeshua.

Dynamic Beyond the Closed

The long biblical tradition was one of hearing God, expressing that hearing in textual form, and applying it in the life of the time. Understanding grew with experience, and we see this inside the Bible itself, which is why both Testaments are crucial for the full understanding of contemporary Christians. The internal biblical process instructs us in how to negotiate difficult ground today. We are to be open to growth and change, "not despite the Bible but because we believe that its rich dialogue...has empowered us to do so."[8]

A rather amazing assertion is in order, therefore, one made possible only because of who God has shown himself to be. We believers live in relation to our sacred Scripture by listening, learning, obeying, and sometimes even finding significant reason to "talk back" to the holy and dynamic text. When we do respond to our reading with critical questions or even disagreements, we must be sure that our voice is in tune with the current voice of the Spirit who is directing the reading and interpreting process. We must beware of alien voices and the tendency to human self-delusion. One good way to avoid such delusion is

---

8. Delwin Brown, *What Does a Progressive Christian Believe?* (NY: Seabury Books, 2008), 25.

to listen to the Spirit's voice as the church together, not as isolated individuals. The corporate approach is typically Jewish. It should include the wisdom of the church of today in sensitive dialogue with the accumulated wisdom of the church's past.

Of course, there is danger that talking back to the Bible will elevate human arrogance over divine revelation. Even so, on occasion the community of Christian faith over the centuries has come to a corporate judgment that something that appears on the surface of the biblical text is not all that God would have wanted. What was lying beneath the text had become clearer to God's people over time, not out of any disrespect for the biblical text, but out of great appreciation for the God who continues to illumine the meaning of the text in changed circumstances. An example will be helpful.

Christians now condemn human slavery and the second-class status of women as inappropriate in God's eyes. These are condoned in the Bible, at least on the surface of the text. Jacob successfully encountered and wrestled with God face to face, getting his name changed to Israel. But many of today's Christians would not get past the report of how Jacob got to the place of wresting: "That same night he got up and took his two wives..." (Gen. 32:22). Mention of two wives is immediately troubling since it is not accompanied by criticism from Yahweh.

The surface of this text passes no judgment on the practice of polygamy. What the Bible does establish authoritatively, when one goes below the surface, are the key guidelines of appropriate, ongoing conversation with the biblical text. We are invited to be fresh dialogue participants in our new time and place of reading the text and listening for God's voice. Part of what must be taken into account is that several voices in the Final Testament speak of family life for believers in Yeshua, with no hint of the acceptability of multiple wives.

The Bible provides the essential historical background and the kinds of truth options, worship intentions, and lifestyles that are acceptable to God. The Bible grounds our "creativity" without eliminating it. The Bible inspires our hearts, takes us to the feet of Yahweh who is all in all, and invites our transformation into the likeness of Yeshua, who best reveals the heart of Yahweh. It reminds us that Yeshua left behind important promises for the encouragement and enlightenment of disciples in all time to come.

First, Yeshua promised that would remain with his disciples always (Matt. 28:20). Second, he told them that there was still more to be said and that even greater things would get accomplished, but "you can't bear them now" (Jn. 16:12). The good news was that Yeshua would send his Spirit upon them. He said that "when the Spirit of truth comes, he will guide you into all the truth.... He will glorify me, because he will take what is mine and declare it to you" (Jn. 16:13-14). In other words, not all has been said inside the canon of Scripture—and God will continue to speak.

More will be shared by the Spirit as time goes on and the community of Yeshua receives the Spirit, walks in the Spirit, and is taught by the Spirit. A guideline is clear as this process of learning goes forward. Whatever is learned over time will have been taught by the Spirit, the promised teacher who is none other than the Spirit *of Yeshua*. So, whatever else is yet to be said by God, it will be in accord with and only an extension of what already has been said biblically in Israel and Yeshua. If it is not, its origin is not the Spirit of God. When tends to be highlighted is what was beneath the surface of the biblical text all the time but recognized only over time and with the Spirit's help.

There is danger in this ongoing process, obviously. Human subjectivity can easily replace God's true voice and claim a divine source for its own "insights." For example, John Wesley was anxious to honor the living voice of God through the current work of the Holy Spirit. He also was particularly concerned with claims to having received new insight into biblical meaning that had "the appearance of *enthusiasm*: overvaluing *feelings* and *inward impressions*; mistaking the mere work of *imagination* for the voice of the Spirit; expecting the end without the means; and undervaluing *reason, knowledge*, and *wisdom* in general."[9] There have to be safeguards that eliminate erratic humanness without obstructing the current freedom and work of the divine Spirit. Wesley's attempt to find this balance is key to his continuing significance in the world of Christian theology.

Fresh "revelations from God" can be mere human delusions. Two typical responses to this danger, however, each go too far in opposite directions. One excessive response is the ultra-conservative one, grasping tightly to known truth and eliminating the ongoing work of the Spirit. The opposite excessive response might be termed the ultra-liberal one, placing so much stress on the subjective side of the faith that the objective side is seriously compromised. The Bible must be allowed to discipline all supposed "inner lights," but in ways that do not end the possibility of legitimate ones occurring. God's work

---

9. David B. McEwan, "The Living and Written Voice of God: John Wesley's Reading, Understanding, and Application of Scripture," in *Wesleyan Theological Journal*, 46:1 (Spring 2011), 107.

among us is both *informative* and *transformative*, objective and subjective.

We spoke in the last chapter about reactionary conseratives like Harold Lindsell. That is one excessive position. The other, ultra-liberal, is well illustrated by Rudolf Bultmann. This influential biblical scholar assumed that, by engaging the Final Testament, one is encouraged to have an "existential" encounter with God that can transform human existence. For him, the historic biblical revelation is fallible and its objective truth claims mere symbols, even "myths," with their original historical references now of secondary importance at best. What matters now is that the biblical text still can function as living vehicles for salvation and authentic living.

This excessive line of thought argues that Christianity began as a "charismatic" movement that later hardened into "confessionalism." Modern people often find it difficult to believe many things in the Bible in an intellectual way, so they hunt for their subjective significance. Even conservatives with a Pietist tradition sometimes say, "Isn't getting saved really the point?" "Pentecostals" are accused regularly of being all emotion with little doctrinal content or concern. But is not emotion, real life, and current meaning the most important of all points? The point of valuing history is directing today with maximum wisdom.

We must recognize the danger lying on all sides of this delicate paradox of Word and Spirit, the objective and the subjective, biblical information and contemporary transformation. There is an important point to be made on the "objective" side of things—the burden of chapter twelve. But there also is a crucial point to be made on the "subjective" side of things, the burden of this chapter. The Spirit of Christ carries forward the original biblical message, telling us the things of Christ (Jn. 14:16-17, 26). The Spirit never replaces the original Word with something brand new, but interprets it and illumines our minds to become aware of the Word's current significance. The possibilities of meaning "are not limited to the original intent of the text, although that is always the anchor of interpretation. Fresh insights can arise from the interaction of the Spirit and the Word. We read the text and in it seek the will of the Lord for today."[10]

Christians are called to be Spirit people who trust God for the needed light yet to break forth on God's Word, enabling contemporary people to read the biblical text and, by the wisdom and power of

---

10. Clark Pinnock and Barry Callen, *The Scripture Principle*, 189.

God's Spirit, be illumined about its current meaning and applications. So we pray with these hymn lines:

> Come, Holy Ghost, for moved by Thee,
> Thy prophets wrote and spoke;
> Unlock the truth, Thyself the key,
> Unseal the sacred book.[11]

As God is graciously open to us, we must become open to God. We will read the Word again and again and ask hard questions about its meaning for today. A central biblical keynote is *incarnation*—the spiritual life enfleshed in the concrete realities of this world as it now is.

The Foundational Testament takes human history very seriously, with strong emphasis on God's mercy and justice being realized in the here and now. The Final Testament's very center is Yeshua, Yahweh birthed in the midst of our sordid world at its most raw. Yeshua was Yahweh actually with us for our salvation. That divine with-us continues through the ongoing ministry of the Spirit of Yeshua as believers now live in dramatically changed circumstances.

Difficult questions inevitably arise and demand answers if believers are to be effective disciples in this world and not merely hopeful disciples waiting for the glories of the world to come. The Final Testament asserts this: "Jesus Christ discloses to us the oneness of God with the world and the manner of God's working in it.... We affirm the incarnation of God in the entire creation, not just humanity—fully God, fully at one with the full creation."[12] Beyond the assertion come hard questions. For instance:

> 1. Is there one and only one way to salvation, being put fully right with God? Yeshua said he was "the way." Are there other ways? What about Jews loyal to Yahweh who do not accept Yeshua as the final revelation of God?
>
> 2. Part of today's social/religious environment is "pluralism." There is a widespread attitude that people should "live and let live." This clashes with the overarching paradigm of the biblical record, that God is one, alone. The Christian doctrine of "Trinity"

---

11. From "Come Holy Ghost, Our Hearts Inspire" in *The Book of Praise* (Presbyterian Church in Canada, 1972).
12. Delwin Brown, *What Does a Progressive Christian Believe?*, 96-97.

is particularly difficult for Jews and Moslems. Is Allah the same God as Yahweh? Even if the answer is "yes," questions remain. Yahweh, when known through Yeshua, is pictured as the suffering servant (Isa. 53). Allah, at times at least, is pictured differently. For that matter, so is Yahweh at points on the surface of the text of the Foundational Testament.

3. How should Christians be active in protecting this world's environment? Population growth, mass pollution from over industrialization, and pure human greed are assaulting the land, oceans, and skies. Exactly what should Christians be doing about it?

4. What should Christians think about the State of Israel? Is God still in covenant with the Jewish people? Does God condone, commend, or condemn strong military action taken by a particular political entity against her neighbors?

These and other questions are not answered easily, or in the same ways by all Christians, Jews, and Moslems. One thing, however, has always been answered with one voice by at least Jews and Christians. It is the acknowledgment and glad celebration of the *One God For All*, the God from whom four gracious truth streams continuously flow. In light of this central affirmation and its related truth streams, I conclude this book with two "J"s.

The first is Jonah. He appears briefly in the Foundational Testament as a most reluctant prophet. His compelling story is a repudiation of any arrogance that may emerge among God's people. It is a sharp rebuke of provincial pride that has a tendency to instruct God in what he should do about "outsiders." Jonah's story is about the one God whose world mission and redeeming grace are intended for all people, without ethnic, political, or geographical boundaries—even if some of God's "evangelists" act as if it were otherwise.

This worldwide vision of God's love contradicts claims that arise too often in Jewish and Christian communities: "We have God in our camp, on our team, packaged, as it were, in our church; our concerns are God's concerns...; and we have a formula, a ritual, a cultus, a program of worship which guarantees God's exclusively favorable relationship to us."[13] In fact, God functions as God knows God, not necessarily as Jonah or we assume God is and should do.

---

13. Davie Napier, *Song of the Vineyard*, 311.

The second "J" is Jude and the benediction that ends his little letter in the Final Testament. It celebrates the Water Source, the Overarching Paradigm, the theological center, that which lies beneath the surface of the whole biblical text, ties together the two Testaments, and is the heart of the Judeo-Christian tradition. It is *One God For All*. Reads this benediction (Jude 24-25):

> Now to him who is able to keep you from falling, and to make you stand without blemish in the presence of his glory with rejoicing, to the only God our Savior, through Jesus Christ our Lord, be glory, majesty, power, and authority, before all time and now and forever. Amen.

www.ingramcontent.com/pod-product-compliance
Lightning Source LLC
Chambersburg PA
CBHW021809220426
43662CB00006B/245